THE NEW FOLGER LIBRARY SHAKESPEARE

Designed to make Shakespeare's great plays available to all readers, the New Folger Library edition of Shakespeare's plays provides accurate texts in modern spelling and punctuation, as well as scene-by-scene action summaries, full explanatory notes, many pictures clarifying Shakespeare's language, and notes recording all significant departures from the early printed versions. Each play is prefaced by a brief introduction, by a guide to reading Shakespeare's language, and by accounts of his life and theater. Each play is followed by an annotated list of further readings and by a "Modern Perspective" written by an expert on that particular play.

Barbara A. Mowat is Director of Research *emerita* at the Folger Shakespeare Library, Consulting Editor of *Shakespeare Quarterly,* and author of *The Dramaturgy of Shakespeare's Romances* and of essays on Shakespeare's plays and their editing.

Paul Werstine is Professor of English at the Graduate School and at King's University College at Western University. He is general editor of the New Variorum Shakespeare and author of *Early Modern Playhouse Manuscripts and the Editing of Shakespeare* and of many papers and articles on the printing and editing of Shakespeare's plays.

Folger Shakespeare Library

The Folger Shakespeare Library in Washington, D.C., is a privately funded research library dedicated to Shakespeare and the civilization of early modern Europe. It was founded in 1932 by Henry Clay and Emily Jordan Folger, and incorporated as part of Amherst College in Amherst, Massachusetts, one of the nation's oldest liberal arts colleges, from which Henry Folger had graduated in 1879. In addition to its role as the world's preeminent Shakespeare collection and its emergence as a leading center for Renaissance studies, the Folger Shakespeare Library offers a wide array of cultural and educational programs and services for the general public.

EDITORS

BARBARA A. MOWAT
Director of Research emerita
Folger Shakespeare Library

PAUL WERSTINE
Professor of English
King's University College at Western University, Canada

FOLGER SHAKESPEARE LIBRARY

The Taming of the Shrew

By

WILLIAM SHAKESPEARE

AN UPDATED EDITION

EDITED BY BARBARA A. MOWAT
AND PAUL WERSTINE

SIMON & SCHUSTER PAPERBACKS
NEW YORK LONDON TORONTO SYDNEY NEW DELHI

Simon & Schuster
Avenue of the Americas
New York, NY 10020

This Simon & Schuster trade paperback edition October 2014

SIMON & SCHUSTER and colophon are registered trademarks of Simon & Schuster, Inc.

For information about special discounts for bulk purchases, please contact Simon & Schuster Special Sales at 1-866-506-1949 or business@simonandschuster.com

The Simon & Schuster Speakers Bureau can bring authors to your live event. For more information or to book an event, contact the Simon & Schuster Speakers Bureau at 1-866-248-3049 or visit our website at www.simonspeakers.com.

Manufactured in the United States of America

10 9 8 7 6

ISBN 978-1-4767-7739-9
ISBN 978-1-4767-8851-7 (ebook)

From the Director of the Folger Shakespeare Library

It is hard to imagine a world without Shakespeare. Since their composition more than four hundred years ago, Shakespeare's plays and poems have traveled the globe, inviting those who see and read his works to make them their own.

Readers of the New Folger Editions are part of this ongoing process of "taking up Shakespeare," finding our own thoughts and feelings in language that strikes us as old or unusual and, for that very reason, new. We still struggle to keep up with a writer who could think a mile a minute, whose words paint pictures that shift like clouds. These expertly edited texts, presented here with accompanying explanatory notes and up-to-date critical essays, are distinctive because of what they do: they allow readers not simply to keep up, but to engage deeply with a writer whose works invite us to think, and think again.

These New Folger Editions of Shakespeare's plays are also special because of where they come from. The Folger Shakespeare Library in Washington, DC, where the Editions are produced, is the single greatest documentary source of Shakespeare's works. An unparalleled collection of early modern books, manuscripts, and artwork connected to Shakespeare, the Folger's holdings have been consulted extensively in the preparation of these texts. The Editions also reflect the expertise gained through the regular performance of Shakespeare's works in the Folger's Elizabethan Theater.

I want to express my deep thanks to editors Barbara Mowat and Paul Werstine for creating these indispensable editions of Shakespeare's works, which incorporate the best of textual scholarship with a richness of commentary that is both inspired and engaging. Readers who want to know more about Shakespeare and his plays can follow the paths these distinguished scholars have tread by visiting the Folger itself, where a range of physical and digital resources (available online) exist to supplement the material in these texts. I commend to you these words, and hope that they inspire.

Michael Witmore
Director, Folger Shakespeare Library

Contents

Editors' Preface

In recent years, ways of dealing with Shakespeare's texts and with the interpretation of his plays have been undergoing significant change. This edition, while retaining many of the features that have always made the Folger Shakespeare so attractive to the general reader, at the same time reflects these current ways of thinking about Shakespeare. For example, modern readers, actors, and teachers have become interested in the differences between, on the one hand, the early forms in which Shakespeare's plays were first published and, on the other hand, the forms in which editors through the centuries have presented them. In response to this interest, we have based our edition on what we consider the best early printed version of a particular play (explaining our rationale in a section called "An Introduction to This Text") and have marked our changes in the text—unobtrusively, we hope, but in such a way that the curious reader can be aware that a change has been made and can consult the "Textual Notes" to discover what appeared in the early printed version.

Current ways of looking at the plays are reflected in our brief introductions, in many of the commentary notes, in the annotated lists of "Further Reading," and especially in each play's "Modern Perspective," an essay written by an outstanding scholar who brings to the reader his or her fresh assessment of the play in the light of today's interests and concerns.

As in the Folger Library General Reader's Shakespeare, which the New Folger Library Shakespeare replaces, we include explanatory notes designed to help make Shakespeare's language clearer to a modern reader, and we place the notes on the page facing the text that they explain. We also follow the earlier edition in including illustrations—of objects, of clothing, of mythological figures—from books and manuscripts in the Folger Library collection. We provide fresh accounts of the life of Shakespeare, of the publishing of his plays, and of the theaters in which his plays were performed, as well as an introduction to the text itself. We also include a section called "Reading Shakespeare's Language," in which we try to help readers learn to "break the code" of Elizabethan poetic language.

For each section of each volume, we are indebted to a host of generous experts and fellow scholars. The "Reading Shakespeare's Language" sections, for example, could not have been written had not Arthur King, of Brigham Young University, and Randal Robinson, author of *Unlocking Shakespeare's Language,* led the way in untangling Shakespearean language puzzles and shared their insights and methodologies generously with us. "Shakespeare's Life" profited by the careful reading given it by S. Schoenbaum, "Shakespeare's Theater" was read and strengthened by Andrew Gurr, William Ingram, and John Astington, and "The Publication of Shakespeare's Plays" is indebted to the comments of Peter W. M. Blayney. We, as editors, take sole responsibility for any errors in our editions.

We are grateful to the authors of the "Modern Perspectives," to Leeds Barroll and David Bevington for their generous encouragement; to the Huntington and Newberry Libraries for fellowship support; to King's University College for the grants it has provided to Paul Werstine; to the Social Sciences and Humanities Research Council of Canada, which has provided him with Research Time Stipends; to R. J. Shroyer of Western University for essential computer support;

and to the Folger Institute's Center for Shakespeare Studies for its fortuitous sponsorship of a workshop on "Shakespeare's Texts for Students and Teachers" (funded by the National Endowment for the Humanities and led by Richard Knowles of the University of Wisconsin), a workshop from which we learned an enormous amount about what is wanted by college and high-school teachers of Shakespeare today.

In preparing this preface for the publication of *The Taming of the Shrew* in 1992, we wrote: "Our biggest debt is to the Folger Shakespeare Library: to Werner Gundersheimer, Director of the Library, who has made possible our edition; to Jean Miller, the Library's Art Curator, who combed the Library holdings for illustrations, and to Julie Ainsworth, Head of the Photography Department, who carefully photographed them; to Peggy O'Brien, Director of Education, who gave us expert advice about the needs being expressed by Shakespeare teachers and students (and to Martha Christian and other "master teachers" who used our texts in manuscript in their classrooms); to the staff of the Academic Programs Division, especially Paul Menzer (who drafted "Further Reading" material), Mary Tonkinson, Lena Cowen Orlin, Molly Haws, and Jessica Hymowitz; and, finally, to the staff of the Library Reading Room, whose patience and support have been invaluable."

As we revise the play for publication in 2014, we add to the above our gratitude to Michael Witmore, Director of the Folger Shakespeare Library, who brings to our work a gratifying enthusiasm and vision; to Gail Kern Paster, Director of the Library from 2002 until 2011, whose interest and support have been unfailing and whose scholarly expertise continues to be an invaluable resource; to Stephen Llano, our production editor at Simon & Schuster, whose expertise, attention to detail, and wisdom have been essential to this project from the very beginning and to Jonathan Evans and Alysha Bullock, who, as they take over from Stephen on his retirement, are demonstrating their own expertise and professional skills; to Deborah Curren-Aquino, who provides extensive editorial and production support; to Alice Falk for her expert copyediting; to Christina LeMaster and Rebecca Niles for crucial production assistance; to the Folger's Photography Department; to Michael Poston for unfailing computer support; to Kate Lawson for help with Further Reading; and, for especially helpful conversations about *The Shrew* and *A Shrew*, to David Schalkwyk, Director of Research at the Folger from 2009 to 2013. Among the editions we consulted, we found Ann Thompson's updated New Cambridge edition and Barbara Hodgdon's Arden edition especially useful. Finally, we once again express our gratitude to the late Jean Miller for the wonderful images she unearthed from the Folger collection and to the ever-supportive staff of the Library Reading Room.

Barbara A. Mowat and Paul Werstine
2014

Shakespeare's *The Taming of the Shrew*

Love and marriage are the concerns of Shakespeare's *The Taming of the Shrew.* The play offers us some strikingly different models of the process of attracting and choosing a mate and then coming to terms with the mate one has chosen. Some of these models may still seem attractive to us, some not. Lucentio's courtship of and marriage to Bianca are prompted by his idealized love of an apparently ideal woman. When she first appears, Bianca is silent and perfectly obedient to her father. Lucentio then speaks of her as if she were a goddess come to earth. Because her father denies all men the opportunity openly to court Bianca, Lucentio spontaneously throws off his social status as a gentleman in order to disguise himself as a lowly tutor, the only kind of man that Bianca's father, Baptista, will let near her. All that matters to Lucentio is winning Bianca's heart. To marry her—even in secret and in shared defiance of her father—is surely, he believes, to be happy.

An alternative style of wooing adopted by Petruchio in quest of Katherine is notably free of idealism. Petruchio is concerned with money. He takes money from all Bianca's suitors for wooing her older sister, Katherine, who, Baptista has dictated, must be married before Bianca. When Petruchio comes to see Katherine, he first arranges with her father the dowry to be acquired by marrying her. Assured of the money, Petruchio is ready to marry Katherine even against her will. Katherine is the shrew named in the play's title; and, according to all the men but Petruchio, her bad temper denies her the status of "ideal woman" accorded Bianca by Lucen-

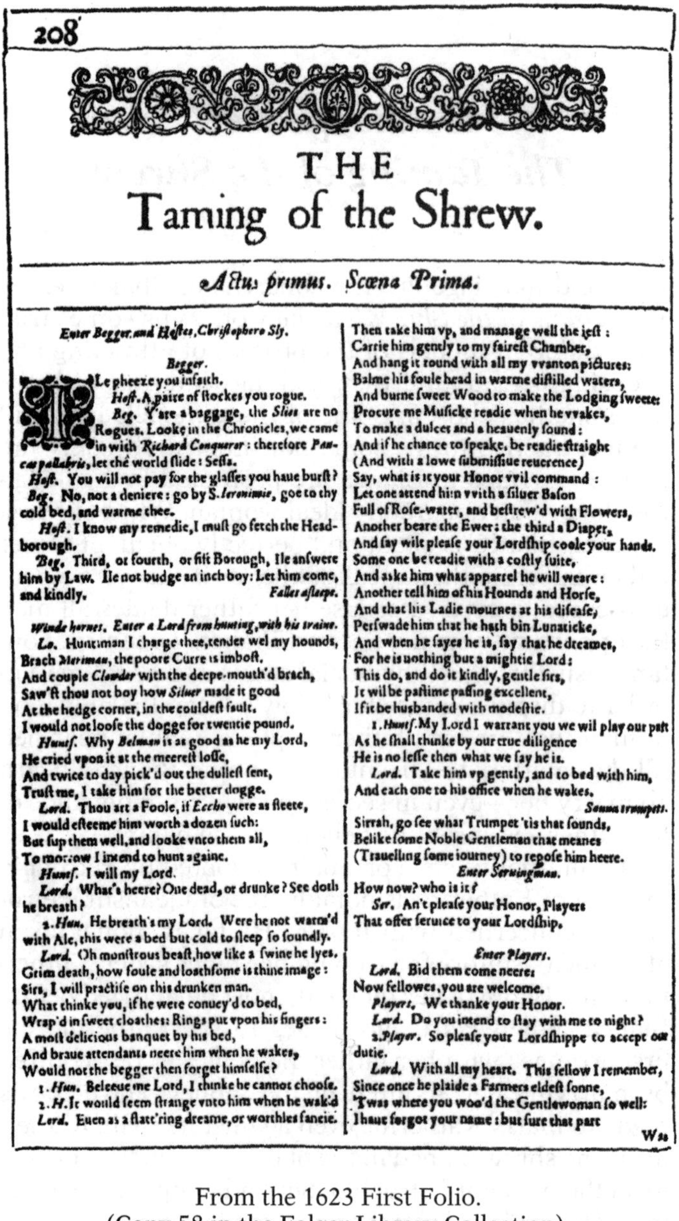
208

THE Taming of the Shrevv.

Actus primus. Scœna Prima.

Enter Begger and Hostes, Christophero Sly.

Begger.

I'Le pheeze you infaith.

Host. A paire of stockes you rogue.

Beg. Y'are a baggage, the *Slies* are no Rogues. Looke in the Chronicles, we came in with *Richard Conqueror*: therefore *Paucas pallabris*, let the world slide: Sessa.

Host. You will not pay for the glasses you haue burst?

Beg. No, not a deniere: go by S. *Ieronimie*, goe to thy cold bed, and warme thee.

Host. I know my remedie, I must go fetch the Headborough.

Beg. Third, or fourth, or fift Borough, Ile answere him by Law. Ile not budge an inch boy: Let him come, and kindly. *Falles asleepe.*

Winde hornes. Enter a Lord from hunting, with his traine.

Lo. Huntsman I charge thee, tender wel my hounds,
Brach *Meriman*, the poore Curre is imbost,
And couple *Clowder* with the deepe-mouth'd brach,
Saw'st thou not boy how *Siluer* made it good
At the hedge corner, in the couldest fault,
I would not loose the dogge for twentie pound.

Huntſ. Why *Belman* is as good as he my Lord,
He cried vpon it at the meerest losse,
And twice to day pick'd out the dullest sent,
Trust me, I take him for the better dogge.

Lord. Thou art a Foole, if *Eccho* were as fleete,
I would esteeme him worth a dozen such:
But sup them well, and looke vnto them all,
To morrow I intend to hunt againe.

Huntſ. I will my Lord.

Lord. What's heere? One dead, or drunke? See doth he breath?

2. Hun. He breath's my Lord. Were he not warm'd with Ale, this were a bed but cold to sleep so soundly.

Lord. Oh monstrous beast, how like a swine he lyes.
Grim death, how foule and loathsome is thine image:
Sirs, I will practise on this drunken man.
What thinke you, if he were conuey'd to bed,
Wrap'd in sweet cloathes: Rings put vpon his fingers:
A most delicious banquet by his bed,
And braue attendants neere him when he wakes,
Would not the begger then forget himselfe?

1. Hun. Beleeue me Lord, I thinke he cannot choose.

2. H. It would seem strange vnto him when he wak'd

Lord. Euen as a flatt'ring dreame, or worthles fancie.
Then take him vp, and manage well the iest:
Carrie him gently to my fairest Chamber,
And hang it round with all my vvanton pictures:
Balme his foule head in warme distilled waters,
And burne sweet Wood to make the Lodging sweete:
Procure me Musicke readie when he vvakes,
To make a dulcet and a heauenly sound:
And if he chance to speake, be readie straight
(And with a lowe submissiue reuerence)
Say, what is it your Honor vvil command:
Let one attend him vvith a siluer Bason
Full of Rose-water, and bestrew'd with Flowers,
Another beare the Ewer: the third a Diaper,
And say wilt please your Lordship coole your hands.
Some one be readie with a costly suite,
And aske him what apparrel he will weare:
Another tell him of his Hounds and Horse,
And that his Ladie mournes at his disease,
Perswade him that he hath bin Lunaticke,
And when he sayes he is, say that he dreames,
For he is nothing but a mightie Lord:
This do, and do it kindly, gentle sirs,
It wil be pastime passing excellent,
If it be husbanded with modestie.

1. Huntſ. My Lord I warrant you we wil play our part
As he shall thinke by our true diligence
He is no lesse then what we say he is.

Lord. Take him vp gently, and to bed with him,
And each one to his office when he wakes.

Sound trumpets.

Sirrah, go see what Trumpet 'tis that sounds,
Belike some Noble Gentleman that meanes
(Trauelling some iourney) to repose him heere.

Enter Seruingman.

How now? who is it?

Ser. An't please your Honor, Players
That offer seruice to your Lordship.

Enter Players.

Lord. Bid them come neere:
Now fellowes, you are welcome.

Players. We thanke your Honor.

Lord. Do you intend to stay with me to night?

2. Player. So please your Lordshippe to accept our dutie.

Lord. With all my heart. This fellow I remember,
Since once he plaide a Farmers eldest sonne,
'Twas where you woo'd the Gentlewoman so well:
I haue forgot your name: but sure that part

Was

From the 1623 First Folio.
(Copy 58 in the Folger Library Collection).

tio. Yet by the end of the play, Katherine, whether she has been tamed or not, certainly acts much changed. Petruchio then claims to have the more successful marriage. But is the marriage of Petruchio and Katherine a superior match—have they truly learned to love each other?—or is it based on terror and deception?

And what of the plot about Christopher Sly, the drunken tinker, with which the play opens, and which we, following editorial tradition, call "The Induction"? The play about Katherine, Petruchio, Bianca, and Bianca's suitors actually begins as a comedy put on for the entertainment of the deceived Christopher Sly—that is, as a play-within-a-play. If we were to take *Taming*'s first two scenes as an opening frame within which the taming play is set, our questions about Katherine's transformation or about Petruchio's taming methods would perhaps need to be reformulated. If, that is, there existed a closing frame (as in other versions, in which the Sly figure watches the whole entertainment and learns from it how to tame his shrewish wife), we might respond to the play-within-the-play as a kind of parody on marriage customs and male fantasies about how women should and should not behave. Because *The Taming of the Shrew* exists in only one early printed form (the one in the 1623 First Folio), and because that printing lacks a closing frame for the Sly story, the opening Sly scenes are considered a prologue rather than part of a frame—though some productions borrow the closing frame from the anonymous T*aming of a Shrew.* (See Appendix, "Framing Dialogue in *The Taming of a Shrew* [1594]," pages 233–45.) This basic question about how seriously we are to take its plots and characters may be the most intriguing question presented us by *The Taming of the Shrew.*

After you have read the play, we invite you to read "*The Taming of the Shrew:* A Modern Perspective" by Professor Karen Newman of Brown University.

". . . fair Padua, nursery of arts." (1.1.2)

From Pietro Bertelli, *Theatrum vrbium Italicarum* . . . (1599).

Reading Shakespeare's Language: *The Taming of the Shrew*

For many people today, reading Shakespeare's language can be a problem—but it is a problem that can be solved. Those who have studied Latin (or even French or German or Spanish), and those who are used to reading poetry, will have little difficulty understanding the language of Shakespeare's poetic drama. Others, however, need to develop the skills of untangling unusual sentence structures and of recognizing and understanding poetic compressions, omissions, and wordplay. And even those skilled in reading unusual sentence structures may have occasional trouble with Shakespeare's words. More than four hundred years of "static"—caused by changes in language and life—intervene between his speaking and our hearing. Most of his immense vocabulary is still in use, but a few of his words are no longer used, and many of his words now have meanings quite different from those they had in the sixteenth century. In the theater, most of these difficulties are solved for us by actors who study the language and articulate it for us so that the essential meaning is heard—or, when combined with stage action, is at least *felt*. When reading on one's own, one must do what each actor does: go over the lines (often with a dictionary close at hand) until the puzzles are solved and the lines yield up their poetry and the characters speak in words and phrases that are, suddenly, rewarding and wonderfully memorable.

Shakespeare's Words

As you begin to read the opening scenes of a play by Shakespeare, you may notice occasional unfamiliar words. Some are unfamiliar simply because we no longer use them. In the opening scenes of *The Taming of the Shrew,* for example, you will find the words *feeze you* (i.e., fix you, do for you), *an* (i.e., if), *bestraught* (i.e., distracted), and *iwis* (i.e., certainly). Words of this kind are explained in notes to the text and will become familiar the more of Shakespeare's plays you read.

In *The Taming of the Shrew,* as in all of Shakespeare's writing, more problematic are the words that we still use but that now have different meanings. In the opening scenes of *The Taming of the Shrew,* for example, the word *heavy* has the meaning of "grave," the word *envious* is used where we would say "malicious," *brave* where we would say "splendid," *idle* where we would say "silly," and *curst* where we would say "bad-tempered." Such words will be explained in the notes to the text, but they, too, will become familiar as you continue to read Shakespeare's language.

Some words are strange not because of the "static" introduced by changes in language over the past centuries but because these are words that Shakespeare uses to build a dramatic world that has its own space and time. *The Taming of the Shrew* is a particularly complicated example of Shakespeare's construction of a dramatic world in that he creates one world in what we call the "Induction"—a world inhabited by an English beggar and an English lord and his attendants—and then creates a second, Italian, world for the main body of the play. In the Induction we find *rogues, stocks,* and *headboroughs,* as well as references to deep-mouthed brachs, wanton pictures, obeisances, and embracements. In the opening scenes of the main body of the play, the setting in Italy and the story's focus on wooing are created through repeated references to Padua, to Lombardy, to Pisa, to dowries, to Ovid, to poesy, and to Minerva, and through such Italian phrases as *Mi perdonato* and *basta.* These "local" references create the Padua that Kate, Petruchio, Lucentio, and Bianca inhabit and will become increasingly familiar to you as you get further into the play.

Shakespeare's Sentences

In an English sentence, meaning is quite dependent on the place given each word. "The dog bit the boy" and "The boy bit the dog" mean very different things, even though the individual words are the same. Because English places such importance on the positions of words in sentences, on the way words are arranged, unusual arrangements can puzzle a reader. Shakespeare frequently shifts his sentences away from "normal" English arrangements—often in order to create the rhythm he seeks, sometimes in order to use a line's poetic rhythm to emphasize a particular word, sometimes to give a character his or her own speech patterns or to allow the character to speak in a special way. When we attend a good performance of the play, the actors will have worked out the sentence structures and will articulate the sentences so that the meaning is clear. When reading the play, we need to do as the actor does: that is, when puzzled by a character's speech, we check to see if words are being presented in an unusual sequence.

Shakespeare often places the verb before the subject (e.g., instead of "he goes," we find "goes he"). In the Induction to *The Taming of the Shrew,* we find such a construction when Christopher Sly is told "Hence comes it that your kindred shuns your house" (Ind.2.28) (instead of "Hence it comes that . . ."); Hortensio uses this same kind of construction when, at 1.1.87–88, he says, "*Sorry am I* that our goodwill effects / Bianca's grief." Such inversions rarely cause much confusion. More problematic is Shakespeare's frequent placing of the object before the subject and verb (e.g., instead of "I hit him," we might find "him I hit"). Baptista's "Schoolmasters will I keep" (1.1.96) is an example of such an inversion, as are Lucentio's "Vincentio's son . . . / It shall become" (1.1.14–15), and Petruchio's "Crowns in my purse I have" (1.2.58). Occasionally in *The Taming of the Shrew* (which is one of Shakespeare's very early plays), the subject-verb-object sequencing is unusually contorted, as in Baptista's "For how I firmly am resolved you know" (1.1.49, where the normal sentence order would be "For you know how I am firmly resolved"). Here, and elsewhere, the inversions serve primarily to create regular iambic pentameter lines.

Inversions are not the only unusual sentence structures in Shakespeare's language. Often in his sentences words that would normally appear together are separated from each other. (Again, this is often done to create a particular rhythm or to stress a particular word.) Take, for example, Hortensio's "Her only fault, and that is faults enough, / Is that she is intolerable curst" (1.2.89–90); here the phrase "and that is faults enough" separates the subject ("fault") from its verb ("Is"). Or take Lucentio's lines that begin at 1.1.153, "*I found* the effect of love-in-idleness, / *And* now in plainness *do confess* to thee / That art to me as secret and as dear / As Anna to the Queen of Carthage was: / Tranio, *I burn, I pine!*" Here the normal construction "I found . . . and . . . do confess . . . : I burn, I pine" is interrupted by the insertion of a series of phrases and clauses. In order to create sentences that seem more like the English of everyday speech, you can rearrange the words, putting together the word clusters ("her fault is that," "do confess: I burn, I pine"). The result will usually be an increase in clarity but a loss of rhythm or a shift in emphasis.

Locating and rearranging words that "belong together" is especially necessary in passages with long delaying or expanding interruptions. Tranio uses such an interrupted construction when he says to Lucentio at 1.1.217–22

In brief, sir, *sith it your pleasure is,*
And I am tied to be obedient
(For so your father charged me at our parting:
"Be serviceable to my son," quoth he,
Although I think 'twas in another sense),
I am content to be Lucentio.

In some plays (*Hamlet,* for instance), long interrupted sentences are used to catch the audience up in the narrative or are used as a characterizing device. In *The Taming of the Shrew,* the interruptions are more often simply extra bits of detail. Lucentio's opening speech in 1.1, for instance, includes descriptive details for almost every city or person named:

Tranio, since for [i.e., because of] the great desire I had
To see fair Padua, *nursery of arts,*
I am arrived for [i.e., have arrived in] fruitful Lombardy,
The pleasant garden of great Italy,
And by my father's love and leave am armed
With his goodwill and thy good company.
My trusty servant *well approved in all,*
Here let us breathe [i.e., remain] and haply institute
A course of learning and ingenious studies.

> Pisa, *renownèd for grave citizens,*
> Gave me my being, and my father first,
> *A merchant of great traffic through the world,*
> Vincentio, *come of the Bentivolii.*
> Vincentio's son, *brought up in Florence,*
> It shall become to serve all hopes conceived
> To deck his fortune with his virtuous deeds.

Such descriptive details lengthen the sentences and, in combination with such inversions as "Vincentio's son . . . It shall become," give the verse a formal quality that marks it off both from the play's prose passages and from the much simpler and more straightforward verse of the Induction.

In several passages in *The Taming of the Shrew,* Shakespeare not only interrupts with details but piles up detail to create extraordinary speeches (see, for example, the description of Petruchio's wedding clothes and his horse [3.2.42–62] and the description of the wedding itself [3.2.160–67]). Such speeches are hard to appreciate when read silently (especially since so many of the words he selects here are no longer in our vocabularies), but come wonderfully alive as grotesque, farcical verbal riffs when delivered aloud.

Shakespearean Wordplay

Shakespeare plays with language so often and so variously that entire books are written on the topic. Here we will mention only two kinds of wordplay, puns and metaphors. A pun is a play on words that sound the same but that have different meanings. In *The Taming of the Shrew* the scene that introduces us to Petruchio includes a long argument between Petruchio and his servant Grumio (1.2.5–21, 38–44) that turns on the word *knock* and the phrase *knock me,* by which Petruchio means "knock for me [on the gate]," but which Grumio interprets as "hit me." In 1.1, when Kate enters she says to Baptista, "I pray you, sir, is it your will / To make a stale [i.e., laughingstock] of me amongst these mates?" *Mates* here means "fellows." Hortensio replies with "'Mates,' maid? How mean you that? No mates for you / Unless you were of gentler, milder mold," where *mates* means "husbands." The first scene between Kate and Petruchio (2.1.190–293) is built around a whole series of puns, beginning with puns on the name Kate (delicacies are known as "cates") and including puns on *sounded, movables, bear, light, take, crest, crab, arms,* and *tale/tail.* (In the glosses to this text, puns are often indicated by numbered meanings; e.g., *crab* [at 2.1.243] is glossed as "(1) crab apple; (2) sour-faced person.") In all of Shakespeare's plays, one must stay alert to the sounds of words and to the possibility of double meanings. In *The Taming of the Shrew,* many scenes are funny only if we hear the puns.

A metaphor is a play on words in which one object or idea is expressed as if it were something else, something with which it is said to share common features. *The Taming of the Shrew* is not rich in metaphoric language, but at one point, when Petruchio describes his method of "taming" Kate (at 4.1.190–96), he uses metaphor in a powerful and significant way:

My falcon now is sharp and passing empty,
And, till she stoop, she must not be full-gorged,
For then she never looks upon her lure.
Another way I have to man my haggard,
To make her come and know her keeper's call.
That is, to watch her, as we watch these kites
That bate and beat and will not be obedient.

Here, in an extended metaphor, Kate is a falcon being tamed by its master, a "haggard" (i.e., a female hawk) being "manned," being made to "stoop." The language is taken from manuals for the training of hawks, and the metaphor works out in careful detail Petruchio's image of himself as trainer and Kate as the hawk he is taming.

Implied Stage Action

Finally, in reading Shakespeare's plays we must always remember that what we are reading is a performance script. The dialogue is written to be spoken by actors who, at the same time, are moving, gesturing, picking up objects, weeping, shaking their fists. Some stage action is described in what are called "stage directions"; some is suggested within the dialogue itself. We must learn to be alert to such signals as we stage the play in our imaginations. When, in *The Taming of the Shrew* 1.1.212–13, Lucentio says, "Tranio, at once / Uncase thee. Take my colored hat and cloak," it is clear, from later dialogue in the scene, that they here exchange clothes; in 1.2.28–29, when Hortensio says, "Rise, Grumio, rise," it is equally clear that at some previous point Grumio has fallen. At several places in *The Taming of the Shrew,* signals to the reader are not quite so clear. When, after Kate and Petruchio's first meeting, Petruchio claims, untruthfully, that he and she have fallen in love and agreed to marry, and he says (2.1.333) "Give me thy hand, Kate," it is not at all clear that she does as he asks; nor do we know exactly what should happen a few lines later when her father says, "Give me your hands." Since he then says to Petruchio, "'Tis a match," we can assume that Petruchio, at least, gives Baptista his hand, but the actor playing Katherine—and we as readers—must decide whether Katherine allows him to join their hands or refuses to do so. Even more interesting challenges are offered by the final scene of the play, where Katherine, having spoken eloquently about the proper duties of a wife, concludes her speech by saying to the other women: "place your hands below your husband's foot; / In token of which duty, if he please, / My hand is ready, may it do him ease" (5.2.193–95). Katherine may here stoop and place her hand under Petruchio's foot—this is the case in many productions. If she does, the picture of her subjugation (or her happy acceptance of her new role) is quite different than if she merely offers to do so. The text leaves open interesting possibilities for staging this moment.

It is immensely rewarding to work carefully with Shakespeare's language—with the words, the sentences, the wordplay, and the implied stage action—as readers for the past four centuries have discovered. It may be more pleasurable to attend a good performance of a play—though not everyone has thought so. But the joy of being able to stage a Shakespeare play in one's imagination, to return to passages that continue to yield further meanings (or further questions) the more one reads them—these are pleasures that, for many, rival (or at least augment) those of the performed text, and certainly make it worth considerable effort to "break the code" of Elizabethan poetic drama and let free the remarkable language that makes up a Shakespeare text.

Shakespeare's Life

Surviving documents that give us glimpses into the life of William Shakespeare show us a playwright, poet, and actor who grew up in the market town of Stratford-upon-Avon, spent his professional life in London, and returned to Stratford a wealthy landowner. He was born in April 1564, died in April 1616, and is buried inside the chancel of Holy Trinity Church in Stratford.

We wish we could know more about the life of the world's greatest dramatist. His plays and poems are testaments to his wide reading—especially to his knowledge of Virgil, Ovid, Plutarch, Holinshed's *Chronicles*, and the Bible—and to his mastery of the English language, but we can only speculate about his education. We know that the King's New School in Stratford-upon-Avon was considered excellent. The school was one of the English "grammar schools" established to educate young men, primarily in Latin grammar and literature. As in other schools of the time, students began their studies at the age of four or five in the attached "petty school," and there learned to read and write in English, studying primarily the catechism from the Book of Common Prayer. After two years in the petty school, students entered the lower form (grade) of the grammar school, where they began the serious study of Latin grammar and Latin texts that would occupy most of the remainder of their school days. (Several Latin texts that Shakespeare used repeatedly in writing his plays and poems were texts that schoolboys memorized and recited.) Latin comedies were introduced early in the lower form; in the upper form, which the boys entered at age ten or eleven, students wrote their own Latin orations and declamations, studied Latin

Title page of a 1573 Latin and Greek catechism for children.
From Alexander Nowell, *Catechismus paruus pueris primum Latine* . . . (1573).

historians and rhetoricians, and began the study of Greek using the Greek New Testament.

Since the records of the Stratford "grammar school" do not survive, we cannot prove that William Shakespeare attended the school; however, every indication (his father's position as an alderman and bailiff of Stratford, the playwright's own knowledge of the Latin classics, scenes in the plays that recall grammar-school experiences—for example, *The Merry Wives of Windsor,* 4.1) suggests that he did. We also lack generally accepted documentation about Shakespeare's life after his schooling ended and his professional life in London began. His marriage in 1582 (at age eighteen) to Anne Hathaway and the subsequent births of his daughter Susanna (1583) and the twins Judith and Hamnet (1585) are recorded, but how he supported himself and where he lived are not known. Nor do we know when and why he left Stratford for the London theatrical world, nor how he rose to be the important figure in that world that he had become by the early 1590s.

We do know that by 1592 he had achieved some prominence in London as both an actor and a playwright. In that year was published a book by the playwright Robert Greene attacking an actor who had the audacity to write blank-verse drama and who was "in his own conceit [i.e., opinion] the only Shake-scene in a country." Since Greene's attack includes a parody of a line from one of Shakespeare's early plays, there is little doubt that it is Shakespeare to whom he refers, a "Shake-scene" who had aroused Greene's fury by successfully competing with university-educated dramatists like Greene himself. It was in 1593 that Shakespeare became a published poet. In that year he published his long narrative poem *Venus and Adonis*; in 1594, he followed it with *The Rape of Lucrece.* Both poems were dedicated to the young earl of Southampton (Henry Wriothesley), who may have become Shakespeare's patron.

It seems no coincidence that Shakespeare wrote these narrative poems at a time when the theaters were closed because of the plague, a contagious epidemic disease that devastated the population of London. When the theaters reopened in 1594, Shakespeare apparently resumed his double career of actor and playwright and began his long (and seemingly profitable) service as an acting-company shareholder. Records for December of 1594 show him to be a leading member of the Lord Chamberlain's Men. It was this company of actors, later named the King's Men, for whom he would be a principal actor, dramatist, and shareholder for the rest of his career.

So far as we can tell, that career spanned about twenty years. In the 1590s, he wrote his plays on English history as well as several comedies and at least two tragedies (*Titus Andronicus* and *Romeo and Juliet*). These histories, comedies, and tragedies are the plays credited to him in 1598 in a work, *Palladis Tamia*, that in one chapter compares English writers with "Greek, Latin, and Italian Poets." There the author, Francis Meres, claims that Shakespeare is comparable to the Latin dramatists Seneca for tragedy and Plautus for comedy, and calls him "the most excellent in both kinds for the stage." He also names him "Mellifluous and honey-tongued Shakespeare": "I say," writes Meres, "that the Muses would speak with Shakespeare's fine filed phrase, if they would speak English." Since Meres also mentions Shakespeare's "sugared sonnets among his private friends," it is assumed that many of Shakespeare's sonnets (not published until 1609) were also written in the 1590s.

In 1599, Shakespeare's company built a theater for themselves across the river from London, naming it the Globe. The plays that are considered by many to be Shakespeare's major tragedies (*Hamlet, Othello, King Lear*, and *Macbeth*) were written while the company was resident in this theater, as were such comedies as *Twelfth Night* and *Measure for Measure*. Many of Shakespeare's plays were performed at court (both for Queen Elizabeth I and, after her death in 1603, for King James I), some were presented at the Inns of Court (the residences of London's legal societies), and some were doubtless performed in other towns, at the universities, and at great houses when the King's Men went on tour; otherwise, his plays from 1599 to 1608 were, so far as we know, performed only at the Globe. Between 1608 and 1612, Shakespeare wrote several plays—among them *The Winter's Tale* and *The Tempest*—presumably for the company's new indoor Blackfriars theater, though the plays were performed also at the Globe and at court. Surviving documents describe a performance of *The Winter's Tale* in 1611 at the Globe, for example, and performances of *The Tempest* in 1611 and 1613 at the royal palace of Whitehall.

Shakespeare seems to have written very little after 1612, the year in which he probably wrote *King Henry VIII*. (It was at a performance of *Henry VIII* in 1613 that the Globe caught fire and burned to the ground.) Sometime between 1610 and 1613, according to many biographers, he returned to live in Stratford-upon-Avon, where he owned a large house and considerable property, and where his wife and his two daughters lived. (His son Hamnet had died in 1596.) However, other biographers suggest that Shakespeare did not leave London for good until much closer to the time of his death. During his professional years in London, Shakespeare had presumably derived income from the acting company's profits as well as from his own career as an actor, from the sale of his play manuscripts to the

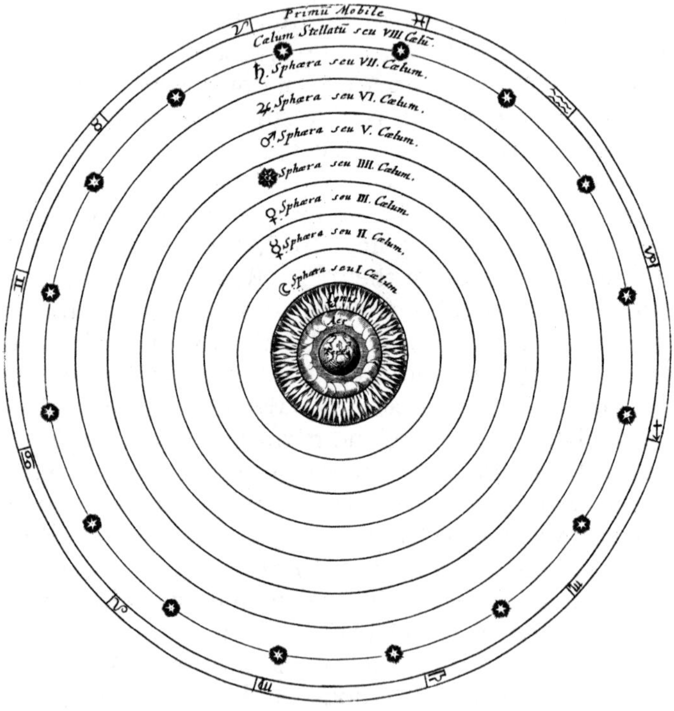

Ptolemaic universe.
From Marcus Manilius, *The sphere of* . . . (1675).

acting company, and, after 1599, from his shares as an owner of the Globe. It was presumably that income, carefully invested in land and other property, that made him the wealthy man that surviving documents show him to have become. It is also assumed that William Shakespeare's growing wealth and reputation played some part in inclining the Crown, in 1596, to grant John Shakespeare, William's father, the coat of arms that he had so long sought. William Shakespeare died in Stratford on April 23, 1616 (according to the epitaph carved under his bust in Holy Trinity Church) and was buried on April 25. Seven years after his death, his collected plays were published as *Mr. William Shakespeares Comedies, Histories, & Tragedies* (the work now known as the First Folio).

The years in which Shakespeare wrote were among the most exciting in English history. Intellectually, the discovery, translation, and printing of Greek and Roman classics were making available a set of works and worldviews that interacted complexly with Christian texts and beliefs. The result was a questioning, a vital intellectual ferment, that provided energy for the period's amazing dramatic and literary output and that fed directly into Shakespeare's plays. The Ghost in *Hamlet*, for example, is wonderfully complicated in part because he is a figure from Roman tragedy—the spirit of the dead returning to seek revenge—who at the same time inhabits a Christian hell (or purgatory); Hamlet's description of humankind reflects at one moment the Neoplatonic wonderment at mankind ("What a piece of work is a man!") and, at the next, the Christian view of the human condition ("And yet, to me, what is this quintessence of dust?").

As intellectual horizons expanded, so also did geographical and cosmological horizons. New worlds—both North and South America—were explored, and in them were found human beings who lived and worshiped in ways radically different from those of Renaissance Europeans and Englishmen. The universe during these years also seemed to shift and expand. Copernicus had earlier theorized that the earth was not the center of the cosmos but revolved as a planet around the sun. Galileo's telescope, created in 1609, allowed scientists to see that Copernicus had been correct: the universe was not organized with the earth at the center, nor was it so nicely circumscribed as people had, until that time, thought. In terms of expanding horizons, the impact of these discoveries on people's beliefs—religious, scientific, and philosophical—cannot be overstated.

London, too, rapidly expanded and changed during the years (from the early 1590s to around 1610) that Shakespeare lived there. London—the center of England's government, its economy, its royal court, its overseas trade—was, during these years, becoming an exciting metropolis, drawing to it thousands of new citizens every year. Troubled by overcrowding, by poverty, by recurring epidemics of the plague, London was also a mecca for the wealthy and the aristocratic, and for those who sought advancement at court, or power in government or finance or trade. One hears in Shakespeare's plays the voices of London—the struggles for power, the fear of venereal disease, the language of buying and selling. One hears as well the voices of Stratford-upon-Avon—references to the nearby Forest of Arden, to sheepherding, to small-town gossip, to village fairs and markets. Part of the richness of Shakespeare's work is the influence felt there of the various worlds in which he lived: the world of metropolitan London, the world of small-town and rural England, the world of the theater, and the worlds of craftsmen and shepherds.

That Shakespeare inhabited such worlds we know from surviving London and Stratford documents, as well as from the evidence of the plays and poems themselves. From such records we can sketch the dramatist's life. We know from his works that he was a voracious reader. We know from legal and business documents that he was a multifaceted theater man who became a wealthy landowner. We know a bit about his family life and a fair amount about his legal and financial dealings. Most scholars today depend upon such evidence as they draw their picture of the world's greatest playwright. Such, however, has not always been the case. Until the late eighteenth century, the William Shakespeare who lived in most biographies was the creation of legend and tradition. This was the Shakespeare who was supposedly caught poaching deer at Charlecote, the estate of Sir Thomas Lucy close by Stratford; this was the Shakespeare who fled from Sir Thomas's vengeance and made his way in London by taking care of horses outside a playhouse; this was the Shakespeare who reportedly could barely read, but whose natural gifts were extraordinary, whose father was a butcher who allowed his gifted son sometimes to help in the butcher shop, where William supposedly killed calves "in a high style," making a speech for the occasion. It was this legendary William Shakespeare whose Falstaff (in *1* and *2 Henry IV*) so pleased Queen Elizabeth that she demanded a play about Falstaff in love, and demanded that it be written in fourteen days (hence the existence of *The Merry Wives of Windsor*). It was this legendary Shakespeare who reached the top of his acting career in the roles of the Ghost in *Hamlet* and old Adam in *As You Like It*—and who died of a fever contracted by drinking too hard at "a merry meeting" with the poets Michael Drayton and Ben Jonson. This legendary Shakespeare is a rambunctious, undisciplined man, as attractively "wild" as his plays were seen by earlier generations to be. Unfortunately, there is no trace of evidence to support these wonderful stories.

Perhaps in response to the disreputable Shakespeare of legend—or perhaps in response to the fragmentary and, for some, all-too-ordinary Shakespeare documented by surviving records—some people since the mid-nineteenth century have argued that William Shakespeare could not have written the plays that bear his name. These persons have put forward some dozen names as more likely authors, among them Queen Elizabeth, Sir Francis Bacon, Edward de Vere (earl of Oxford), and Christopher Marlowe. Such attempts to find what for these people is a more believable author of the plays is a tribute to the regard in which the plays are held. Unfortunately for their claims, the documents that exist that provide evidence for the facts of Shakespeare's life tie him inextricably to the body of plays and poems that bear his name. Unlikely as it seems to those who want the works to have been written by an aristocrat, a university graduate, or an "important" person, the plays and poems seem clearly to have been produced by a man from Stratford-upon-Avon with a very good "grammar-school" education and a life of experience in London and in the world of the London theater. How this particular man produced the works that dominate the cultures of much of the world almost four hundred years after his death is one of life's mysteries—and one that will continue to tease our imaginations as we continue to delight in his plays and poems.

Shakespeare's Theater

The actors of Shakespeare's time are known to have performed plays in a great variety of locations. They played at court (that is, in the great halls of such royal residences as Whitehall, Hampton Court, and Greenwich); they played in halls at the universities of Oxford and Cambridge, and at the Inns of Court (the residences in London of the legal societies); and they also played in the private houses of great lords and civic officials. Sometimes acting companies went on tour from London into the provinces, often (but not only) when outbreaks of bubonic plague in the capital forced the closing of theaters to reduce the possibility of contagion in crowded audiences. In the provinces the actors usually staged their plays in churches (until around 1600) or in guildhalls. While surviving records show only a handful of occasions when actors played at inns while on tour, London inns were important playing places up until the 1590s.

The building of theaters in London had begun only shortly before Shakespeare wrote his first plays in the 1590s. These theaters were of two kinds: outdoor or public playhouses that could accommodate large numbers of playgoers, and indoor or private theaters for much smaller audiences. What is usually regarded as the first London outdoor public playhouse was called simply the Theatre. James Burbage—the father of Richard Burbage, who was perhaps the most famous actor in Shakespeare's company—built it in 1576 in an area north of the city of London called Shoreditch. Among the more famous of the other public playhouses that capitalized on the new fashion were the Curtain and the Fortune (both also built north of the city), the Rose,

A stylized representation of the Globe theater.
From Claes Jansz Visscher, *Londinum florentissima Britanniae urbs* . . . [c. 1625].

the Swan, the Globe, and the Hope (all located on the Bankside, a region just across the Thames south of the city of London). All these playhouses had to be built outside the jurisdiction of the city of London because many civic officials were hostile to the performance of drama and repeatedly petitioned the royal council to abolish it.

The theaters erected on the Bankside (a region under the authority of the Church of England, whose head was the monarch) shared the neighborhood with houses of prostitution and with the Paris Garden, where the blood sports of bearbaiting and bullbaiting were carried on. There may have been no clear distinction between playhouses and buildings for such sports, for we know that the Hope was used for both plays and baiting and that Philip Henslowe, owner of the Rose and, later, partner in the ownership of the Fortune, was also a partner in a monopoly on baiting. All these forms of entertainment were easily accessible to Londoners by boat across the Thames or over London Bridge.

Evidently Shakespeare's company prospered on the Bankside. They moved there in 1599. Threatened by difficulties in renewing the lease on the land where their first theater (the Theatre) had been built, Shakespeare's company took advantage of the Christmas holiday in 1598 to dismantle the Theatre and transport its timbers across the Thames to the Bankside, where, in 1599, these timbers were used in the building of the Globe. The weather in late December 1598 is recorded as having been especially harsh. It was so cold that the Thames was "nigh [nearly] frozen," and there was heavy snow. Perhaps the weather aided Shakespeare's company in eluding their landlord, the snow hiding their activity and the freezing of the Thames allowing them to slide the timbers across to the Bankside without paying tolls for repeated trips over London Bridge.

Attractive as this narrative is, it remains just as likely that the heavy snow hampered transport of the timbers in wagons through the London streets to the river. It also must be remembered that the Thames was, according to report, only "nigh frozen," and therefore did not necessarily provide solid footing. Whatever the precise circumstances of this fascinating event in English theater history, Shakespeare's company was able to begin playing at their new Globe theater on the Bankside in 1599. After this theater burned down in 1613 during the staging of Shakespeare's *Henry VIII* (its thatch roof was set alight by cannon fire called for in performance), Shakespeare's company immediately rebuilt on the same location. The second Globe seems to have been a grander structure than its predecessor. It remained in use until the beginning of the English Civil War in 1642, when Parliament officially closed the theaters. Soon thereafter it was pulled down.

The public theaters of Shakespeare's time were very different buildings from our theaters today. First of all, they were open-air playhouses. As recent excavations of the Rose and the Globe confirm, some were polygonal or roughly circular in shape; the Fortune, however, was square. The most recent estimates of their size put the diameter of these buildings at 72 feet (the Rose) to 100 feet (the Globe), but we know that they held vast audiences of two or three thousand, who must have been squeezed together quite tightly. Some of these spectators paid extra to sit or stand in the two or three levels of roofed galleries that extended, on the upper levels, all the way around the theater and surrounded an open space. In this space were the stage and, perhaps, the tiring house (what we would call dressing rooms), as well as the so-called yard. In the yard stood the spectators who chose to pay less, the ones whom Hamlet contemptuously called "groundlings." For a roof they had only the sky, and so they were exposed to all kinds of weather. They stood on a floor that was sometimes made of mortar and sometimes of ash mixed with the shells of hazelnuts, which, it has recently been discovered, were standard flooring material in the period.

Unlike the yard, the stage itself was covered by a roof. Its ceiling, called "the heavens," is thought to have been elaborately painted to depict the sun, moon, stars, and planets. The exact size of the stage remains hard to determine. We have a single sketch of part of the interior of the Swan. A Dutchman named Johannes de Witt visited this theater around 1596 and sent a sketch of it back to his friend, Arend van Buchel. Because van Buchel found de Witt's letter and sketch of interest, he copied both into a book. It is van Buchel's copy, adapted, it seems, to the shape and size of the page in his book, that survives. In this sketch, the stage appears to be a large rectangular platform that thrusts far out into the yard, perhaps even as far as the center of the circle formed by the surrounding galleries. This drawing, combined with the specifications for the size of the stage in the building contract for the Fortune, has led scholars to conjecture that the stage on which Shakespeare's plays were performed must have measured approximately 43 feet in width and 27 feet in depth, a vast acting area. But the digging up of a large part of the Rose by late-twentieth-century archaeologists has provided evidence of a quite different stage design. The Rose stage was a platform tapered at the corners and much shallower than what seems to be depicted in the van Buchel sketch. Indeed, its measurements seem to be about 37.5 feet across at its widest point and only 15.5 feet deep. Because the surviving indications of stage size and design differ from each other so much, it is possible that the stages in other theaters, like the Theatre, the Curtain, and the Globe (the outdoor playhouses where we know that Shakespeare's plays were performed), were different from those at both the Swan and the Rose.

After about 1608 Shakespeare's plays were staged not only at the Globe but also at an indoor or private playhouse in Blackfriars. This theater had been constructed in 1596 by James Burbage in an upper hall of a former Dominican priory or monastic house. Although Henry VIII had dissolved all English monasteries in the 1530s (shortly after he had founded the Church of England), the area remained under church, rather than hostile civic, control. The hall that Burbage had purchased and renovated was a large one in which Parliament had once met. In the private theater that he constructed, the stage, lit by candles, was built across the narrow end of the hall, with boxes flanking it. The rest of the hall offered seating room only. Because there was no provision for standing room, the largest audience it could hold was less than a thousand, or about a quarter of what the Globe could accommodate. Admission to Blackfriars was correspondingly more expensive. Instead of a penny to stand in the yard at the Globe, it cost a minimum of sixpence to get into Blackfriars. The best seats at the Globe (in the Lords' Room in the gallery above and behind the stage) cost sixpence; but the boxes flanking the stage at Blackfriars were half a crown, or five times sixpence. Some spectators who were particularly interested in displaying themselves paid even more to sit on stools on the Blackfriars stage.

Whether in the outdoor or indoor playhouses, the stages of Shakespeare's time were different from ours. They were not separated from the audience by the dropping of a curtain between acts and scenes. Therefore the playwrights of the time had to find other ways of signaling to the audience that one scene (to be imagined as occurring in one location at a given time) had ended and the next (to be imagined at perhaps a different location at a later time) had begun. The customary way used by Shakespeare and many of his contemporaries was to have everyone on stage exit at the end of one scene and have one or more different characters enter to begin the next. In a few cases, where characters remain onstage from one scene to another, the dialogue or stage action makes the change of location clear, and the characters are generally to be imagined as having moved from one place to another. For example, in *Romeo and Juliet*, Romeo and his friends remain onstage in Act 1 from scene 4 to scene 5, but they are represented as having moved between scenes from the street that leads to Capulet's house into Capulet's house itself. The new location is signaled in part by the appearance onstage of Capulet's servingmen carrying table napkins, something they would not take into the streets. Playwrights had to be quite resourceful in the use of hand properties, like the napkin, or in the use of dialogue to specify where the action was taking place in their plays because, in contrast to most of today's theaters, the playhouses of Shakespeare's time did not fill the stage with scenery to make the setting precise. A consequence of this difference was that the playwrights of Shakespeare's time did not have to specify exactly where the action of their plays was set when they did not choose to do so, and much of the action of their plays is tied to no specific place.

Usually Shakespeare's stage is referred to as a "bare stage," to distinguish it from the stages of the last two or three centuries with their elaborate sets. But the stage in Shakespeare's time was not completely bare. Philip Henslowe, owner of the Rose, lists in his inventory of stage properties a rock, three tombs, and two mossy banks. Stage directions in plays of the time also call for such things as thrones (or “states”), banquets (presumably tables with plaster replicas of food on them), and beds and tombs to be pushed onto the stage. Thus the stage often held more than the actors.

The actors did not limit their performing to the stage alone. Occasionally they went beneath the stage, as the Ghost appears to do in the first act of *Hamlet.* From there they could emerge onto the stage through a trapdoor. They could retire behind the hangings across the back of the stage, as, for example, the actor playing Polonius does when he hides behind the arras. Sometimes the hangings could be drawn back during a performance to “discover” one or more actors behind them. When performance required that an actor appear “above,” as when Juliet is imagined to stand at the window of her chamber in the famous and misnamed “balcony scene,” then the actor probably climbed the stairs to the gallery over the back of the stage and temporarily shared it with some of the spectators. The stage was also provided with ropes and winches so that actors could descend from, and reascend to, the “heavens.”

Perhaps the greatest difference between dramatic performances in Shakespeare’s time and ours was that in Shakespeare’s England the roles of women were played by boys. (Some of these boys grew up to take male roles in their maturity.) There were no women in the acting companies. It was not so in Europe, and it had not always been so in the history of the English stage. There are records of women on English stages in the thirteenth and fourteenth centuries, two hundred years before Shakespeare’s plays were performed. After the accession of James I in 1603, the queen of England and her ladies took part in entertainments at court called masques, and with the reopening of the theaters in 1660 at the restoration of Charles II, women again took their place on the public stage.

The chief competitors of such acting companies as the one to which Shakespeare belonged and for which he wrote were companies of exclusively boy actors. The competition was most intense in the early 1600s. There were then two principal children's companies: the Children of Paul's (the choirboys from St. Paul's Cathedral, whose private playhouse was near the cathedral); and the Children of the Chapel Royal (the choirboys from the monarch's private chapel, who performed at the Blackfriars theater built by Burbage in 1596). In *Hamlet* Shakespeare writes of "an aerie [nest] of children, little eyases [hawks], that cry out on the top of question and are most tyrannically clapped for 't. These are now the fashion and . . . berattle the common stages [attack the public theaters]." In the long run, the adult actors prevailed. The Children of Paul's dissolved around 1606. By about 1608 the Children of the Chapel Royal had been forced to stop playing at the Blackfriars theater, which was then taken over by the King's Men, Shakespeare's own troupe.

Acting companies and theaters of Shakespeare's time seem to have been organized in various ways. For example, with the building of the Globe, Shakespeare's company apparently managed itself, with the principal actors, Shakespeare among them, having the status of "sharers" and the right to a share in the takings, as well as the responsibility for a part of the expenses. Five of the sharers, including Shakespeare, owned the Globe. As actor, as sharer in an acting company and in ownership of theaters, and as playwright, Shakespeare was about as involved in the theatrical industry as one could imagine. Although Shakespeare and his fellows prospered, their status under the law was conditional upon the protection of powerful patrons. "Common players"—those who did not have patrons or masters—were classed in the language of the law with "vagabonds and sturdy beggars." So the actors had to secure for themselves the official rank of servants of patrons. Among the patrons under whose protection Shakespeare's company worked were the lord chamberlain and, after the accession of King James in 1603, the king himself.

In the early 1990s we began to learn a great deal more about the theaters in which Shakespeare and his contemporaries performed—or, at least, began to open up new questions about them. At that time about 70 percent of the Rose had been excavated, as had about 10 percent of the second Globe, the one built in 1614. Excavation was halted at that point, but London has come to value the sites of its early playhouses, and takes what opportunities it can to explore them more deeply, both on the Bankside and in Shoreditch. Information about the playhouses of Shakespeare's London is therefore a constantly changing resource.

The Publication of Shakespeare's Plays

Eighteen of Shakespeare's plays found their way into print during the playwright's lifetime, but there is nothing to suggest that he took any interest in their publication. These eighteen appeared separately in editions in quarto or, in the case of *Henry VI, Part 3,* octavo format. The quarto pages are not much larger than a modern mass-market paperback book, and the octavo pages are even smaller; these little books were sold unbound for a few pence. The earliest of the quartos that still survive were printed in 1594, the year that both *Titus Andronicus* and a version of the play now called *Henry VI, Part 2* became available. While almost every one of these early quartos displays on its title page the name of the acting company that performed the play, only about half provide the name of the playwright, Shakespeare. The first quarto edition to bear the name Shakespeare on its title page is *Love's Labor's Lost* of 1598. A few of the quartos were popular with the book-buying public of Shakespeare's lifetime; for example, quarto *Richard II* went through five editions between 1597 and 1615. But most of the quartos were far from best sellers; *Love's Labor's Lost* (1598), for instance, was not reprinted in quarto until 1631. After Shakespeare's death, two more of his plays appeared in quarto format: *Othello* in 1622 and *The Two Noble Kinsmen,* coauthored with John Fletcher, in 1634.

In 1623, seven years after Shakespeare's death, *Mr. William Shakespeares Comedies, Histories, & Tragedies* was published. This printing offered readers in a single book thirty-six of the thirty-eight plays now thought to have been written by Shakespeare, including eighteen that had never been printed before. And it offered them in a style that was then reserved for serious literature and scholarship. The plays were arranged in double columns on pages nearly a foot high. This large page size is called "folio," as opposed to the smaller "quarto," and the 1623 volume is usually called the Shakespeare First Folio. It is reputed to have sold for the lordly price of a pound. (One copy at the Folger Shakespeare Library is marked fifteen shillings—that is, three-quarters of a pound.)

In a preface to the First Folio entitled "To the great Variety of Readers," two of Shakespeare's former fellow actors in the King's Men, John Heminge and Henry Condell, wrote that they themselves had collected their dead companion's plays. They suggested that they had seen his own papers: "we have scarce received from him a blot in his papers." The title page of the Folio declared that the plays within it had been printed "according to the True Original Copies." Comparing the Folio to the quartos, Heminge and Condell disparaged the quartos, advising their readers that "before you were abused with divers stolen and surreptitious copies, maimed, and deformed by the frauds and stealths of injurious impostors." Many Shakespeareans of the eighteenth and nineteenth centuries believed Heminge and Condell and regarded the Folio plays as superior to anything in the quartos.

Once we begin to examine the Folio plays in detail, it becomes less easy to take at face value the word of Heminge and Condell about the superiority of the Folio texts. For example, of the first nine plays in the Folio (one-quarter of the entire collection), four were essentially reprinted from earlier quarto printings that Heminge and Condell had disparaged, and four have now been identified as printed from copies written in the hand of a professional scribe of the 1620s named Ralph Crane; the ninth, *The Comedy of Errors*, was apparently also printed from a manuscript, but one whose origin cannot be readily identified. Evidently, then, eight of the first nine plays in the First Folio were not printed, in spite of what the Folio title page announces, "according to the True Original Copies," or Shakespeare's own papers, and the source of the ninth is unknown. Since today's editors have been forced to treat Heminge and Condell's pronouncements with skepticism, they must choose whether to base their own editions upon quartos or the Folio on grounds other than Heminge and Condell's story of where the quarto and Folio versions originated.

Editors have often fashioned their own narratives to explain what lies behind the quartos and Folio. They have said that Heminge and Condell meant to criticize only a few of the early quartos, the ones that offer much shorter and sometimes quite different, often garbled, versions of plays. Among the examples of these are the 1600 quarto of *Henry V* (the Folio offers a much fuller version) or the 1603 *Hamlet* quarto. (In 1604 a different, much longer form of the play got into print as a quarto.) Early twentieth-century editors speculated that these questionable texts were produced when someone in the audience took notes from the plays' dialogue during performances and then employed "hack poets" to fill out the notes. The poor results were then sold to a publisher and presented in print as Shakespeare's plays. More recently this story has given way to another in which the shorter versions are said to be re-creations from memory of Shakespeare's plays by actors who wanted to stage them in the provinces but lacked manuscript copies. Most of the quartos offer much better texts than these so-called bad quartos. Indeed, in most of the quartos we find texts that are at least equal to or better than what is printed in the Folio. Many Shakespeare enthusiasts persuaded themselves that most of the quartos were set into type directly from Shakespeare's own papers, although there is nothing on which to base this conclusion except the desire for it to be true. Thus speculation continues about how the Shakespeare plays got to be printed. All that we have are the printed texts.

The book collector who was most successful in bringing together copies of the quartos and the First Folio was Henry Clay Folger, founder of the Folger Shakespeare Library in Washington, D.C. While it is estimated that there survive around the world only about 230 copies of the First Folio, Mr. Folger was able to acquire more than seventy-five copies, as well as a large number of fragments, for the library that bears his name. He also amassed a substantial number of quartos. For example, only fourteen copies of the First Quarto of *Love's Labor's Lost* are known to exist, and three are at the Folger Shakespeare Library. As a consequence of Mr. Folger's labors, scholars visiting the Folger Shakespeare Library have been able to learn a great deal about sixteenth- and seventeenth-century printing and, particularly, about the printing of Shakespeare's plays. And Mr. Folger did not stop at the First Folio, but collected many copies of later editions of Shakespeare, beginning with the Second Folio (1632), the Third (1663–64), and the Fourth (1685). Each of these later folios was based on its immediate predecessor and was edited anonymously. The first editor of Shakespeare whose name we know was Nicholas Rowe, whose first edition came out in 1709. Mr. Folger collected this edition and many, many more by Rowe's successors, and the collecting and scholarship continue.

An Introduction to This Text

The Taming of the Shrew was first printed in the 1623 collection of Shakespeare's plays now known as the First Folio.

The present edition is based directly upon that printing.* (For a brief discussion of a play printed in 1594 as *A Pleasant Conceited Historie, called The Taming of a Shrew*, see Appendix, "Framing Dialogue in *The Taming of a Shrew* (1594)," below, pages 233–45.) For the convenience of the reader, we have modernized the punctuation and the spelling of the Folio. Sometimes we go so far as to modernize certain old forms of words; for example, when *a* means "he," we change it to *he;* we change *mo* to *more* and *ye* to *you.* It is not our practice in editing any of the plays to modernize words that sound distinctly different from modern forms. For example, when the early printed texts read *sith* or *apricocks* or *porpentine,* we have not modernized to *since, apricots, porcupine.* When the forms *an, and,* or *and if* appear instead of the modern form *if,* we have reduced *and* to *an* but have not changed any of these forms to their modern equivalent, *if.* We also modernize and, where necessary, correct passages in foreign languages, unless an error in the early printed text can be reasonably explained as a joke.

Whenever we change the wording of the First Folio or add anything to its stage directions, we mark the change by enclosing it in superior half-brackets (⌜ ⌝). We want our readers to be immediately aware when

*We have also consulted the computerized text of the First Folio provided by the Text Archive of the Oxford University Computing Centre, to which we are grateful.

we have intervened. (Only when we correct an obvious typographical error in the First Folio does the change not get marked.) Whenever we change the First Folio's wording or its punctuation so that meaning changes, we list the change in the textual notes at the back of the book, even if all we have done is fix an obvious error.

We regularize a number of the proper names, as is the usual practice in editions of the play. For example, the Folio sometimes calls Katherine "Katherina." Except where the verse requires "Katherina," we print Katherine throughout this text.

This edition differs from many earlier ones in its efforts to aid the reader in imagining the play as a performance. Thus stage directions are written with reference to the stage. Whenever it is reasonably certain, in our view, that a speech is accompanied by a particular action, we provide a stage direction describing the action. (Occasional exceptions to this rule occur when the action is so obvious that to add a stage direction would insult the reader.) Stage directions for the entrance of characters in mid-scene are, with rare exceptions, placed so that they immediately precede the characters' participation in the scene, even though these entrances may appear somewhat earlier in the early printed texts. Whenever we move a stage direction, we record this change in the textual notes. Latin stage directions (e.g., *Exeunt*) are translated into English (e.g., *They exit*).

We expand the often severely abbreviated forms of names used as speech headings in early printed texts into the full names of the characters. We also regularize the speakers' names in speech headings, using only a single designation for each character, even though the early printed texts sometimes use a variety of designations. Variations in the speech headings of the early printed texts are recorded in the textual notes.

In the present edition, as well, we mark with a dash any change of address within a speech, unless a stage direction intervenes. When the *-ed* ending of a word is to be pronounced, we mark it with an accent. Like editors for the last two centuries, we print metrically linked lines in the following way:

PETRUCHIO
I am content.
KATHERINE Are you content to stay?

However, when there are a number of short verse-lines that can be linked in more than one way, we do not, with rare exceptions, indent any of them.

The Explanatory Notes

The notes that appear on the pages facing the text are designed to provide readers with the help that they may need to enjoy the play. Whenever the meaning of a word in the text is not readily accessible in a good contemporary dictionary, we offer the meaning in a note. Sometimes we provide a note even when the relevant meaning is to be found in the dictionary but when the word has acquired since Shakespeare's time other potentially confusing meanings. In our notes, we try to offer modern synonyms for Shakespeare's words. We also try to indicate to the reader the connection between the word in the play and the modern synonym. For example, Shakespeare sometimes uses the word *head* to mean "source," but, for modern readers, there may be no connection evident between these two words. We provide the connection by explaining Shakespeare's usage as follows: "**head:** fountainhead, source." On some occasions, a whole phrase or clause needs explanation. Then we rephrase in our own words the difficult passage, and add at the end synonyms for individual words in the passage. When scholars have been unable to determine the meaning of a word or phrase, we acknowledge the uncertainty. Biblical quotations are from the Geneva Bible (1560), with spelling modernized.

THE TAMING OF THE SHREW

Characters in the Play

CHRISTOPHER SLY, a beggar
Hostess of an alehouse
A Lord
Huntsmen of the Lord
Page (disguised as a lady)
Players
Servingmen
Messenger
} *characters in the Induction*

BAPTISTA MINOLA, father to Katherine and Bianca
KATHERINE, his elder daughter
BIANCA, his younger daughter

PETRUCHIO, suitor to Katherine

GREMIO
HORTENSIO (later disguised as the teacher Litio)
LUCENTIO (later disguised as the teacher Cambio)
} *suitors to Bianca*

VINCENTIO, Lucentio's father

TRANIO (later impersonating Lucentio)
BIONDELLO
} *servants to Lucentio*

A Merchant (later disguised as Vincentio)

GRUMIO
CURTIS
NATHANIEL
PHILLIP
JOSEPH
NICHOLAS
PETER } *servants to Petruchio*

Widow

Tailor
Haberdasher
Officer

Servants to Baptista and Petruchio

THE TAMING OF THE SHREW

INDUCTION

Ind.1 Christopher Sly, a drunken beggar, is driven out of an alehouse by its hostess. A great lord, returning from the hunt, finds Sly in a drunken sleep and decides to play an elaborate trick on him. The lord orders his servants to place Sly in a luxurious bedroom and, when the beggar awakes, to tell him he is a great lord who has long been out of his mind. A troupe of traveling actors present themselves to the lord, who, by way of further elaborating his trick, instructs them to stage a play for Sly.

---

1. **feeze you:** fix you, do for you

2. **stocks:** a heavy timber frame with holes for the ankles used to punish disturbers of the peace (See picture, page 12.)

4. **chronicles:** histories, such as Holinshed's *Chronicles* (1577 and 1587), often used by Shakespeare

4–5. **Richard Conqueror:** i.e., William the **Conqueror**

5. **paucas pallabris:** i.e., *pocas palabras,* Spanish for "few words," i.e., enough

6. **Sessa:** perhaps French *cessez* or Spanish *cesa,* both meaning "stop" or "be silent"

9. **denier:** small copper coin of little value; **Saint Jeronimy:** St. Jerome (**Jeronimy** may confuse Jerome with Hieronimo, the hero of Kyd's play *The Spanish Tragedy.*)

12. **headborough:** constable

13. **Third . . . borough:** "Thirdborough" was another term for constable.

(continued)

⌜INDUCTION⌝

Scene 1

Enter Beggar (Christopher Sly) and Hostess.

SLY I'll feeze you, in faith.

HOSTESS A pair of stocks, you rogue!

SLY You're a baggage! The Slys are no rogues. Look in the chronicles. We came in with Richard Conqueror. Therefore, *paucas pallabris,* let the world slide. Sessa!

HOSTESS You will not pay for the glasses you have burst?

SLY No, not a denier. Go, by ⌜Saint⌝ Jeronimy! Go to thy cold bed and warm thee. ⌜*He lies down.*⌝

HOSTESS I know my remedy. I must go fetch the headborough. ⌜*She exits.*⌝

SLY Third, or fourth, or fifth borough, I'll answer him by law. I'll not budge an inch, boy. Let him come, and kindly. *Falls asleep.*

Wind horns ⌜within.⌝ Enter a Lord from hunting, with his train.

LORD

Huntsman, I charge thee tender well my hounds.
⌜Breathe⌝ Merriman (the poor cur is embossed)
And couple Clowder with the deep-mouthed brach.
Saw'st thou not, boy, how Silver made it good
At the hedge corner, in the coldest fault?
I would not lose the dog for twenty pound!

14. **boy:** See longer note, page 223.

15. **kindly:** i.e., welcome

15 SD. **Wind:** blow; **within:** offstage

16. **tender well:** take good care of

17. **Breathe Merriman:** let **Merriman** get his breath back; **embossed:** exhausted

19. **made it good:** i.e., picked up the scent

20. **in . . . fault:** i.e., when the scent was lost

23. **it:** i.e., the scent; **at the merest loss:** i.e., when the scent seemed absolutely lost (*Merely* means "entirely.")

36. **thine image:** i.e., sleep, which looks like death

37. **practice on:** play a trick on

39. **sweet:** fragrant

42. **brave:** splendidly dressed

44. **cannot choose:** i.e., will have no other choice

Hunting with hounds. (IND.1.29; IND.2.44–46)
From George Turberville, *The noble art of . . . hunting . . .* (1611).

FIRST HUNTSMAN
Why, Bellman is as good as he, my lord.
He cried upon it at the merest loss,
And twice today picked out the dullest scent.
Trust me, I take him for the better dog.

LORD
Thou art a fool. If Echo were as fleet,
I would esteem him worth a dozen such.
But sup them well, and look unto them all.
Tomorrow I intend to hunt again.

FIRST HUNTSMAN I will, my lord.

⌜*First Huntsman exits.*⌝

LORD, ⌜*noticing Sly*⌝
What's here? One dead, or drunk? See doth he breathe.

SECOND HUNTSMAN
He breathes, my lord. Were he not warmed with ale,
This were a bed but cold to sleep so soundly.

LORD
O monstrous beast, how like a swine he lies!
Grim death, how foul and loathsome is thine image!
Sirs, I will practice on this drunken man.
What think you, if he were conveyed to bed,
Wrapped in sweet clothes, rings put upon his fingers,
A most delicious banquet by his bed,
And brave attendants near him when he wakes,
Would not the beggar then forget himself?

⌜THIRD⌝ HUNTSMAN
Believe me, lord, I think he cannot choose.

SECOND HUNTSMAN
It would seem strange unto him when he waked.

LORD
Even as a flatt'ring dream or worthless fancy.
Then take him up, and manage well the jest.

50. **Balm:** anoint
54. **straight:** immediately
55. **reverence:** bow
59. **diaper:** small towel
65. **disease:** trouble, disturbance
67. **when . . . is:** i.e., when he says he is now mad
69. **kindly:** (1) naturally—with no sign that you are feigning; (2) in a friendly way
70. **passing:** surpassingly
71. **husbanded with modesty:** conducted with restraint
73. **As:** i.e., so that
76. **office:** assigned part; **he:** i.e., Sly
77. **Sirrah:** a term of address to a social inferior

A ewer and basin. (IND.1.57, 59)
From Bartolomeo Scappi, *Opera* . . . (1605).

Carry him gently to my fairest chamber,
And hang it round with all my wanton pictures;
Balm his foul head in warm distillèd waters,
And burn sweet wood to make the lodging sweet;
Procure me music ready when he wakes
To make a dulcet and a heavenly sound.
And if he chance to speak, be ready straight
And, with a low, submissive reverence,
Say "What is it your Honor will command?"
Let one attend him with a silver basin
Full of rosewater and bestrewed with flowers,
Another bear the ewer, the third a diaper,
And say "Will 't please your Lordship cool your
hands?"
Someone be ready with a costly suit,
And ask him what apparel he will wear.
Another tell him of his hounds and horse,
And that his lady mourns at his disease.
Persuade him that he hath been lunatic,
And when he says he is, say that he dreams,
For he is nothing but a mighty lord.
This do, and do it kindly, gentle sirs.
It will be pastime passing excellent
If it be husbanded with modesty.

⌜THIRD⌝ HUNTSMAN

My lord, I warrant you we will play our part
As he shall think by our true diligence
He is no less than what we say he is.

LORD

Take him up gently, and to bed with him,
And each one to his office when he wakes.

⌜Sly is carried out.⌝

Sound trumpets ⌜within.⌝

Sirrah, go see what trumpet 'tis that sounds.

⌜Servingman exits.⌝

78. **Belike:** probably; **means:** intends
81. **An 't:** if it; **players:** actors
87. **So please:** if it **please; duty:** respect
89. **Since once:** the time when
91. **sure:** certainly
92. **aptly fitted:** well cast
93. **Soto:** The earliest surviving play with a character named **Soto** is John Fletcher's *Women Pleased* (1619). It is likely that the reference here is to a lost play, since only a fraction of the drama of Shakespeare's time survives.
95. **in happy time:** i.e., at just the right moment
96. **The rather for:** i.e., especially because
97. **cunning:** skill
99. **doubtful of your modesties:** i.e., suspicious about how well you can control yourselves
100. **over-eying of:** observing
102. **merry passion:** i.e., laughter

"A pair of stocks." (IND.1.2)
From T[homas] F[ella,] *A book of diverse devices* (1585–1622).

Belike some noble gentleman that means
(Traveling some journey) to repose him here.

Enter Servingman.

How now? Who is it?

SERVINGMAN An 't please your Honor, players
That offer service to your Lordship.

LORD
Bid them come near.

Enter Players.

Now, fellows, you are welcome.

PLAYERS We thank your Honor.

LORD
Do you intend to stay with me tonight?

⌜FIRST PLAYER⌝
So please your Lordship to accept our duty.

LORD
With all my heart. This fellow I remember
Since once he played a farmer's eldest son.—
'Twas where you wooed the gentlewoman so well.
I have forgot your name, but sure that part
Was aptly fitted and naturally performed.

⌜SECOND PLAYER⌝
I think 'twas Soto that your Honor means.

LORD
'Tis very true. Thou didst it excellent.
Well, you are come to me in happy time,
The rather for I have some sport in hand
Wherein your cunning can assist me much.
There is a lord will hear you play tonight;
But I am doubtful of your modesties,
Lest, over-eying of his odd behavior
(For yet his Honor never heard a play),
You break into some merry passion,
And so offend him. For I tell you, sirs,
If you should smile, he grows impatient.

106. **veriest antic:** the most peculiar person

107. **buttery:** storeroom for food and drink

109. **want:** lack; **affords:** can provide

110. **Bartholomew:** pronounced "Bartelmy"

111. **see him:** arrange for him to be; **in all suits:** in every way

113–14. **him . . . him . . . him:** i.e., the page

114. **as he will:** i.e., if he wishes to

115. **He bear:** i.e., he should conduct

117. **accomplishèd:** performed

119. **tongue:** voice

124. **with . . . bosom: with** his (the page's) **head** lowered onto Sly's breast

125. **him:** i.e., the page; **as being:** i.e., **as** if he were

127. **esteemed him:** i.e., thought himself to be

131. **shift:** trick

132. **napkin:** handkerchief; **close conveyed:** secretly carried

133. **Shall . . . eye:** despite his inability to cry, will force his eyes to water

135. **Anon:** soon

136. **usurp:** take on

⌜FIRST PLAYER⌝
Fear not, my lord, we can contain ourselves
Were he the veriest antic in the world.

LORD, ⌜*to a Servingman*⌝
Go, sirrah, take them to the buttery
And give them friendly welcome every one.
Let them want nothing that my house affords.
One exits with the Players.
Sirrah, go you to Bartholomew, my page,
And see him dressed in all suits like a lady.
That done, conduct him to the drunkard's chamber,
And call him "Madam," do him obeisance.
Tell him from me, as he will win my love,
He bear himself with honorable action,
Such as he hath observed in noble ladies
Unto their lords, by them accomplishèd.
Such duty to the drunkard let him do
With soft low tongue and lowly courtesy,
And say "What is 't your Honor will command,
Wherein your lady and your humble wife
May show her duty and make known her love?"
And then with kind embracements, tempting kisses,
And with declining head into his bosom,
Bid him shed tears, as being overjoyed
To see her noble lord restored to health,
Who, for this seven years, hath esteemed him
No better than a poor and loathsome beggar.
And if the boy have not a woman's gift
To rain a shower of commanded tears,
An onion will do well for such a shift,
Which (in a napkin being close conveyed)
Shall in despite enforce a watery eye.
See this dispatched with all the haste thou canst.
Anon I'll give thee more instructions.
A Servingman exits.
I know the boy will well usurp the grace,

139. **how . . . will:** i.e., the way **my men** should; **stay:** stop, keep

141. **do homage:** show respect

142. **Haply:** perhaps

143. **over-merry spleen:** excess of laughter (The **spleen** was thought to be the seat of laughter, as well as of other strong emotions.)

Ind.2 The newly awakened Sly is offered delicacies and fine clothes. When he demands his usual ale and beef, the lord and servants tell him that he has been suffering from delusions. After they inform him that he has a beautiful wife, he asks to see her. The lord's page, who impersonates the wife, persuades Sly to watch the play that is about to begin.

---

1. **small:** thin, weak, and therefore cheap

2. **sack:** costly dry Spanish wine, such as sherry

3. **conserves:** candied fruit

6. **An if:** i.e., **if**

7. **conserves of beef:** salted **beef**

9. **doublets:** i.e., jackets (See picture, page 198.)

12. **overleather:** upper leather of a shoe

13. **idle humor:** groundless fantasy

Voice, gait, and action of a gentlewoman.
I long to hear him call the drunkard "husband"!
And how my men will stay themselves from
laughter
When they do homage to this simple peasant,
I'll in to counsel them. Haply my presence
May well abate the over-merry spleen
Which otherwise would grow into extremes.

⌜*They exit.*⌝

⌜Scene 2⌝

Enter aloft ⌜*Christopher Sly,*⌝ *the drunkard, with Attendants, some with apparel, basin and ewer, and other appurtenances, and Lord* ⌜*dressed as an Attendant.*⌝

SLY For God's sake, a pot of small ale.

FIRST SERVINGMAN
Will 't please your Lord drink a cup of sack?

SECOND SERVINGMAN
Will 't please your Honor taste of these conserves?

THIRD SERVINGMAN
What raiment will your Honor wear today?

SLY I am Christophero Sly! Call not me "Honor" nor "Lordship." I ne'er drank sack in my life. An if you give me any conserves, give me conserves of beef. Ne'er ask me what raiment I'll wear, for I have no more doublets than backs, no more stockings than legs, nor no more shoes than feet, nay sometime more feet than shoes, or such shoes as my toes look through the overleather.

LORD, ⌜*as* ATTENDANT⌝
Heaven cease this idle humor in your Honor!
O, that a mighty man of such descent,
Of such possessions, and so high esteem
Should be infusèd with so foul a spirit!

18. **Burton Heath:** perhaps Barton-on-the-Heath, a village about a dozen miles from Shakespeare's native Stratford

19. **cardmaker:** maker of cards used to comb wool

20. **bearherd:** keeper of a tame, performing bear (See picture, page 26.)

21. **alewife:** woman alehousekeeper

21–22. **Wincot:** another village near Stratford

23. **on the score:** on account (Charges for drink were cut or scored on a stick or tally.) **sheer ale: ale** alone; or, perhaps, "small **ale**"; **score me up:** chalk **me up**

25. **bestraught:** distracted, insane

30. **bethink thee:** think; **birth:** lineage, inherited position

31. **ancient:** former

32. **dreams:** fantasies

34. **office:** assignment

35. **Apollo:** here, patron god of music (See picture, page 82.)

39. **Semiramis:** queen of Assyria, noted for her sexual escapades

40. **bestrew:** cover with flowers or rushes

41. **trapped:** dressed in trappings

43. **hawking:** hunting for birds with trained hawks

45–46. **Thy hounds . . . Earth:** i.e., the sound of the hounds' barking will strike the sky and then return to echo from the Earth **welkin:** sky

47. **course:** hunt hares with **greyhounds** (which hunt by sight, not scent)

48. **breathèd stags: stags** with good wind or endurance; **roe:** small deer

SLY What, would you make me mad? Am not I Christopher Sly, old Sly's son of Burton Heath, by birth a peddler, by education a cardmaker, by transmutation a bearherd, and now by present profession a tinker? Ask Marian Hacket, the fat alewife of Wincot, if she know me not! If she say I am not fourteen pence on the score for sheer ale, score me up for the lying'st knave in Christendom. What, I am not bestraught! Here's—

THIRD SERVINGMAN
O, this it is that makes your lady mourn.

SECOND SERVINGMAN
O, this is it that makes your servants droop.

LORD, ⌜*as* ATTENDANT⌝
Hence comes it that your kindred shuns your house,
As beaten hence by your strange lunacy.
O noble lord, bethink thee of thy birth,
Call home thy ancient thoughts from banishment,
And banish hence these abject lowly dreams.
Look how thy servants do attend on thee,
Each in his office ready at thy beck.
Wilt thou have music? Hark, Apollo plays, *Music.*
And twenty cagèd nightingales do sing.
Or wilt thou sleep? We'll have thee to a couch
Softer and sweeter than the lustful bed
On purpose trimmed up for Semiramis.
Say thou wilt walk, we will bestrew the ground.
Or wilt thou ride? Thy horses shall be trapped,
Their harness studded all with gold and pearl.
Dost thou love hawking? Thou hast hawks will soar
Above the morning lark. Or wilt thou hunt?
Thy hounds shall make the welkin answer them
And fetch shrill echoes from the hollow Earth.

FIRST SERVINGMAN
Say thou wilt course. Thy greyhounds are as swift
As breathèd stags, ay, fleeter than the roe.

49. **pictures:** These are presumably the "wanton **pictures**" mentioned by the lord in Induction 1, now, in lines 49–60, described as pictures of seductions and rapes based on stories told in Ovid's *Metamorphoses:* the story of Venus and Adonis, of Jove and Io, of Apollo and Daphne. **straight:** immediately

50. **Adonis:** a mortal loved by **Cytherea** (i.e., Venus)

51. **sedges:** marsh grass

52. **wanton:** move playfully and lovingly

54. **Io:** a maiden raped by Jove and transformed into a heifer

55. **beguilèd and surprised:** tricked and captured

56. **As lively . . . done:** i.e., **painted as** vividly **as** if it were **the** actual **deed**

57. **Daphne:** a maiden desired and pursued by Apollo (She escaped by being transformed into a laurel tree; see picture, page 24.)

60. **workmanly:** expertly

63. **this waning age:** a reference to the belief that the world, originally innocent and virtuous (the Golden Age), had ever since declined and was continuing to wane

65. **envious floods:** malicious streams; **o'errun:** overran

67. **yet:** even now

71. **savors:** odors

74. **our:** Sly now uses the royal "we."

75. **smallest:** thinnest, weakest, cheapest (An attendant may exit at this point to bring "the lady" and fetch the ale.)

77. **wit:** mind

SECOND SERVINGMAN

Dost thou love pictures? We will fetch thee straight
Adonis painted by a running brook,
And Cytherea all in sedges hid,
Which seem to move and wanton with her breath,
Even as the waving sedges play with wind.

LORD, ⌜*as* ATTENDANT⌝

We'll show thee Io as she was a maid
And how she was beguilèd and surprised,
As lively painted as the deed was done.

THIRD SERVINGMAN

Or Daphne roaming through a thorny wood,
Scratching her legs that one shall swear she bleeds,
And at that sight shall sad Apollo weep,
So workmanly the blood and tears are drawn.

LORD, ⌜*as* ATTENDANT⌝

Thou art a lord, and nothing but a lord;
Thou hast a lady far more beautiful
Than any woman in this waning age.

FIRST SERVINGMAN

And till the tears that she hath shed for thee
Like envious floods o'errun her lovely face,
She was the fairest creature in the world—
And yet she is inferior to none.

SLY

Am I a lord, and have I such a lady?
Or do I dream? Or have I dreamed till now?
I do not sleep: I see, I hear, I speak,
I smell sweet savors, and I feel soft things.
Upon my life, I am a lord indeed
And not a tinker, nor Christopher Sly.
Well, bring our lady hither to our sight,
And once again a pot o' the smallest ale.

SECOND SERVINGMAN

Will 't please your Mightiness to wash your hands?
O, how we joy to see your wit restored!

78. **knew but:** only **knew**

79. **These:** i.e., **these** last

81. **fay:** faith

82. **of:** in

83. **idle:** silly

84. **goodly:** splendid

86. **house:** alehouse

87. **present . . . leet:** accuse her before the court of the lord of the manor

88–89. **stone jugs . . . quarts:** Customers preferred **sealed quarts,** which bore official stamps (seals) guaranteeing the quantity they contained, rather than **stone** jars that could hold indeterminate quantities.

91. **Ay:** yes; **woman's:** hostess's

93. **reckoned up:** named one after another

94. **Greete:** a hamlet in Gloucestershire, near Stratford (The Folio reading, "Greece," seems to be a misreading.)

98. **amends:** recovery

100. **Thou . . . by it:** i.e., I will reward you for it

102. **Marry:** i.e., indeed (originally an oath on the name of the Virgin Mary); **fare:** eat (wordplay on **fares** [line 101], which means "does"); **cheer:** food and drink

106. **goodman:** the term with which a lower-class wife addressed her husband

O, that once more you knew but what you are!
These fifteen years you have been in a dream,
Or, when you waked, so waked as if you slept.

SLY
These fifteen years! By my fay, a goodly nap.
But did I never speak of all that time?

FIRST SERVINGMAN
Oh, yes, my lord, but very idle words.
For though you lay here in this goodly chamber,
Yet would you say you were beaten out of door,
And rail upon the hostess of the house,
And say you would present her at the leet
Because she brought stone jugs and no sealed quarts.
Sometimes you would call out for Cicely Hacket.

SLY Ay, the woman's maid of the house.

THIRD SERVINGMAN
Why, sir, you know no house, nor no such maid,
Nor no such men as you have reckoned up,
As Stephen Sly and old John Naps of ⌜Greete,⌝
And Peter Turph and Henry Pimpernell,
And twenty more such names and men as these,
Which never were, nor no man ever saw.

SLY Now, Lord be thanked for my good amends!

ALL Amen.

SLY I thank thee. Thou shalt not lose by it.

Enter ⌜Page as⌝ Lady, with Attendants.

⌜PAGE, *as*⌝ LADY How fares my noble lord?

SLY Marry, I fare well, for here is cheer enough. Where is my wife?

⌜PAGE, *as*⌝ LADY
Here, noble lord. What is thy will with her?

SLY
Are you my wife, and will not call me "husband"?
My men should call me "lord." I am your goodman.

114. **above:** more than
116. **abandoned:** banished
123. **In peril . . . malady:** because of the danger that you will again fall ill
125. **stands:** will serve (There is a bawdy pun on **stands** when it is repeated in the next line.)
126. **tarry:** wait
130. **players:** actors; **amendment:** recovery
132. **hold . . . meet:** regard it to be most suitable

Apollo and Daphne. (IND.2.57, 59)
From Natale Conti, . . . *Mythologiae* . . . (1616).

⌜PAGE, *as*⌝ LADY
My husband and my lord, my lord and husband,
I am your wife in all obedience.

SLY
I know it well.—What must I call her?

LORD, ⌜*as* ATTENDANT⌝ "Madam."

SLY "Alice Madam," or "Joan Madam"?

LORD
"Madam," and nothing else. So lords call ladies.

SLY
Madam wife, they say that I have dreamed
And slept above some fifteen year or more.

⌜PAGE, *as*⌝ LADY
Ay, and the time seems thirty unto me,
Being all this time abandoned from your bed.

SLY
'Tis much.—Servants, leave me and her alone.—
Madam, undress you, and come now to bed.

⌜PAGE, *as*⌝ LADY
Thrice noble lord, let me entreat of you
To pardon me yet for a night or two;
Or if not so, until the sun be set.
For your physicians have expressly charged,
In peril to incur your former malady,
That I should yet absent me from your bed.
I hope this reason stands for my excuse.

SLY Ay, it stands so that I may hardly tarry so long; but I would be loath to fall into my dreams again. I will therefore tarry in despite of the flesh and the blood.

Enter a Messenger.

MESSENGER
Your Honor's players, hearing your amendment,
Are come to play a pleasant comedy,
For so your doctors hold it very meet,

133. **Seeing:** i.e., **seeing** that

135. **nurse of frenzy:** nourisher of madness or delirium

138. **bars:** prevents

140. **comonty:** i.e., comedy; **gambold:** i.e., frolic, merrymaking

143. **household stuff:** goods belonging to a household (with wordplay on **stuff** [line 142], which means "literary or artistic matter")

144. **history:** i.e., story

147 SD. For the two induction scenes in *The Taming of a Shrew* (1594), see Appendix, "Framing Dialogue," A and B, pages 234–40, below.

A bearherd. (IND.2.20)
From Jacobus a. Bruck, *Emblemata moralia . . .* (1615).

Seeing too much sadness hath congealed your blood,
And melancholy is the nurse of frenzy.
Therefore they thought it good you hear a play
And frame your mind to mirth and merriment,
Which bars a thousand harms and lengthens life.

SLY Marry, I will. Let them play it. ⌜*Messenger exits.*⌝ Is not a comonty a Christmas gambold or a tumbling trick?

⌜PAGE, *as*⌝ LADY
No, my good lord, it is more pleasing stuff.

SLY What, household stuff?

⌜PAGE, *as*⌝ LADY It is a kind of history.

SLY Well, we'll see 't. Come, madam wife, sit by my side, and let the world slip. We shall ne'er be younger.

⌜*They sit.*⌝

THE TAMING OF THE SHREW

ACT 1

1.1 Lucentio has come with his servant Tranio to Padua to study philosophy. They witness an encounter between Baptista and his daughters, in which Baptista announces that Bianca cannot marry until the elder and bad-tempered Katherine does. Bianca's suitors decide to search for a husband for Katherine. Meanwhile Lucentio has fallen in love with Bianca and decides to have Tranio impersonate him so that Lucentio, in the disguise of a schoolmaster, can secretly woo Bianca. The two men exchange clothes.

---

0 SD. **Flourish:** a fanfare of trumpets

1. **for:** because of

2. **nursery of arts: Padua** was famous for its university. **arts:** i.e., the liberal **arts**

3. **am arrived for:** i.e., have **arrived** in

5. **leave:** permission

7. **well approved:** found perfectly reliable

8. **breathe:** pause, rest, remain; **haply:** perhaps; **institute:** i.e., begin

9. **ingenious:** liberal

10. **grave:** worthy and serious

11. **my father first:** i.e., **my father** before me

12. **of great traffic:** i.e., trading extensively

13. **come of:** descended from

14–16. **Vincentio's son . . . deeds:** i.e., it will be fitting for me, **Vincentio's son,** to fulfill all expectations by adorning my good **fortune** with good **deeds**

17. **the:** i.e., this

19–20. **Will I apply . . . achieved:** i.e., **I will** devote myself to **that part of philosophy that** deals with the **happiness achieved** through **virtue**

⌜ACT 1⌝

⌜Scene 1⌝

Flourish. Enter Lucentio and his man Tranio.

LUCENTIO

Tranio, since for the great desire I had
To see fair Padua, nursery of arts,
I am arrived for fruitful Lombardy,
The pleasant garden of great Italy,
And by my father's love and leave am armed
With his goodwill and thy good company.
My trusty servant well approved in all,
Here let us breathe and haply institute
A course of learning and ingenious studies.
Pisa, renownèd for grave citizens,
Gave me my being, and my father first,
A merchant of great traffic through the world,
⌜Vincentio,⌝ come of the Bentivolii.
Vincentio's son, brought up in Florence,
It shall become to serve all hopes conceived
To deck his fortune with his virtuous deeds.
And therefore, Tranio, for the time I study
Virtue, and that part of philosophy
Will I apply that treats of happiness
By virtue specially to be achieved.
Tell me thy mind, for I have Pisa left
And am to Padua come, as he that leaves

23. **plash:** pool, puddle

25. **Mi perdonato:** pardon me (Italian)

26. **affected:** i.e., of the same feeling

30. **discipline:** course of instruction

31. **stoics:** persons who put aside all pleasures, refusing to give in to emotion and desire (There is a play here on the word **stocks,** i.e., unfeeling people.)

32. **devote:** devoted; **Aristotle's checks:** the self-restraint that the Greek philosopher Aristotle (384–322 B.C.E.) advocated

33. **As:** i.e., so that; **Ovid:** Roman love poet (In his *Art of Love,* Ovid names himself the Professor of Love.) **be:** becomes; **abjured:** renounced

34. **Balk logic:** chop **logic,** bandy terms (with wordplay on **balk** as "avoid" and **logic** as a philosophical discipline)

35. **practice . . . talk:** i.e., instead of studying **rhetoric** in the university, **practice rhetoric** by talking with friends

36. **Music . . . quicken you:** i.e., **use music and** poetry **to** enliven **you**

38. **your stomach serves you:** you have an appetite for them

40. **affect:** like

41. **Gramercies:** thanks

42. **Biondello:** an (absent) servant of Lucentio's

43. **put us in readiness:** prepare ourselves

45 SD. **pantaloon:** ridiculous old man, a stock character in Italian comedy of the period (See picture, page 34.)

46. **stay awhile:** wait a minute

47. **show:** entertainment, spectacle

A shallow plash to plunge him in the deep
And with satiety seeks to quench his thirst.

TRANIO

⌜*Mi perdonato,*⌝ gentle master mine.
I am in all affected as yourself,
Glad that you thus continue your resolve
To suck the sweets of sweet philosophy.
Only, good master, while we do admire
This virtue and this moral discipline,
Let's be no stoics nor no stocks, I pray,
Or so devote to Aristotle's checks
As Ovid be an outcast quite abjured.
Balk logic with acquaintance that you have,
And practice rhetoric in your common talk;
Music and poesy use to quicken you;
The mathematics and the metaphysics—
Fall to them as you find your stomach serves you.
No profit grows where is no pleasure ta'en.
In brief, sir, study what you most affect.

LUCENTIO

Gramercies, Tranio, well dost thou advise.
If, Biondello, thou wert come ashore,
We could at once put us in readiness
And take a lodging fit to entertain
Such friends as time in Padua shall beget.

Enter Baptista with his two daughters, Katherine and Bianca; Gremio, a pantaloon, ⌜*and*⌝ *Hortensio,* ⌜*suitors*⌝ *to Bianca.*

But stay awhile! What company is this?

TRANIO

Master, some show to welcome us to town.

Lucentio ⌜*and*⌝ *Tranio stand by.*

BAPTISTA, ⌜*to Gremio and Hortensio*⌝

Gentlemen, importune me no farther,
For how I firmly am resolved you know:

50. **bestow:** give in marriage

54. **Leave:** permission

55. **cart:** Women who transgressed community standards were shamed by being paraded through the streets in open carts.

58. **stale:** laughingstock; also, prostitute (Prostitutes were among those "carted.") **mates:** fellows

59. **mates:** spouses

63. **Iwis:** certainly; **it:** i.e., marriage; **her:** i.e., Katherine's

65. **noddle:** head (slang)

66. **paint:** i.e., scratch until it bleeds

69. **pastime toward:** entertainment about to take place

70. **wonderful froward:** amazingly ungovernable

Pantaloon. (1.1.45 SD)
From Otto van Veen,
Quinti Horatii Flacci emblemata . . . (1612).

That is, not to bestow my youngest daughter
Before I have a husband for the elder.
If either of you both love Katherine,
Because I know you well and love you well,
Leave shall you have to court her at your pleasure.

GREMIO
To cart her, rather. She's too rough for me.—
There, there, Hortensio, will you any wife?

KATHERINE, ⌜*to Baptista*⌝
I pray you, sir, is it your will
To make a stale of me amongst these mates?

HORTENSIO
"Mates," maid? How mean you that? No mates for you,
Unless you were of gentler, milder mold.

KATHERINE
I' faith, sir, you shall never need to fear.
Iwis it is not halfway to her heart.
But if it were, doubt not her care should be
To comb your noddle with a three-legged stool
And paint your face and use you like a fool.

HORTENSIO
From all such devils, good Lord, deliver us!

GREMIO And me too, good Lord.

TRANIO, ⌜*aside to Lucentio*⌝
Husht, master, here's some good pastime toward;
That wench is stark mad or wonderful froward.

LUCENTIO, ⌜*aside to Tranio*⌝
But in the other's silence do I see
Maid's mild behavior and sobriety.
Peace, Tranio.

TRANIO, ⌜*aside to Lucentio*⌝
Well said, master. Mum, and gaze your fill.

BAPTISTA, ⌜*to Gremio and Hortensio*⌝
Gentlemen, that I may soon make good
What I have said—Bianca, get you in,

79. **peat:** pet, favorite
79–80. **It is . . . eye:** she should make herself cry
80. **an:** if
82. **subscribe:** give in, submit
83. **instruments:** musical **instruments**
85. **Minerva:** goddess of wisdom, also credited with inventing musical instruments
86. **strange:** uncooperative, unfriendly
89. **mew her up:** cage her
90. **for:** because of
91. **her . . . her:** i.e., Bianca . . . Katherine's
99. **Prefer:** recommend; **cunning:** learned
103. **commune:** talk over together (Accent on first syllable.)
105. **belike:** perhaps

Minerva. (1.1.85)
From Ottavio Rossi,
Le memorie bresciane . . . (1616).

And let it not displease thee, good Bianca,
For I will love thee ne'er the less, my girl.

KATHERINE
A pretty peat! It is best
Put finger in the eye, an she knew why.

BIANCA
Sister, content you in my discontent.—
Sir, to your pleasure humbly I subscribe.
My books and instruments shall be my company,
On them to look and practice by myself.

LUCENTIO, ⌜*aside to Tranio*⌝
Hark, Tranio, thou mayst hear Minerva speak!

HORTENSIO
Signior Baptista, will you be so strange?
Sorry am I that our goodwill effects
Bianca's grief.

GREMIO Why will you mew her up,
Signior Baptista, for this fiend of hell,
And make her bear the penance of her tongue?

BAPTISTA
Gentlemen, content you. I am resolved.—
Go in, Bianca. ⌜*Bianca exits.*⌝
And for I know she taketh most delight
In music, instruments, and poetry,
Schoolmasters will I keep within my house
Fit to instruct her youth. If you, Hortensio,
Or, Signior Gremio, you know any such,
Prefer them hither. For to cunning men
I will be very kind, and liberal
To mine own children in good bringing up.
And so, farewell.—Katherine, you may stay,
For I have more to commune with Bianca. *He exits.*

KATHERINE
Why, and I trust I may go too, may I not?
What, shall I be appointed hours as though, belike,
I knew not what to take and what to leave? Ha!
She exits.

107. **Devil's dam: Devil's** mother (in proverbs, said to be worse than the Devil)

108. **hold:** restrain; **Their love:** perhaps, our love of women (Some editors print this as "There! Love. . . .")

109. **but . . . nails:** i.e., that we cannot wait patiently

110. **fast . . . out:** i.e., quietly go without reward (literally, without sustenance)

110–11. **Our cake's . . . sides:** proverbial for "we've both lost"

114. **wish:** recommend

117. **brooked parle:** i.e., allowed for discussion; **advice:** careful consideration; **toucheth:** concerns

126–27. **so very a fool: so** entirely **a fool** as

129. **alarums:** brawlings

130. **an:** if

131. **light on:** i.e., find

132. **and:** if (there were)

133. **had as lief:** would just as soon

134. **high cross: cross** at the town center

137. **bar in law:** legal barrier (i.e., Baptista's insistence that Katherine must be married before Bianca)

138–39. **so far . . . maintained:** kept up in a **friendly** manner to this extent and no further

141. **have to 't afresh:** i.e., compete anew, go to it again

142. **Happy . . . dole:** i.e., may the winner find happiness; or, may the best man win

GREMIO You may go to the Devil's dam! Your gifts are so good here's none will hold you.—Their love is not so great, Hortensio, but we may blow our nails together and fast it fairly out. Our cake's dough on both sides. Farewell. Yet for the love I bear my sweet Bianca, if I can by any means light on a fit man to teach her that wherein she delights, I will wish him to her father.

HORTENSIO So will I, Signior Gremio. But a word, I pray. Though the nature of our quarrel yet never brooked parle, know now upon advice, it toucheth us both (that we may yet again have access to our fair mistress and be happy rivals in Bianca's love) to labor and effect one thing specially.

GREMIO What's that, I pray?

HORTENSIO Marry, sir, to get a husband for her sister.

GREMIO A husband? A devil!

HORTENSIO I say "a husband."

GREMIO I say "a devil." Think'st thou, Hortensio, though her father be very rich, any man is so very a fool to be married to hell?

HORTENSIO Tush, Gremio. Though it pass your patience and mine to endure her loud alarums, why, man, there be good fellows in the world, an a man could light on them, would take her with all faults, and money enough.

GREMIO I cannot tell. But I had as lief take her dowry with this condition: to be whipped at the high cross every morning.

HORTENSIO Faith, as you say, there's small choice in rotten apples. But come, since this bar in law makes us friends, it shall be so far forth friendly maintained till by helping Baptista's eldest daughter to a husband we set his youngest free for a husband, and then have to 't afresh. Sweet Bianca! Happy man be his dole! He that runs fastest gets the ring. How say you, Signior Gremio?

144–45. **would I . . . wooing:** i.e., I wish **I had** already **given** Katherine's wooer **the best horse in Padua** as encouragement **to begin his wooing**

153. **I found . . . love-in-idleness:** i.e., I fell in love (Lucentio plays with the idea that idleness begets love, "love-in-idleness" being the name of a flower whose juice in one's eyes, according to Shakespeare's *A Midsummer Night's Dream,* causes one to love the next thing that one sees.)

155. **to me as secret:** as much in my confidence

156. **Anna to the Queen of Carthage:** In Virgil's *Aeneid,* Dido, **queen of Carthage**, has a sister, **Anna,** to whom the queen reveals her love for Aeneas.

158. **achieve not:** do not succeed in obtaining

162. **rated:** chided, scolded

164. **Redime . . . minimo:** i.e., ransom yourself from capture as cheaply as possible (Latin)

165. **Gramercies:** thanks; **Go forward:** continue (with your counsel); **contents:** i.e., makes me content

167. **longly:** long; perhaps also longingly

168. **marked not:** did not notice; **pith:** essence

170. **daughter of Agenor:** Europa, whom Jove, in the form of a bull, took to Crete (The story is told in Ovid's *Metamorphoses.*) See picture, page 42.

GREMIO I am agreed, and would I had given him the best horse in Padua to begin his wooing that would thoroughly woo her, wed her, and bed her, and rid the house of her. Come on.

⌜Gremio and Hortensio⌝ exit.
Tranio and Lucentio remain onstage.

TRANIO
I pray, sir, tell me, is it possible
That love should of a sudden take such hold?

LUCENTIO
O Tranio, till I found it to be true,
I never thought it possible or likely.
But see, while idly I stood looking on,
I found the effect of love-in-idleness,
And now in plainness do confess to thee
That art to me as secret and as dear
As Anna to the Queen of Carthage was:
Tranio, I burn, I pine! I perish, Tranio,
If I achieve not this young modest girl.
Counsel me, Tranio, for I know thou canst.
Assist me, Tranio, for I know thou wilt.

TRANIO
Master, it is no time to chide you now.
Affection is not rated from the heart.
If love have touched you, naught remains but so:
Redime te ⌜captum⌝ quam queas minimo.

LUCENTIO
Gramercies, lad. Go forward. This contents;
The rest will comfort, for thy counsel's sound.

TRANIO
Master, you looked so longly on the maid,
Perhaps you marked not what's the pith of all.

LUCENTIO
O yes, I saw sweet beauty in her face,
Such as the daughter of Agenor had,
That made great Jove to humble him to her hand
When with his knees he kissed the Cretan strand.

176. **her:** i.e., Bianca's

183. **curst and shrewd:** bad-tempered and loud

185. **maid:** maiden, virgin

186. **mewed:** caged

187. **Because:** i.e., so that

189. **advised:** i.e., aware (literally, informed)

191. **marry:** i.e., indeed; **'tis plotted:** i.e., I've a scheme

193. **for my hand:** i.e., I'll bet **my hand**

194. **meet . . . one:** i.e., coincide perfectly

Europa, "daughter of Agenor,"
borne by "great Jove." (1.1.170–71)
From Gabriele Simeoni, *La vita . . .* (1559).

TRANIO
Saw you no more? Marked you not how her sister
Began to scold and raise up such a storm
That mortal ears might hardly endure the din?

LUCENTIO
Tranio, I saw her coral lips to move,
And with her breath she did perfume the air.
Sacred and sweet was all I saw in her.

TRANIO, ⌜*aside*⌝
Nay, then 'tis time to stir him from his trance.—
I pray, awake, sir! If you love the maid,
Bend thoughts and wits to achieve her. Thus it stands:
Her elder sister is so curst and shrewd
That till the father rid his hands of her,
Master, your love must live a maid at home,
And therefore has he closely mewed her up,
Because she will not be annoyed with suitors.

LUCENTIO
Ah, Tranio, what a cruel father's he!
But art thou not advised he took some care
To get her cunning schoolmasters to instruct her?

TRANIO
Ay, marry, am I, sir—and now 'tis plotted!

LUCENTIO
I have it, Tranio!

TRANIO Master, for my hand,
Both our inventions meet and jump in one.

LUCENTIO
Tell me thine first.

TRANIO You will be schoolmaster
And undertake the teaching of the maid:
That's your device.

LUCENTIO It is. May it be done?

TRANIO
Not possible. For who shall bear your part

202. **Keep house:** establish a household; **ply his book:** i.e., study **ply:** apply himself to

204. **Basta:** Italian for "enough"; **have it full:** i.e., have worked out a whole plan

209. **port:** style of life fitting my station

211. **meaner:** less socially important

213. **Uncase thee:** i.e., undress; **colored hat and cloak:** See longer note, page 223.

214. **waits on:** serves

215. **charm . . . tongue: first** conjure **him to** stay quiet

217. **sith:** since

218. **tied:** bound, obligated

220. **serviceable:** diligent in service; **quoth:** said

226. **Whose sudden sight:** i.e., the **sudden sight** of whom; **thralled:** enthralled, enslaved

229. **how now:** an interjection that here means "what's going on" (literally, "how is it now")

And be in Padua here Vincentio's son,
Keep house, and ply his book, welcome his friends,
Visit his countrymen and banquet them?

LUCENTIO
Basta, content thee, for I have it full.
We have not yet been seen in any house,
Nor can we be distinguished by our faces
For man or master. Then it follows thus:
Thou shalt be master, Tranio, in my stead,
Keep house, and port, and servants, as I should.
I will some other be, some Florentine,
Some Neapolitan, or meaner man of Pisa.
'Tis hatched, and shall be so. Tranio, at once
Uncase thee. Take my colored hat and cloak.
⌜*They exchange clothes.*⌝
When Biondello comes, he waits on thee,
But I will charm him first to keep his tongue.

TRANIO So had you need.
In brief, sir, sith it your pleasure is,
And I am tied to be obedient
(For so your father charged me at our parting:
"Be serviceable to my son," quoth he,
Although I think 'twas in another sense),
I am content to be Lucentio,
Because so well I love Lucentio.

LUCENTIO
Tranio, be so, because Lucentio loves,
And let me be a slave, t' achieve that maid
Whose sudden sight hath thralled my wounded eye.

Enter Biondello.

Here comes the rogue.—Sirrah, where have you
been?

BIONDELLO
Where have I been? Nay, how now, where are you?

230. **fellow: fellow** servant
233. **frame:** adjust
235. **count'nance:** appearance, manner
236. **for:** i.e., to make good
238. **descried:** identified, recognized
239. **becomes:** is becoming or appropriate
242. **Ne'er a whit:** i.e., not a bit
246. **So could I:** i.e., **I** too would like to change **into Lucentio; faith:** a mild oath
255. **rests:** remains
256. **make:** become
258 SD. **Presenters:** characters in the Induction (who "presented" the play). This bit of dialogue between Sly, a Servingman, and the Page does not appear in *A Shrew.* (See Appendix, "Framing Dialogue in *The Taming of a Shrew* [1594]," pages 233–46.) In *The Shrew*, this is Sly's final appearance.
259. **mind:** pay attention to

Master, has my fellow Tranio stolen your clothes?
Or you stolen his? Or both? Pray, what's the news?

LUCENTIO
Sirrah, come hither. 'Tis no time to jest,
And therefore frame your manners to the time.
Your fellow, Tranio here, to save my life,
Puts my apparel and my count'nance on,
And I for my escape have put on his;
For in a quarrel since I came ashore
I killed a man and fear I was descried.
Wait you on him, I charge you, as becomes,
While I make way from hence to save my life.
You understand me?

BIONDELLO Ay, sir. ⌜*Aside.*⌝ Ne'er a whit.

LUCENTIO
And not a jot of "Tranio" in your mouth.
Tranio is changed into Lucentio.

BIONDELLO
The better for him. Would I were so too.

TRANIO
So could I, faith, boy, to have the next wish after,
That Lucentio indeed had Baptista's youngest
daughter.
But, sirrah, not for my sake, but your master's, I
advise
You use your manners discreetly in all kind of
companies.
When I am alone, why then I am Tranio;
But in all places else, ⌜your⌝ master Lucentio.

LUCENTIO Tranio, let's go. One thing more rests, that thyself execute, to make one among these wooers. If thou ask me why, sufficeth my reasons are both good and weighty. *They exit.*

The Presenters above ⌜speak.⌝

FIRST SERVINGMAN
My lord, you nod. You do not mind the play.

264. **Would:** i.e., I wish
264 SD. **mark:** i.e., watch

1.2 Petruchio, with his servant Grumio, has just arrived in Padua. His friend Hortensio suggests that Petruchio woo Katherine. Petruchio enthusiastically agrees. He agrees also to present Hortensio, in disguise, to Baptista as a music teacher named Litio. Gremio appears with Lucentio, who is disguised as a teacher named Cambio. Last of all comes Tranio, now impersonating Lucentio and declaring his intention to woo Bianca. Gremio, Hortensio, and Tranio (as Lucentio) agree to help Petruchio win Katherine.

---

0 SD. **man:** i.e., servant
2. **of all:** especially
3. **approvèd:** tried, tested
4. **trow:** think
7. **rebused:** Grumio's error for "abused"
8. **knock me:** i.e., **knock** (rap on the gate) for **me** (This begins extensive wordplay on **knock me** as [1] an old dative form meaning **knock,** and [2] an ordinary verb plus object meaning "hit me.")
12. **rap me: rap; pate:** head
13–15. **I . . . worst:** i.e., if **I** were to hit **you first, I know who** would afterward get **the worst** of it
17. **ring it:** perhaps, use the ring fastened to the door as a knocker (with a pun on "wring")
18. **sol, fa:** notes on the scale; **sing it:** i.e., wail
19. **mistress:** perhaps a printer's error for "masters," or perhaps addressed to Sly's "wife"
21. **villain:** scoundrel, rascal

SLY Yes, by Saint Anne, do I. A good matter, surely. Comes there any more of it?

⌜PAGE, *as*⌝ LADY My lord, 'tis but begun.

SLY 'Tis a very excellent piece of work, madam lady. Would 'twere done.

They sit and mark.

⌜Scene 2⌝

Enter Petruchio and his man Grumio.

PETRUCHIO
Verona, for a while I take my leave
To see my friends in Padua, but of all
My best belovèd and approvèd friend,
Hortensio. And I trow this is his house.
Here, sirrah Grumio, knock, I say.

GRUMIO Knock, sir? Whom should I knock? Is there any man has rebused your Worship?

PETRUCHIO Villain, I say, knock me here soundly.

GRUMIO Knock you here, sir? Why, sir, what am I, sir, that I should knock you here, sir?

PETRUCHIO
Villain, I say, knock me at this gate
And rap me well, or I'll knock your knave's pate.

GRUMIO
My master is grown quarrelsome. I should knock
you first,
And then I know after who comes by the worst.

PETRUCHIO Will it not be?
Faith, sirrah, an you'll not knock, I'll ring it.
I'll try how you can *sol, fa,* and sing it.

He wrings him by the ears. ⌜*Grumio falls.*⌝

GRUMIO Help, mistress, help! My master is mad.

PETRUCHIO Now knock when I bid you, sirrah villain.

25. **part the fray:** i.e., stop the fight

26. **Con tutto il cuore ben trovato:** Italian for "Well found (i.e., welcome) with all [my] heart"

27–28. **Alla . . . Petruchio:** Italian for "Welcome to our house, my much-honored Master Petruchio"

29. **compound:** settle

30. **'leges:** i.e., alleges

31. **Latin:** Grumio seems to be presented as an Englishman who cannot tell the difference between Italian and Latin.

34. **being: (his master) being**

35. **two-and-thirty . . . out:** i.e., not quite right in the head (The allusion is to a card game called "one-in-thirty." According to Grumio, Petruchio is one "pip"—i.e., one mark on the card—over the goal of the game.)

46. **pledge:** guarantor

47. **this':** i.e., this is; **heavy chance:** grave misfortune

48. **ancient:** longtime

Enter Hortensio.

HORTENSIO How now, what's the matter? My old friend Grumio and my good friend Petruchio? How do you all at Verona?

PETRUCHIO
Signior Hortensio, come you to part the fray?
⌜*Con tutto il cuore ben trovato,*⌝ may I say.

HORTENSIO *Alla nostra casa* ⌜*ben*⌝ *venuto,* ⌜*molto honorato*⌝ *signor mio Petruchio.*—Rise, Grumio, rise. We will compound this quarrel. ⌜*Grumio rises.*⌝

GRUMIO Nay, 'tis no matter, sir, what he 'leges in Latin. If this be not a lawful cause for me to leave his service—look you, sir: he bid me knock him and rap him soundly, sir. Well, was it fit for a servant to use his master so, being perhaps, for aught I see, two-and-thirty, a pip out?
Whom, would to God, I had well knocked at first,
Then had not Grumio come by the worst.

PETRUCHIO
A senseless villain, good Hortensio.
I bade the rascal knock upon your gate
And could not get him for my heart to do it.

GRUMIO Knock at the gate? O, heavens, spake you not these words plain: "Sirrah, knock me here, rap me here, knock me well, and knock me soundly"? And come you now with "knocking at the gate"?

PETRUCHIO
Sirrah, begone, or talk not, I advise you.

HORTENSIO
Petruchio, patience. I am Grumio's pledge.
Why, this' a heavy chance 'twixt him and you,
Your ancient, trusty, pleasant servant Grumio.
And tell me now, sweet friend, what happy gale
Blows you to Padua here from old Verona?

PETRUCHIO
Such wind as scatters young men through the world

53. **in a few:** i.e., **in a few** words

56. **maze:** intricate business

57. **Happily:** perhaps; or, with pleasure

58. **Crowns:** i.e., coins

60. **come roundly to thee:** speak to you bluntly

61. **ill-favored:** unattractive (because bad-tempered)

69. **burden:** refrain; or, bass accompaniment

70. **foul:** ugly; **Florentius' love:** Florentius, in John Gower's fourteenth-century *Confessio Amantis,* agrees to marry an old hag, who is later transformed into a young beauty.

71. **Sibyl:** the **Sibyl** of Cumae, who had been granted as many years of life as there are grains in a handful of sand (See picture, page 54.) **curst and shrewd:** bad-tempered

72. **Socrates' Xanthippe:** The wife of Socrates is usually represented as a shrew.

73. **moves:** disturbs, dislodges

80. **aglet-baby:** i.e., doll decked with aglets, or spangles

81. **trot:** hag

83. **withal:** with it

To seek their fortunes farther than at home,
Where small experience grows. But in a few,
Signior Hortensio, thus it stands with me:
Antonio, my father, is deceased,
And I have thrust myself into this maze,
Happily to wive and thrive, as best I may.
Crowns in my purse I have and goods at home,
And so am come abroad to see the world.

HORTENSIO
Petruchio, shall I then come roundly to thee
And wish thee to a shrewd ill-favored wife?
Thou'dst thank me but a little for my counsel—
And yet I'll promise thee she shall be rich,
And very rich. But thou'rt too much my friend,
And I'll not wish thee to her.

PETRUCHIO
Signior Hortensio, 'twixt such friends as we
Few words suffice. And therefore, if thou know
One rich enough to be Petruchio's wife
(As wealth is burden of my wooing dance),
Be she as foul as was Florentius' love,
As old as Sibyl, and as curst and shrewd
As Socrates' Xanthippe, or a worse,
She moves me not, or not removes at least
Affection's edge in me, were she as rough
As are the swelling Adriatic seas.
I come to wive it wealthily in Padua;
If wealthily, then happily in Padua.

GRUMIO, ⌜*to Hortensio*⌝ Nay, look you, sir, he tells you flatly what his mind is. Why, give him gold enough and marry him to a puppet or an aglet-baby, or an old trot with ne'er a tooth in her head, though she have as many diseases as two-and-fifty horses. Why, nothing comes amiss, so money comes withal.

HORTENSIO
Petruchio, since we are stepped thus far in,

85. **that:** i.e., **that** which

91. **shrewd, and froward:** shrewish and perverse

92. **state:** estate, financial status

96. **board her:** i.e., woo her

98, 100. **Minola:** accent on first syllable

106. **give you over:** leave you right now

109. **humor:** whim, mood; **an:** if

111–12. **half a score:** ten

113. **rail . . . tricks:** perhaps, scold in his "rhetorics"; or, use abusive language for which he should be hanged (The passage is very obscure.)

114. **stand him:** i.e., **stand** up to **him** (with a sexual meaning as well)

114–16. **he will . . . cat:** These lines suggest that Petruchio will throw "figures of speech" at Katherine until she is overcome. But they also suggest physical violence and, perhaps, rape.

The Sibyl of Cumae. (1.2.71)
From Philippus de Barberiis, *Quattuor hic compressa . . .* (1495).

I will continue that I broached in jest.
I can, Petruchio, help thee to a wife
With wealth enough, and young and beauteous,
Brought up as best becomes a gentlewoman.
Her only fault, and that is faults enough,
Is that she is intolerable curst,
And shrewd, and froward, so beyond all measure
That, were my state far worser than it is,
I would not wed her for a mine of gold.

PETRUCHIO

Hortensio, peace. Thou know'st not gold's effect.
Tell me her father's name, and 'tis enough;
For I will board her, though she chide as loud
As thunder when the clouds in autumn crack.

HORTENSIO

Her father is Baptista Minola,
An affable and courteous gentleman.
Her name is Katherina Minola,
Renowned in Padua for her scolding tongue.

PETRUCHIO

I know her father, though I know not her,
And he knew my deceasèd father well.
I will not sleep, Hortensio, till I see her,
And therefore let me be thus bold with you
To give you over at this first encounter—
Unless you will accompany me thither.

GRUMIO, ⌜*to Hortensio*⌝ I pray you, sir, let him go while the humor lasts. O' my word, an she knew him as well as I do, she would think scolding would do little good upon him. She may perhaps call him half a score knaves or so. Why, that's nothing; an he begin once, he'll rail in his rope tricks. I'll tell you what, sir, an she stand him but a little, he will throw a figure in her face and so disfigure her with it that she shall have no more eyes to see withal than a cat. You know him not, sir.

118. **Tarry:** wait

119. **keep:** i.e., keeping; or, castle **keep,** the heavily fortified inner tower of a castle

120. **hold:** i.e., his stronghold; his safekeeping

122. **other more:** i.e., others too

124. **Supposing:** i.e., Baptista supposes

125. **For:** i.e., because of; **rehearsed:** itemized

127. **this . . . ta'en:** i.e., **Baptista** has arranged

131. **maid:** maiden, virgin

132. **do me grace:** do me a favor

133. **sober:** subdued in color, dark

135. **Well seen: well** trained

136. **device:** scheme

137. **leave:** opportunity; **make love to:** pay amorous attention to, woo

144. **proper stripling:** handsome youngster (sarcastic reference to Gremio)

A scholar "in sober robes." (1.2.133)
From Geoffrey Whitney, *A choice of emblemes . . .* (1586).

HORTENSIO

Tarry, Petruchio. I must go with thee,
For in Baptista's keep my treasure is.
He hath the jewel of my life in hold,
His youngest daughter, beautiful Bianca,
And her withholds from me ⌜and⌝ other more,
Suitors to her and rivals in my love,
Supposing it a thing impossible,
For those defects I have before rehearsed,
That ever Katherina will be wooed.
Therefore this order hath Baptista ta'en,
That none shall have access unto Bianca
Till Katherine the curst have got a husband.

GRUMIO "Katherine the curst,"
A title for a maid, of all titles the worst.

HORTENSIO

Now shall my friend Petruchio do me grace
And offer me disguised in sober robes
To old Baptista as a schoolmaster
Well seen in music, to instruct Bianca,
That so I may, by this device at least,
Have leave and leisure to make love to her
And unsuspected court her by herself.

GRUMIO Here's no knavery! See, to beguile the old folks, how the young folks lay their heads together!

Enter Gremio and Lucentio, disguised ⌜as Cambio, a schoolmaster.⌝

Master, master, look about you. Who goes there, ha?

HORTENSIO

Peace, Grumio, it is the rival of my love.—
Petruchio, stand by awhile.

⌜*Petruchio, Hortensio, and Grumio stand aside.*⌝

GRUMIO, ⌜*aside*⌝

A proper stripling, and an amorous.

145. **the note:** i.e., perhaps, a list of the **books** mentioned at line 147

146. **bound:** Books were sold unbound. (For a picture of a **bound** book, see below.)

147. **See . . . hand:** i.e., **see** to **that** in **any** case

148. **lectures:** lessons

150. **liberality:** generosity; probably, here, "what Baptista pays you"

151. **mend:** improve; **a largess:** a gift of money; **paper:** probably **the note** mentioned above

152. **them:** i.e., the books

156. **stand:** i.e., rest

157. **as yourself . . . place: as** if you **were** present the whole time

161. **woodcock:** i.e., dupe (A woodcock is a bird easily snared and therefore thought to be foolish. See picture, page 60.)

166. **Trow:** know

172. **warrant:** guarantee

A bound book, with clasps. (1.2.146)
From *Notitia vtraque cum Orientis tum Occidentis . . .* (1552).

GREMIO, ⌜*to Lucentio*⌝
O, very well, I have perused the note.
Hark you, sir, I'll have them very fairly bound,
All books of love. See that at any hand,
And see you read no other lectures to her.
You understand me. Over and beside
Signior Baptista's liberality,
I'll mend it with a largess. Take your paper too.
And let me have them very well perfumed,
For she is sweeter than perfume itself
To whom they go to. What will you read to her?

LUCENTIO, ⌜*as* CAMBIO⌝
Whate'er I read to her, I'll plead for you
As for my patron, stand you so assured,
As firmly as yourself were still in place,
Yea, and perhaps with more successful words
Than you—unless you were a scholar, sir.

GREMIO
O this learning, what a thing it is!

GRUMIO, ⌜*aside*⌝
O this woodcock, what an ass it is!

PETRUCHIO, ⌜*aside*⌝ Peace, sirrah.

HORTENSIO, ⌜*aside*⌝
Grumio, mum. ⌜*Coming forward.*⌝
God save you, Signior Gremio.

GREMIO
And you are well met, Signior Hortensio.
Trow you whither I am going? To Baptista Minola.
I promised to enquire carefully
About a schoolmaster for the fair Bianca,
And by good fortune I have lighted well
On this young man, for learning and behavior
Fit for her turn, well read in poetry
And other books—good ones, I warrant you.

HORTENSIO
'Tis well. And I have met a gentleman

179. **bags:** i.e., moneybags

180. **vent:** express

181. **speak me fair:** respond courteously

182. **indifferent:** equally

184. **Upon agreement . . . liking:** i.e., if we agree to terms that he likes (Hortensio and Gremio are to pay the expenses that Petruchio incurs in his courtship of Katherine; see lines 218–19.)

187. **So said, so done, is well:** i.e., if the deeds match the words, this is good

191. **What countryman?:** i.e., from what country are you?

196. **stomach:** desire, spirit; **to 't:** go to it; **i':** i.e., in

Woodcocks being trapped. (1.2.161)
From Henry Parrot, *Laquei ridiculosi* . . . (1613).

Hath promised me to help ⌜me⌝ to another,
A fine musician to instruct our mistress.
So shall I no whit be behind in duty
To fair Bianca, so beloved of me.

GREMIO
Beloved of me, and that my deeds shall prove.

GRUMIO, ⌜*aside*⌝ And that his bags shall prove.

HORTENSIO
Gremio, 'tis now no time to vent our love.
Listen to me, and if you speak me fair
I'll tell you news indifferent good for either.
⌜*Presenting Petruchio.*⌝
Here is a gentleman whom by chance I met,
Upon agreement from us to his liking,
Will undertake to woo curst Katherine,
Yea, and to marry her, if her dowry please.

GREMIO So said, so done, is well.
Hortensio, have you told him all her faults?

PETRUCHIO
I know she is an irksome, brawling scold.
If that be all, masters, I hear no harm.

GREMIO
No? Sayst me so, friend? What countryman?

PETRUCHIO
Born in Verona, old Antonio's son.
My father dead, my fortune lives for me,
And I do hope good days and long to see.

GREMIO
Oh, sir, such a life with such a wife were strange.
But if you have a stomach, to 't, i' God's name!
You shall have me assisting you in all.
But will you woo this wildcat?

PETRUCHIO Will I live?

GRUMIO
Will he woo her? Ay, or I'll hang her.

206. **ordnance:** heavy guns

209. **'larums:** i.e., alarums, or calls to battle

213. **fear boys with bugs:** frighten little **boys with** bugbears or bogeymen

216. **happily:** opportunely, at just the right time

219. **bear . . . of:** pay his expenses for

223. **readiest:** i.e., shortest

225. **fair:** beautiful

228. **her to—:** Gremio seems to be interrupted here before he finishes the question "you mean not her to woo?" (Some editors print the line as "mean not her too?")

A "chestnut in a farmer's fire." (1.2.212)
From Jacob Cats, *Alle de wercken* . . . (1657–59).

PETRUCHIO
Why came I hither but to that intent?
Think you a little din can daunt mine ears?
Have I not in my time heard lions roar?
Have I not heard the sea, puffed up with winds,
Rage like an angry boar chafèd with sweat?
Have I not heard great ordnance in the field
And heaven's artillery thunder in the skies?
Have I not in a pitchèd battle heard
Loud 'larums, neighing steeds, and trumpets clang?
And do you tell me of a woman's tongue,
That gives not half so great a blow to hear
As will a chestnut in a farmer's fire?
Tush, tush, fear boys with bugs!

GRUMIO
For he fears none.

GREMIO Hortensio, hark.
This gentleman is happily arrived,
My mind presumes, for his own good and yours.

HORTENSIO
I promised we would be contributors
And bear his charge of wooing whatsoe'er.

GREMIO
And so we will, provided that he win her.

GRUMIO
I would I were as sure of a good dinner.

Enter Tranio, ⌜disguised as Lucentio,⌝ and Biondello.

TRANIO, ⌜*as* LUCENTIO⌝
Gentlemen, God save you. If I may be bold,
Tell me, I beseech you, which is the readiest way
To the house of Signior Baptista Minola?

BIONDELLO He that has the two fair daughters—is 't he you mean?

TRANIO, ⌜*as* LUCENTIO⌝ Even he, Biondello.

GREMIO
Hark you, sir, you mean not her to—

229. **What . . . do?:** i.e., **what** business is it of yours?

230. **her that chides:** i.e., Katherine; **at any hand:** in **any** case

233. **ere:** before

235. **An if: if**

236. **get you hence:** i.e., go away

242. **choice:** i.e., chosen

244. **Softly:** gently

250. **Leda's daughter:** the legendarily beautiful Helen of Troy, daughter of the god Jove and the woman Leda

251. **well . . . have:** i.e., **Bianca may well have one more**

252. **make one:** i.e., be one

253. **Paris:** lover of Helen of Troy; **speed:** prevail, succeed

A raging "sea, puffed up with winds." (1.2.204–05)
From Lodovico Dolce, *Imprese nobili* . . . (1583).

TRANIO, ⌜*as* LUCENTIO⌝
Perhaps him and her, sir. What have you to do?

PETRUCHIO
Not her that chides, sir, at any hand, I pray.

TRANIO, ⌜*as* LUCENTIO⌝
I love no chiders, sir. Biondello, let's away.

LUCENTIO, ⌜*aside*⌝
Well begun, Tranio.

HORTENSIO Sir, a word ere you go.
Are you a suitor to the maid you talk of, yea or no?

TRANIO, ⌜*as* LUCENTIO⌝
An if I be, sir, is it any offense?

GREMIO
No, if without more words you will get you hence.

TRANIO, ⌜*as* LUCENTIO⌝
Why sir, I pray, are not the streets as free
For me as for you?

GREMIO But so is not she.

TRANIO, ⌜*as* LUCENTIO⌝
For what reason, I beseech you?

GREMIO
For this reason, if you'll know:
That she's the choice love of Signior Gremio.

HORTENSIO
That she's the chosen of Signior Hortensio.

TRANIO, ⌜*as* LUCENTIO⌝
Softly, my masters. If you be gentlemen,
Do me this right: hear me with patience.
Baptista is a noble gentleman
To whom my father is not all unknown,
And were his daughter fairer than she is,
She may more suitors have, and me for one.
Fair Leda's daughter had a thousand wooers.
Then well one more may fair Bianca have.
And so she shall. Lucentio shall make one,
Though Paris came in hope to speed alone.

254. **What:** an interjection introducing a question or an exclamation

255. **give him head:** i.e., let him run (as if he were a horse); **jade:** a worthless horse (See picture, below.)

257. **as:** i.e., **as** to

262. **let her go by:** leave her alone

263. **Hercules:** Also called Alcides, he was required to undertake **twelve** seemingly impossible labors. (See line 264.)

266. **hearken:** ask

272. **stead:** help

275. **whose hap:** whoever's fortune

276. **so graceless . . . ingrate:** i.e., **be so** ungracious as **to** fail to show his gratitude

277. **conceive:** understand

279. **gratify:** i.e., pay

A jade. (1.2.255; 2.1.212; 4.1.1)
From Cesare Fiaschi, *Trattato dell'imbrigliare* . . . (1614).

GREMIO
What, this gentleman will out-talk us all!

LUCENTIO, ⌜*as* CAMBIO⌝
Sir, give him head; I know he'll prove a jade.

PETRUCHIO
Hortensio, to what end are all these words?

HORTENSIO, ⌜*to Tranio*⌝
Sir, let me be so bold as ask you,
Did you yet ever see Baptista's daughter?

TRANIO, ⌜*as* LUCENTIO⌝
No, sir, but hear I do that he hath two,
The one as famous for a scolding tongue
As is the other for beauteous modesty.

PETRUCHIO
Sir, sir, the first's for me; let her go by.

GREMIO
Yea, leave that labor to great Hercules,
And let it be more than Alcides' twelve.

PETRUCHIO, ⌜*to Tranio*⌝
Sir, understand you this of me, in sooth:
The youngest daughter, whom you hearken for,
Her father keeps from all access of suitors
And will not promise her to any man
Until the elder sister first be wed.
The younger then is free, and not before.

TRANIO, ⌜*as* LUCENTIO⌝
If it be so, sir, that you are the man
Must stead us all, and me amongst the rest,
And if you break the ice and do this ⌜feat,⌝
Achieve the elder, set the younger free
For our access, whose hap shall be to have her
Will not so graceless be to be ingrate.

HORTENSIO
Sir, you say well, and well you do conceive.
And since you do profess to be a suitor,
You must, as we do, gratify this gentleman,
To whom we all rest generally beholding.

282. **Please you:** i.e., if it **please you; contrive:** perhaps, while away, spend; or, perhaps, plot, conspire

283. **quaff carouses:** drink copiously

286. **motion:** proposal

288. **I . . . venuto:** i.e., I will introduce you; I will ensure your welcome **ben venuto:** welcome (Italian)

288 SD. **They exit:** The play familiarly called *A Shrew* includes, at approximately this point, a bit of dialogue between Sly and the disguised lord. See longer note, page 223, and "Framing Dialogue in *The Taming of a Shrew*, C, page 241, below.

". . . eat and drink as friends. . . ." (1.2.285)
From T[homas] F[ella], *A book of diverse devices . . .* (1585–1622).

TRANIO, ⌜*as* LUCENTIO⌝

Sir, I shall not be slack; in sign whereof,
Please you we may contrive this afternoon
And quaff carouses to our mistress' health,
And do as adversaries do in law,
Strive mightily, but eat and drink as friends.

GRUMIO ⌜*and*⌝ BIONDELLO

O excellent motion! Fellows, let's be gone.

HORTENSIO

The motion's good indeed, and be it so.—
Petruchio, I shall be your ⌜*ben*⌝ *venuto.*

They exit.

THE TAMING OF THE SHREW

ACT 2

2.1 Baptista stops Katherine from abusing Bianca and receives a visit from Petruchio, who presents Hortensio (disguised as Litio, a music teacher); Gremio introduces Lucentio (disguised as Cambio, a teacher of languages). Tranio, impersonating Lucentio, announces his wish to marry Bianca, and Petruchio his desire to marry Katherine. Baptista insists that Petruchio must get Katherine's love. Petruchio and Katherine, left alone, enter into a furious bout of wordplay. Petruchio then lies to Baptista, insisting that Katherine loves him but that the couple have agreed that she will pretend to dislike him in public. Katherine's wedding is arranged, and Baptista hears the offers that Gremio and Tranio (as Lucentio) make for Bianca. Tranio-Lucentio outbids Gremio and is awarded Bianca, provided that Vincentio, Lucentio's father, will guarantee the dowry. Tranio-Lucentio sets out to find someone to impersonate Vincentio and provide the guarantee.

---

2. **bondmaid:** i.e., **slave**
3. **goods:** things; articles of clothing
4. **Unbind:** i.e., if you will **unbind**
8. **charge:** command
13. **Minion:** hussy
14. **affect:** like
15. **but . . . him:** i.e., **but** in any case **you shall have him**
16. **belike:** perhaps
17. **fair:** i.e., in beautiful clothes

⌜ACT 2⌝

⌜Scene 1⌝

Enter Katherine and Bianca ⌜*with her hands tied.*⌝

BIANCA
Good sister, wrong me not, nor wrong yourself,
To make a bondmaid and a slave of me.
That I disdain. But for these other goods—
Unbind my hands, I'll pull them off myself,
Yea, all my raiment to my petticoat,
Or what you will command me will I do,
So well I know my duty to my elders.

KATHERINE
Of all thy suitors here I charge ⌜thee⌝ tell
Whom thou lov'st best. See thou dissemble not.

BIANCA
Believe me, sister, of all the men alive
I never yet beheld that special face
Which I could fancy more than any other.

KATHERINE
Minion, thou liest. Is 't not Hortensio?

BIANCA
If you affect him, sister, here I swear
I'll plead for you myself, but you shall have him.

KATHERINE
O, then belike you fancy riches more.
You will have Gremio to keep you fair.

18. **envy:** hate (pronounced "en-vigh´")
27. **hilding:** beast
32. **flouts:** mocks, insults
34. **suffer me:** allow me to be, tolerate me
36. **dance . . . day:** the proverbial misfortune of the unmarried elder daughter on **her** sister's **wedding day**
37. **for:** because of; **lead . . . hell:** the proverbial fate of unmarried women

Women plying their needles. (2.1.26)
From Jan van der Straet, [*The celebrated Roman women*] (1543).

BIANCA

Is it for him you do envy me so?
Nay, then, you jest, and now I well perceive
You have but jested with me all this while.
I prithee, sister Kate, untie my hands.

⌜*Katherine*⌝ *strikes her.*

KATHERINE

If that be jest, then all the rest was so.

Enter Baptista.

BAPTISTA

Why, how now, dame, whence grows this insolence?—
Bianca, stand aside.—Poor girl, she weeps!

⌜*He unties her hands.*⌝

⌜*To Bianca.*⌝ Go ply thy needle; meddle not with her.
⌜*To Katherine.*⌝ For shame, thou hilding of a devilish spirit!
Why dost thou wrong her that did ne'er wrong thee?
When did she cross thee with a bitter word?

KATHERINE

Her silence flouts me, and I'll be revenged!

⌜*She*⌝ *flies after Bianca.*

BAPTISTA

What, in my sight?—Bianca, get thee in.

⌜*Bianca*⌝ *exits.*

KATHERINE

What, will you not suffer me? Nay, now I see
She is your treasure, she must have a husband,
I must dance barefoot on her wedding day
And, for your love to her, lead apes in hell.
Talk not to me. I will go sit and weep
Till I can find occasion of revenge. ⌜*She exits.*⌝

BAPTISTA

Was ever gentleman thus grieved as I?
But who comes here?

41 SD. **habit:** clothing; **mean man: man** of low status

42. **Good morrow: good** morning

49. **Give me leave:** permit me to continue

54. **forward:** eager, presumptuous

57. **entrance:** price of admission; **entertainment:** reception as a **guest** (line 54)

58. **man:** servant

59. **Cunning:** versed, learned; skillful

62. **Accept of:** i.e., **accept**

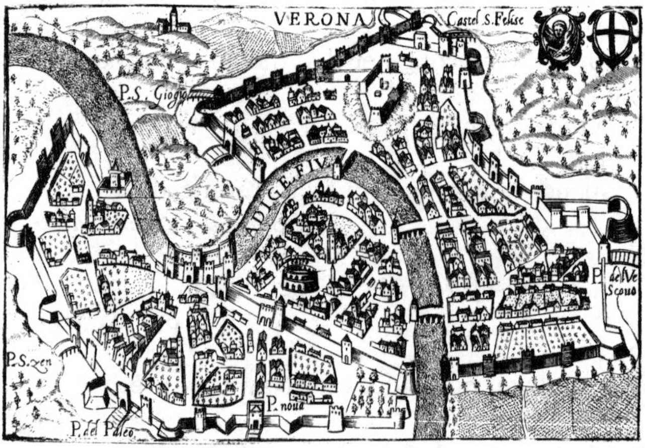

Verona. (1.2.1, 24, 50, 192; 2.1.50)
From Pietro Bertelli, *Theatrum vrbium Italicarum* . . . (1599).

Enter Gremio; Lucentio ⌜disguised as Cambio⌝ in the habit of a mean man; Petruchio with ⌜Hortensio disguised as Litio; and⌝ Tranio ⌜disguised as Lucentio,⌝ with his boy ⌜Biondello⌝ bearing a lute and books.

GREMIO Good morrow, neighbor Baptista.

BAPTISTA Good morrow, neighbor Gremio.—God save you, gentlemen.

PETRUCHIO

And you, good sir. Pray, have you not a daughter
Called Katherina, fair and virtuous?

BAPTISTA

I have a daughter, sir, called Katherina.

GREMIO, ⌜*to Petruchio*⌝

You are too blunt. Go to it orderly.

PETRUCHIO

You wrong me, Signior Gremio. Give me leave.—
I am a gentleman of Verona, sir,
That hearing of her beauty and her wit,
Her affability and bashful modesty,
Her wondrous qualities and mild behavior,
Am bold to show myself a forward guest
Within your house, to make mine eye the witness
Of that report which I so oft have heard,
And, for an entrance to my entertainment,
I do present you with a man of mine,
⌜*Presenting Hortensio, disguised as Litio.*⌝
Cunning in music and the mathematics,
To instruct her fully in those sciences,
Whereof I know she is not ignorant.
Accept of him, or else you do me wrong.
His name is Litio, born in Mantua.

BAPTISTA

You're welcome, sir, and he for your good sake.

66. **is not for your turn:** i.e., **is not** right **for** you

68. **like not of:** i.e., do **not like**

74. **Saving:** with all respect to

76. **Bacare:** corrupt Latin for "get back"

77. **fain:** rather

80. **gift:** i.e., Litio, given to Baptista by Petruchio; **grateful:** gratifying, welcome

86. **the other:** i.e., Litio

91. **walk like a stranger:** perhaps, hang back instead of pressing forward (like Petruchio and Gremio)

But for my daughter Katherine, this I know,
She is not for your turn, the more my grief.

PETRUCHIO
I see you do not mean to part with her,
Or else you like not of my company.

BAPTISTA
Mistake me not. I speak but as I find.
Whence are you, sir? What may I call your name?

PETRUCHIO
Petruchio is my name, Antonio's son,
A man well known throughout all Italy.

BAPTISTA
I know him well. You are welcome for his sake.

GREMIO
Saving your tale, Petruchio, I pray
Let us that are poor petitioners speak too!
Bacare, you are marvelous forward.

PETRUCHIO
O, pardon me, Signior Gremio, I would fain be doing.

GREMIO
I doubt it not, sir. But you will curse your wooing.
⌜*To Baptista.* Neighbor,⌝ this is a gift very grateful, I am sure of it. To express the like kindness, myself, that have been more kindly beholding to you than any, freely give unto ⌜you⌝ this young scholar ⌜*presenting Lucentio, disguised as Cambio*⌝ that hath been long studying at Rheims, as cunning in Greek, Latin, and other languages as the other in music and mathematics. His name is Cambio. Pray accept his service.

BAPTISTA A thousand thanks, Signior Gremio. —Welcome, good Cambio. ⌜*To Tranio as Lucentio.*⌝ But, gentle sir, methinks you walk like a stranger. May I be so bold to know the cause of your coming?

98. **In the preferment of:** granting precedence to
116. **them both:** i.e., Katherine and Bianca
118. **orchard:** garden (See picture, below.)
119. **passing:** very

An orchard. (2.1.118)
From Octavio Boldoni, *Theatrum temporaneum* . . . (1636).

TRANIO, ⌜*as* LUCENTIO⌝
Pardon me, sir, the boldness is mine own,
That being a stranger in this city here
Do make myself a suitor to your daughter,
Unto Bianca, fair and virtuous.
Nor is your firm resolve unknown to me,
In the preferment of the eldest sister.
This liberty is all that I request,
That, upon knowledge of my parentage,
I may have welcome 'mongst the rest that woo
And free access and favor as the rest.
And toward the education of your daughters
I here bestow a simple instrument
And this small packet of Greek and Latin books.
⌜*Biondello comes forward with the gifts.*⌝
If you accept them, then their worth is great.

BAPTISTA
Lucentio is your name. Of whence, I pray?

TRANIO, ⌜*as* LUCENTIO⌝
Of Pisa, sir, son to Vincentio.

BAPTISTA
A mighty man of Pisa. By report
I know him well. You are very welcome, sir.
⌜*To Hortensio as Litio.*⌝ Take you the lute, ⌜*To Lucentio as Cambio.*⌝ and you the set of books.
You shall go see your pupils presently.
Holla, within!

Enter a Servant.

Sirrah, lead these gentlemen
To my daughters, and tell them both
These are their tutors. Bid them use them well.
⌜*Servant exits with Hortensio and Lucentio.*⌝
We will go walk a little in the orchard,
And then to dinner. You are passing welcome,
And so I pray you all to think yourselves.

129. **in possession:** for immediate **possession**

131. **widowhood:** her rights as a widow; **be it:** i.e., if **it be**

133. **specialties:** special contracts

134. **on either hand:** i.e., on both sides

137. **father:** i.e., (future) father-in-law

145. **happy:** fortunate; **speed:** progress

147. **to the proof:** in tested or proven armor, invulnerable

147–48. **as mountains . . . perpetually:** i.e., **as mountains,** which do not shake, even **though winds blow** against them **perpetually**

Apollo. (IND.2.35)
From Johann Basilius Herold, *Heydenweldt* [1554].

PETRUCHIO

Signior Baptista, my business asketh haste,
And every day I cannot come to woo.
You knew my father well, and in him me,
Left solely heir to all his lands and goods,
Which I have bettered rather than decreased.
Then tell me, if I get your daughter's love,
What dowry shall I have with her to wife?

BAPTISTA

After my death, the one half of my lands,
And, in possession, twenty thousand crowns.

PETRUCHIO

And, for that dowry, I'll assure her of
Her widowhood, be it that she survive me,
In all my lands and leases whatsoever.
Let specialties be therefore drawn between us,
That covenants may be kept on either hand.

BAPTISTA

Ay, when the special thing is well obtained,
That is, her love, for that is all in all.

PETRUCHIO

Why, that is nothing. For I tell you, father,
I am as peremptory as she proud-minded;
And where two raging fires meet together,
They do consume the thing that feeds their fury.
Though little fire grows great with little wind,
Yet extreme gusts will blow out fire and all.
So I to her and so she yields to me,
For I am rough and woo not like a babe.

BAPTISTA

Well mayst thou woo, and happy be thy speed.
But be thou armed for some unhappy words.

PETRUCHIO

Ay, to the proof, as mountains are for winds,
That shakes not, though they blow perpetually.

153. **hold with her:** withstand her use

154. **break:** tame, train (a metaphor from horse training)

155. **broke the lute:** Usually in productions Hortensio enters with the lute broken over his head.

156. **did but tell:** only told; **mistook her frets:** placed her fingers the wrong way on the ridges or bars (**frets**) on the neck of the lute

157. **bowed:** curved, bent

159. **fume:** rage (as in "frets and fumes")

162. **pate:** head

163. **amazèd:** astounded

166. **Jack:** rascal

167. **As had she:** i.e., **as** if **she had**

168. **lusty:** lively

169. **ere:** before (The editorial tradition prints "e'er," but we prefer F's "ere.")

173. **apt:** inclined

A lute. (2.1.111)
From Silvestro Pietrasanta,
Symbola heroica . . . (1682).

Enter Hortensio ⌜as Litio⌝ with his head broke.

BAPTISTA
How now, my friend, why dost thou look so pale?

HORTENSIO, ⌜*as* LITIO⌝
For fear, I promise you, if I look pale.

BAPTISTA
What, will my daughter prove a good musician?

HORTENSIO, ⌜*as* LITIO⌝
I think she'll sooner prove a soldier!
Iron may hold with her, but never lutes.

BAPTISTA
Why, then thou canst not break her to the lute?

HORTENSIO, ⌜*as* LITIO⌝
Why, no, for she hath broke the lute to me.
I did but tell her she mistook her frets,
And bowed her hand to teach her fingering,
When, with a most impatient devilish spirit,
"'Frets' call you these?" quoth she. "I'll fume with them!"
And with that word she struck me on the head,
And through the instrument my pate made way,
And there I stood amazèd for a while,
As on a pillory, looking through the lute,
While she did call me "rascal fiddler,"
And "twangling Jack," with twenty such vile terms,
As had she studied to misuse me so.

PETRUCHIO
Now, by the world, it is a lusty wench.
I love her ten times more than ere I did.
O, how I long to have some chat with her!

BAPTISTA, ⌜*to Hortensio as Litio*⌝
Well, go with me, and be not so discomfited.
Proceed in practice with my younger daughter.
She's apt to learn, and thankful for good turns.—
Signior Petruchio, will you go with us,
Or shall I send my daughter Kate to you?

176. **attend:** await

178. **rail:** scold; **plain:** directly, simply

180. **clear:** serene, unclouded

185. **pack:** i.e., **pack** up and leave

187. **deny:** refuse; **crave the day:** beg her to name **the day**

188. **ask the banns:** make public the intention to marry

191. **but:** i.e., but you are

193. **in faith:** a mild oath

194. **curst:** ill-tempered, quarrelsome

196. **super-dainty:** especially choice, precious

197. **dainties:** delicacies to eat, also called "cates"

200. **sounded:** (1) spoken of; (2) measured for depth—hence **deeply** in the next line

202. **moved:** inspired

203. **in good time:** indeed

PETRUCHIO

I pray you do. I'll attend her here—

All but Petruchio exit.

And woo her with some spirit when she comes!
Say that she rail, why then I'll tell her plain
She sings as sweetly as a nightingale.
Say that she frown, I'll say she looks as clear
As morning roses newly washed with dew.
Say she be mute and will not speak a word,
Then I'll commend her volubility
And say she uttereth piercing eloquence.
If she do bid me pack, I'll give her thanks
As though she bid me stay by her a week.
If she deny to wed, I'll crave the day
When I shall ask the banns, and when be marrièd.
But here she comes—and now, Petruchio, speak.

Enter Katherine.

Good morrow, Kate, for that's your name, I hear.

KATHERINE

Well have you heard, but something hard of hearing.
They call me Katherine that do talk of me.

PETRUCHIO

You lie, in faith, for you are called plain Kate,
And bonny Kate, and sometimes Kate the curst.
But Kate, the prettiest Kate in Christendom,
Kate of Kate Hall, my super-dainty Kate
(For dainties are all Kates)—and therefore, Kate,
Take this of me, Kate of my consolation:
Hearing thy mildness praised in every town,
Thy virtues spoke of, and thy beauty sounded
(Yet not so deeply as to thee belongs),
Myself am moved to woo thee for my wife.

KATHERINE

"Moved," in good time! Let him that moved you
hither

206. **movable:** (1) piece of furniture; (2) whimsical person

208. **joint stool:** wooden **stool** made of parts joined or fitted together

210. **bear: bear** burdens

211. **bear:** (1) **bear** children; (2) **bear** the weight of a man in sexual intercourse

212. **jade:** worthless horse (See picture, page 66.)

214. **light:** Since Petruchio is interrupted, it is impossible to say which of the many meanings of **light** might apply here.

215. **light:** quick; **swain:** rustic lover; bumpkin

217. **buzz:** i.e., the sound of a bee (wordplay on **be**)

218. **ta'en:** taken or understood (sarcastic)

219. **buzzard:** (1) a buzzing insect; (2) a stupid person

220. **turtle:** turtle dove, symbolic of love; **buzzard:** a bird of prey; **take:** (1) capture; (2) mistake

A turtle dove. (2.1.220)
From Konrad Gesner, . . . *Historiae animalium* . . . (1585–1604).

Remove you hence. I knew you at the first
You were a movable.

PETRUCHIO
Why, what's a movable?

KATHERINE
A joint stool.

PETRUCHIO
Thou hast hit it. Come, sit on me.

KATHERINE
Asses are made to bear, and so are you.

PETRUCHIO
Women are made to bear, and so are you.

KATHERINE
No such jade as you, if me you mean.

PETRUCHIO
Alas, good Kate, I will not burden thee,
For knowing thee to be but young and light—

KATHERINE
Too light for such a swain as you to catch,
And yet as heavy as my weight should be.

PETRUCHIO
"Should be"—should buzz!

KATHERINE
Well ta'en, and like a buzzard.

PETRUCHIO
O slow-winged turtle, shall a buzzard take thee?

KATHERINE
Ay, for a turtle, as he takes a buzzard.

PETRUCHIO
Come, come, you wasp! I' faith, you are too angry.

KATHERINE
If I be waspish, best beware my sting.

PETRUCHIO
My remedy is then to pluck it out.

KATHERINE
Ay, if the fool could find it where it lies.

233. **try:** test
237. **arms:** i.e., coat of **arms,** the mark of a gentleman
238. **herald:** the officer who regulated and recorded those entitled to coats of arms; **in thy books: in** your herald's **books**; **in** your good **books**, i.e., in your favor
239. **crest:** an identifying heraldic device worn by a knight on his helmet as an accessory to the coat of arms on his shield (See picture, below.) **coxcomb:** fool's cap (See picture, page 94.)
240. **combless:** i.e., peaceful
241. **craven:** coward; a defeated **cock**
243. **crab:** (1) crab apple; (2) sour-faced person
247. **glass:** looking **glass,** mirror
249. **aimed:** guessed; **of:** i.e., by; **young one:** novice
250. **young:** inexperienced

A helmet with a crest. (2.1.239)
From Bonaventura Pistofilo,
Il torneo . . . (1627).

PETRUCHIO
Who knows not where a wasp does wear his sting?
In his tail.
KATHERINE In his tongue.
PETRUCHIO Whose tongue?
KATHERINE
Yours, if you talk of tales, and so farewell.
PETRUCHIO What, with my tongue in your tail?
Nay, come again, good Kate. I am a gentleman—
KATHERINE That I'll try. *She strikes him.*
PETRUCHIO
I swear I'll cuff you if you strike again.
KATHERINE So may you lose your arms.
If you strike me, you are no gentleman,
And if no gentleman, why then no arms.
PETRUCHIO
A herald, Kate? O, put me in thy books.
KATHERINE What is your crest? A coxcomb?
PETRUCHIO
A combless cock, so Kate will be my hen.
KATHERINE
No cock of mine. You crow too like a craven.
PETRUCHIO
Nay, come, Kate, come. You must not look so sour.
KATHERINE
It is my fashion when I see a crab.
PETRUCHIO
Why, here's no crab, and therefore look not sour.
KATHERINE There is, there is.
PETRUCHIO
Then show it me.
KATHERINE Had I a glass, I would.
PETRUCHIO What, you mean my face?
KATHERINE Well aimed of such a young one.
PETRUCHIO
Now, by Saint George, I am too young for you.

254. **sooth:** truth
255. **chafe:** irritate; **tarry:** stay
256. **whit:** bit; **passing:** very
257. **coy:** distant, aloof
258. **a very:** an utter
259. **gamesome:** playful; **passing:** extremely
261. **But . . . speech:** easygoing, not easily excited
262. **askance:** aside (in scorn or contempt)
264. **cross:** inclined to oppose or contradict
266. **conference:** conversation
271. **halt: limp** (line 267)
272. **whom thou keep'st:** i.e., your servants
273. **Dian:** i.e., Diana, the goddess of chastity and of the hunt (See picture, below.)
276. **sportful:** lustful
277. **study:** i.e., prepare; **goodly:** splendid
278. **mother wit:** natural intelligence

Diana. (2.1.273)
From Robert Whitcombe, *Janua divorum* . . . (1678).

KATHERINE
Yet you are withered.
PETRUCHIO 'Tis with cares.
KATHERINE I care not.
PETRUCHIO
Nay, hear you, Kate—in sooth, you 'scape not so.
KATHERINE
I chafe you if I tarry. Let me go.
PETRUCHIO
No, not a whit. I find you passing gentle.
'Twas told me you were rough, and coy, and sullen,
And now I find report a very liar.
For thou art pleasant, gamesome, passing
courteous,
But slow in speech, yet sweet as springtime flowers.
Thou canst not frown, thou canst not look askance,
Nor bite the lip as angry wenches will,
Nor hast thou pleasure to be cross in talk.
But thou with mildness entertain'st thy wooers,
With gentle conference, soft, and affable.
Why does the world report that Kate doth limp?
O sland'rous world! Kate like the hazel twig
Is straight, and slender, and as brown in hue
As hazel nuts, and sweeter than the kernels.
O, let me see thee walk! Thou dost not halt.
KATHERINE
Go, fool, and whom thou keep'st command.
PETRUCHIO
Did ever Dian so become a grove
As Kate this chamber with her princely gait?
O, be thou Dian and let her be Kate,
And then let Kate be chaste and Dian sportful.
KATHERINE
Where did you study all this goodly speech?
PETRUCHIO
It is extempore, from my mother wit.

279. **else:** otherwise

281. **keep you warm:** Proverbial: "He is **wise** enough that can **keep** himself **warm.**"

282. **mean:** intend to do

286. **will you, nill you:** i.e., whether you like it or not

287. **for your turn:** just right for you

292. **wild Kate:** pun on "wildcat"

296. **speed:** succeed

300–301. **In your dumps:** depressed, out of sorts

302. **promise:** assure

306. **face:** brazen

A fool wearing a coxcomb. (2.1.239)
George Wither, *A collection of emblemes* . . . (1635).

KATHERINE
A witty mother, witless else her son.
PETRUCHIO Am I not wise?
KATHERINE Yes, keep you warm.
PETRUCHIO
Marry, so I mean, sweet Katherine, in thy bed.
And therefore, setting all this chat aside,
Thus in plain terms: your father hath consented
That you shall be my wife, your dowry 'greed on,
And, will you, nill you, I will marry you.
Now, Kate, I am a husband for your turn,
For by this light, whereby I see thy beauty,
Thy beauty that doth make me like thee well,
Thou must be married to no man but me.
For I am he am born to tame you, Kate,
And bring you from a wild Kate to a Kate
Conformable as other household Kates.

Enter Baptista, Gremio, ⌜and⌝ Tranio ⌜as Lucentio.⌝

Here comes your father. Never make denial.
I must and will have Katherine to my wife.
BAPTISTA
Now, Signior Petruchio, how speed you with my daughter?
PETRUCHIO How but well, sir? How but well?
It were impossible I should speed amiss.
BAPTISTA
Why, how now, daughter Katherine? In your dumps?
KATHERINE
Call you me daughter? Now I promise you
You have showed a tender fatherly regard,
To wish me wed to one half lunatic,
A madcap ruffian and a swearing Jack,
That thinks with oaths to face the matter out.

307. **Father:** See note to 2.1.137, above.

309. **curst:** quarrelsome, ill-tempered; **for policy:** as a strategem

310. **froward:** strong-willed

311. **hot:** angry

312. **Grissel:** Griselda, the legendary wife who, with superhuman patience, remained obedient and faithful to a cruel husband (Her story is told by Chaucer in *The Clerk's Tale.*)

313. **Lucrece:** After being raped by Tarquin, she committed suicide. (Shakespeare tells her story in his poem *Lucrece.*)

319. **speeding:** success

320. **goodnight our part:** i.e., we'll say good-bye to our suits to Bianca

323. **bargained:** agreed; **'twixt:** between

324. **still:** always

328. **vied:** repeated, piled up

329. **twink:** i.e., twinkling of an eye

332. **meacock:** meek

334. **'gainst:** in preparation for

335. **bid:** invite

336. **fine:** splendidly dressed

337. **give me your hands:** The taking of **hands** before **witnesses** (line 339), along with an exchange of promises, constituted a formal betrothal or precontract of marriage. See page 98 for a picture of such a handfasting.

PETRUCHIO

Father, 'tis thus: yourself and all the world
That talked of her have talked amiss of her.
If she be curst, it is for policy,
For she's not froward, but modest as the dove;
She is not hot, but temperate as the morn.
For patience she will prove a second Grissel,
And Roman Lucrece for her chastity.
And to conclude, we have 'greed so well together
That upon Sunday is the wedding day.

KATHERINE

I'll see thee hanged on Sunday first.

GREMIO Hark, Petruchio, she says she'll see thee hanged first.

TRANIO, ⌈*as* LUCENTIO⌉ Is this your speeding? Nay, then, goodnight our part.

PETRUCHIO

Be patient, gentlemen. I choose her for myself.
If she and I be pleased, what's that to you?
'Tis bargained 'twixt us twain, being alone,
That she shall still be curst in company.
I tell you, 'tis incredible to believe
How much she loves me. O, the kindest Kate!
She hung about my neck, and kiss on kiss
She vied so fast, protesting oath on oath,
That in a twink she won me to her love.
O, you are novices! 'Tis a world to see
How tame, when men and women are alone,
A meacock wretch can make the curstest shrew.—
Give me thy hand, Kate. I will unto Venice
To buy apparel 'gainst the wedding day.—
Provide the feast, father, and bid the guests.
I will be sure my Katherine shall be fine.

BAPTISTA

I know not what to say, but give me your hands.
God send you joy, Petruchio. 'Tis a match.

341. **apace:** quickly

344. **clapped up:** hurriedly arranged

345–48. **Faith, gentlemen . . . the seas:** In these lines Baptista compares himself—and is compared—to a merchant who takes a great gamble to dispose of goods (Katherine) that are wearing out from being long kept in storage. **desperate mart:** risky market **commodity:** goods **fretting:** (1) wearing out (of goods); (2) irritable (of Katherine)

350. **he:** i.e., Petruchio

357–58. **freeze, fry:** references to the supposed cold blood of age and the hot blood of youth

359. **Skipper:** i.e., one young enough that he can skip (term of contempt)

". . . give me your hands." (2.1.337)
From George Wither, *A collection of emblemes . . .* (1635).

GREMIO AND TRANIO, ⌜*as* LUCENTIO⌝
Amen, say we. We will be witnesses.

PETRUCHIO
Father, and wife, and gentlemen, adieu.
I will to Venice. Sunday comes apace.
We will have rings, and things, and fine array,
And kiss me, Kate. We will be married o' Sunday.
Petruchio and Katherine exit ⌜through different doors.⌝

GREMIO
Was ever match clapped up so suddenly?

BAPTISTA
Faith, gentlemen, now I play a merchant's part
And venture madly on a desperate mart.

TRANIO, ⌜*as* LUCENTIO⌝
'Twas a commodity lay fretting by you.
'Twill bring you gain, or perish on the seas.

BAPTISTA
The gain I seek, is quiet ⌜in⌝ the match.

GREMIO
No doubt but he hath got a quiet catch.
But now, Baptista, to your younger daughter.
Now is the day we long have lookèd for.
I am your neighbor and was suitor first.

TRANIO, ⌜*as* LUCENTIO⌝
And I am one that love Bianca more
Than words can witness or your thoughts can guess.

GREMIO
Youngling, thou canst not love so dear as I.

TRANIO, ⌜*as* LUCENTIO⌝
Graybeard, thy love doth freeze.

GREMIO
But thine doth fry!
Skipper, stand back. 'Tis age that nourisheth.

TRANIO, ⌜*as* LUCENTIO⌝
But youth in ladies' eyes that flourisheth.

361. **compound:** settle, reconcile

362. **he of both:** i.e., the one of you two

363. **assure:** promise; guarantee; **dower:** portion of a husband's estate legally assigned to his widow on his death (See longer note, page 224.)

367. **plate:** silver utensils

368. **lave:** wash

369. **hangings:** i.e., wall hangings; **Tyrian tapestry: tapestry woven** in **Tyre**

370. **crowns:** gold coins

371. **arras counterpoints:** counterpanes of rich tapestry fabric

372. **tents:** perhaps, bed curtains

373. **Turkey:** Turkish; **bossed:** i.e., embossed

374. **Valance:** drapery; **gold:** i.e., **gold** thread

377. **milch-kine to the pail:** cows providing milk

378. **Six score:** one hundred twenty

379. **answerable to:** i.e., consistent with; **portion:** proposed **dower** (line 363)

380. **struck in years:** advanced in age

383. **list:** listen

390. **ducats:** gold coins; **by the:** per

391. **Of:** from; **fruitful:** fertile; **jointure:** property which will be hers at his death

392. **pinched you:** put you in a tight spot

BAPTISTA

Content you, gentlemen. I will compound this strife.
'Tis deeds must win the prize, and he of both
That can assure my daughter greatest dower
Shall have my Bianca's love.
Say, Signior Gremio, what can you assure her?

GREMIO

First, as you know, my house within the city
Is richly furnishéd with plate and gold,
Basins and ewers to lave her dainty hands;
My hangings all of Tyrian tapestry;
In ivory coffers I have stuffed my crowns,
In cypress chests my arras counterpoints,
Costly apparel, tents, and canopies,
Fine linen, Turkey cushions bossed with pearl,
Valance of Venice gold in needlework,
Pewter and brass, and all things that belongs
To house or housekeeping. Then, at my farm
I have a hundred milch-kine to the pail,
Six score fat oxen standing in my stalls,
And all things answerable to this portion.
Myself am struck in years, I must confess,
And if I die tomorrow this is hers,
If whilst I live she will be only mine.

TRANIO, ⌜*as* LUCENTIO⌝

That "only" came well in. ⌜*To Baptista.*⌝ Sir, list to me:
I am my father's heir and only son.
If I may have your daughter to my wife,
I'll leave her houses three or four as good,
Within rich Pisa walls, as any one
Old Signior Gremio has in Padua,
Besides two thousand ducats by the year
Of fruitful land, all which shall be her jointure.—
What, have I pinched you, Signior Gremio?

395. **argosy:** largest of trading ships

396. **Marcellus' road:** sheltered anchorage outside the harbor at Marseilles

399. **galliasses:** large ships propelled with both sails and oars

400. **tight:** watertight, sound; **assure:** promise

407. **outvied:** outbid (a metaphor from card playing picked up in line 424 with **gamester** and again at line 429)

409. **let . . . assurance:** i.e., if **your father** provides **her** the guarantee

412. **cavil:** meaningless objection

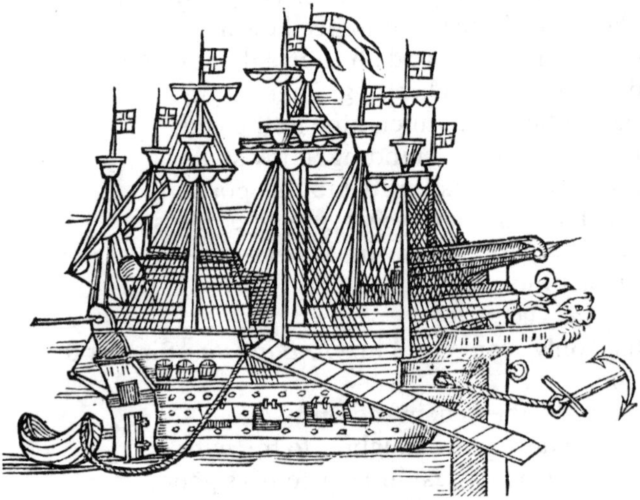

An argosy. (2.1.395)
From Robert Hitchcock, *A pollitique platt* . . . (1580).

GREMIO

Two thousand ducats by the year of land?
⌜*Aside.*⌝ My land amounts not to so much in all.—
That she shall have, besides an argosy
That now is lying in Marcellus' road.
⌜*To Tranio.*⌝ What, have I choked you with an argosy?

TRANIO, ⌜*as* LUCENTIO⌝

Gremio, 'tis known my father hath no less
Than three great argosies, besides two galliasses
And twelve tight galleys. These I will assure her,
And twice as much whate'er thou off'rest next.

GREMIO

Nay, I have offered all. I have no more,
And she can have no more than all I have.
⌜*To Baptista.*⌝ If you like me, she shall have me and
mine.

TRANIO, ⌜*as* LUCENTIO⌝

Why, then, the maid is mine from all the world,
By your firm promise. Gremio is outvied.

BAPTISTA

I must confess your offer is the best,
And, let your father make her the assurance,
She is your own; else—you must pardon me—
If you should die before him, where's her dower?

TRANIO, ⌜*as* LUCENTIO⌝

That's but a cavil. He is old, I young.

GREMIO

And may not young men die as well as old?

BAPTISTA

Well, gentlemen, I am thus resolved:
On Sunday next, you know
My daughter Katherine is to be married.
⌜*To Tranio as Lucentio.*⌝ Now, on the Sunday
following, shall Bianca
Be bride to you, if you make this assurance.
If not, to Signior Gremio.
And so I take my leave, and thank you both.

424. **gamester:** gambler, betting on his father's generosity; **were:** i.e., would be

426. **Set foot under thy table:** i.e., be reduced to a guest in your house; **toy:** joke

428. **A vengeance on:** a mild oath

429. **faced . . . ten:** i.e., bluffed it without even a face card (See note to 2.1.407.)

431. **supposed:** pretend, counterfeit

434. **get:** i.e., beget

435. **sire:** father; **of:** i.e., in

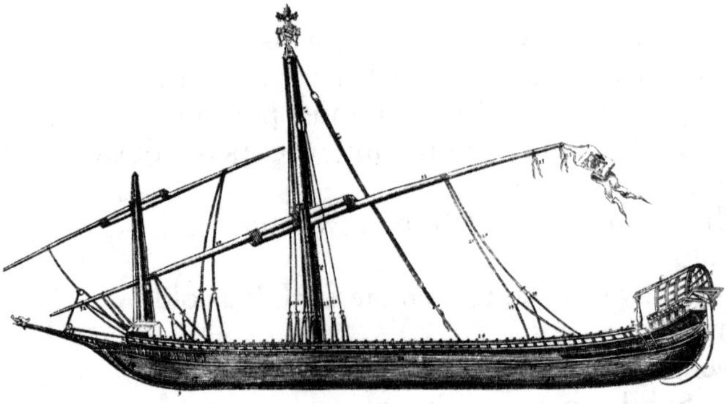

A galley. (2.1.400)
From Bartolomeo Crescentio, *Nautica Mediterranea* . . . (1607).

GREMIO

Adieu, good neighbor. ⌜*Baptista*⌝ *exits.*
Now I fear thee not.
Sirrah young gamester, your father were a fool
To give thee all and in his waning age
Set foot under thy table. Tut, a toy!
An old Italian fox is not so kind, my boy.
⌜*Gremio*⌝ *exits.*

TRANIO

A vengeance on your crafty withered hide!—
Yet I have faced it with a card of ten.
'Tis in my head to do my master good.
I see no reason but supposed Lucentio
Must get a father, called "supposed Vincentio"—
And that's a wonder. Fathers commonly
Do get their children. But in this case of wooing,
A child shall get a sire, if I fail not of my cunning.
He exits.

THE TAMING OF THE SHREW

ACT 3

3.1 Under cover of their disguises as schoolmasters, first Lucentio (as Cambio) and then Hortensio (as Litio) try for Bianca's love. Hortensio notices Lucentio-Cambio's affection for Bianca and determines to abandon her if she shows any interest in such a social inferior as Hortensio believes Cambio to be.

---

1. **forbear:** stop

3. **withal:** i.e., with

4. **this:** i.e., Bianca

6. **leave:** permission; **to have prerogative:** i.e., to go first

8. **Your lecture . . . much:** i.e., your lesson will be given equal time

9. **Preposterous:** literally, putting first what belongs last (Music is to follow work, not precede it.)

10. **ordained:** instituted, created

12. **usual pain:** i.e., daily labor

14. **serve in:** i.e., perform, present

15. **Sirrah:** here, an insulting form of address; **bear these braves:** endure these taunts

18. **breeching scholar:** young student liable to be breeched (i.e., whipped)

19. **'pointed:** i.e., appointed

ACT 3

⌜Scene 1⌝

Enter Lucentio ⌜as Cambio,⌝ Hortensio ⌜as Litio,⌝ and Bianca.

LUCENTIO, ⌜*as* CAMBIO⌝
Fiddler, forbear. You grow too forward, sir.
Have you so soon forgot the entertainment
Her sister Katherine welcomed you withal?

HORTENSIO, ⌜*as* LITIO⌝ But, wrangling pedant, this is
The patroness of heavenly harmony.
Then give me leave to have prerogative,
And when in music we have spent an hour,
Your lecture shall have leisure for as much.

LUCENTIO, ⌜*as* CAMBIO⌝
Preposterous ass, that never read so far
To know the cause why music was ordained.
Was it not to refresh the mind of man
After his studies or his usual pain?
Then give me leave to read philosophy,
And, while I pause, serve in your harmony.

HORTENSIO, ⌜*as* LITIO⌝
Sirrah, I will not bear these braves of thine.

BIANCA
Why, gentlemen, you do me double wrong
To strive for that which resteth in my choice.
I am no breeching scholar in the schools.
I'll not be tied to hours, nor 'pointed times,

23. **the whiles:** in the meantime

30–31. **Hic . . . senis:** "Here flowed the Simois; here is the Sigeian land; / Here had stood old Priam's high palace" (Ovid).

32. **Conster:** construe, interpret

35. **thus:** i.e., as the tutor Cambio

37. **bearing my port:** assuming my social position

38. **pantaloon:** i.e., Gremio (See note to 1.1.45 SD.)

41. **jars:** is out of tune

42–43. **Spit . . . again:** an ironic twist on the proverbial "**Spit** on your hands **and** try **again**"

50. **base knave:** i.e., Cambio

But learn my lessons as I please myself.
And, to cut off all strife, here sit we down.
⌜*To Hortensio.*⌝ Take you your instrument, play you the whiles;
His lecture will be done ere you have tuned.

HORTENSIO, ⌜*as* LITIO⌝
You'll leave his lecture when I am in tune?

LUCENTIO, ⌜*aside*⌝
That will be never. ⌜*To Hortensio.*⌝ Tune your instrument. ⌜*Hortensio steps aside to tune his lute.*⌝

BIANCA Where left we last?

LUCENTIO, ⌜*as* CAMBIO⌝ Here, madam:
⌜*Showing her a book.*⌝
Hic ibat Simois, hic est ⌜*Sigeia*⌝ *tellus,*
Hic steterat Priami regia celsa senis.

BIANCA Conster them.

LUCENTIO *Hic ibat,* as I told you before, *Simois,* I am Lucentio, *hic est,* son unto Vincentio of Pisa, ⌜*Sigeia*⌝ *tellus,* disguised thus to get your love, *Hic steterat,* and that "Lucentio" that comes a-wooing, *Priami,* is my man Tranio, *regia,* bearing my port, *celsa senis,* that we might beguile the old pantaloon.

HORTENSIO, ⌜*as* LITIO⌝ Madam, my instrument's in tune.

BIANCA Let's hear. ⌜*He plays.*⌝ Oh fie, the treble jars!

LUCENTIO, ⌜*as* CAMBIO⌝ Spit in the hole, man, and tune again. ⌜*Hortensio tunes his lute again.*⌝

BIANCA Now let me see if I can conster it. *Hic ibat Simois,* I know you not; *hic est* ⌜*Sigeia*⌝ *tellus,* I trust you not; *Hic* ⌜*steterat*⌝ *Priami,* take heed he hear us not; *regia,* presume not; *celsa senis,* despair not.

HORTENSIO, ⌜*as* LITIO⌝
Madam, 'tis now in tune. ⌜*He plays again.*⌝

LUCENTIO, ⌜*as* CAMBIO⌝ All but the bass.

HORTENSIO, ⌜*as* LITIO⌝
The bass is right. 'Tis the base knave that jars.

52. **for my life:** i.e., I would bet **my life**

53. **Pedascule:** corrupt Latin for "little pedant" (pronounced with four syllables)

55. **Aeacides:** Lucentio is pretending to interpret Ovid to Bianca. The reference to **Aeacides** ("descendant of Aeacus") follows in Ovid the passage quoted at lines 30–31.

61. **pleasant:** merry

62. **give me leave:** let me alone

65. **withal:** as well; **but:** unless

68. **learn:** i.e., teach; **order:** system

70. **gamut:** the musical scale devised in the eleventh century (The notes—known as A, B, C, etc.—were sung to the syllables *re, mi, fa, sol, la,* and *ut* [see lines 76–81]. The "gamut" was also the ground note of the scale.)

73. **drawn:** set out

⌜*Aside.*⌝ How fiery and forward our pedant is.
Now for my life the knave doth court my love!
Pedascule, I'll watch you better yet.

⌜BIANCA, *to Lucentio*⌝
In time I may believe, yet I mistrust.

⌜LUCENTIO⌝
Mistrust it not, for sure Aeacides
Was Ajax, called so from his grandfather.

⌜BIANCA⌝
I must believe my master; else, I promise you,
I should be arguing still upon that doubt.
But let it rest.—Now, Litio, to you.
Good master, take it not unkindly, pray,
That I have been thus pleasant with you both.

HORTENSIO, ⌜*as* LITIO, *to Lucentio*⌝
You may go walk, and give me leave awhile.
My lessons make no music in three parts.

LUCENTIO, ⌜*as* CAMBIO⌝
Are you so formal, sir? Well, I must wait
⌜*Aside.*⌝ And watch withal, for, but I be deceived,
Our fine musician groweth amorous.
⌜*He steps aside.*⌝

HORTENSIO, ⌜*as* LITIO⌝
Madam, before you touch the instrument,
To learn the order of my fingering
I must begin with rudiments of art,
To teach you gamut in a briefer sort,
More pleasant, pithy, and effectual
Than hath been taught by any of my trade.
And there it is in writing fairly drawn.

BIANCA
Why, I am past my gamut long ago.

HORTENSIO
Yet read the gamut of Hortensio.
⌜*Giving her a paper.*⌝

83. **nice:** hard to please
84. **To:** i.e., as to
89. **Faith:** a mild oath
91. **Methinks:** it seems to me
92. **humble:** common, low, base
93. **stale:** decoy, lure (term from falconry)

94–95. **Seize . . . changing:** i.e., Let anyone who wants you capture you. **If I once find** you untrue, I will get even with you by turning to someone else. **list:** please, wish **be quit with:** get even with

3.2 Petruchio is late arriving for his wedding, to Katherine's great embarrassment. When he finally presents himself, he is dressed in ridiculous clothes. At the wedding, according to Gremio's report, Petruchio behaves rudely and abusively. He refuses to attend the supper that traditionally follows a wedding, and he insists on taking Katherine away as well. Over her protests, he forces her to go with him, making a show of defending her against the interference of her family and friends.

---

1. **'pointed:** i.e., appointed

BIANCA ⌜*reads*⌝
"*Gamut* I am, the ground of all accord:
⌜*A re,*⌝ to plead Hortensio's passion;
⌜*B mi,*⌝ Bianca, take him for thy lord,
⌜*C fa ut,*⌝ that loves with all affection;
D sol re, one clef, two notes have I;
E la mi, show pity or I die."
Call you this "gamut"? Tut, I like it not.
Old fashions please me best. I am not so nice
To ⌜change⌝ true rules for ⌜odd⌝ inventions.

Enter a ⌜Servant.⌝

⌜SERVANT⌝
Mistress, your father prays you leave your books
And help to dress your sister's chamber up.
You know tomorrow is the wedding day.

BIANCA
Farewell, sweet masters both. I must be gone.

LUCENTIO
Faith, mistress, then I have no cause to stay.
⌜*Bianca, the Servant, and Lucentio exit.*⌝

HORTENSIO
But I have cause to pry into this pedant.
Methinks he looks as though he were in love.
Yet if thy thoughts, Bianca, be so humble
To cast thy wand'ring eyes on every stale,
Seize thee that list! If once I find thee ranging,
Hortensio will be quit with thee by changing.
He exits.

⌜Scene 2⌝

Enter Baptista, Gremio, Tranio ⌜as Lucentio,⌝ Katherine, Bianca, ⌜Lucentio as Cambio,⌝ and others, Attendants.

BAPTISTA, ⌜*to Tranio*⌝
Signior Lucentio, this is the 'pointed day

5. **want:** lack; **attends:** awaits; is present and ready to serve

8. **forsooth:** in truth

10. **rudesby:** rude, disorderly fellow; **spleen:** impulsiveness, changeableness

12. **frantic:** lunatic, insane

13. **blunt:** rude

14. **noted for:** known as

16. **proclaim the banns:** announce the intended marriage

21. **Patience . . . too:** Editors have correctly noted that the speeches assigned to Tranio-as-Lucentio in the first half of this scene suggest a closer relationship between the character and Petruchio than the play otherwise indicates. See note to 3.2.130, below.

22. **means but:** only **means**

23. **Whatever . . . word: whatever** accident prevents **him from** keeping **his** promise to be married

24. **passing:** very

25. **withal:** at the same time, notwithstanding; **honest:** of honorable character, morally upright

27. **to weep:** i.e., for weeping

29. **humor:** temperament

That Katherine and Petruchio should be married,
And yet we hear not of our son-in-law.
What will be said? What mockery will it be,
To want the bridegroom when the priest attends
To speak the ceremonial rites of marriage?
What says Lucentio to this shame of ours?

KATHERINE
No shame but mine. I must, forsooth, be forced
To give my hand, opposed against my heart,
Unto a mad-brain rudesby, full of spleen,
Who wooed in haste and means to wed at leisure.
I told you, I, he was a frantic fool,
Hiding his bitter jests in blunt behavior,
And, to be noted for a merry man,
He'll woo a thousand, 'point the day of marriage,
Make friends, invite, and proclaim the banns,
Yet never means to wed where he hath wooed.
Now must the world point at poor Katherine
And say "Lo, there is mad Petruchio's wife,
If it would please him come and marry her."

TRANIO, ⌜*as* LUCENTIO⌝
Patience, good Katherine, and Baptista too.
Upon my life, Petruchio means but well,
Whatever fortune stays him from his word.
Though he be blunt, I know him passing wise;
Though he be merry, yet withal he's honest.

KATHERINE
Would Katherine had never seen him, though!
She exits weeping.

BAPTISTA
Go, girl. I cannot blame thee now to weep,
For such an injury would vex a very saint,
Much more a shrew of ⌜thy⌝ impatient humor.

Enter Biondello.

BIONDELLO Master, master, news! And such ⌜old⌝ news as you never heard of!

41. **what to:** i.e., **what** about

43. **jerkin:** short jacket; **turned:** i.e., **turned** inside out in order to get more wear out of them

44. **candle-cases:** places to throw candle ends

47. **chapeless:** without the metal plate (*chape*) on its sheath; **points:** laces to hold up stockings

48. **hipped:** lame in the hip

48–49. **of no kindred:** i.e., that do not match

49. **glanders:** swelling glands and nasal discharge

50. **like . . . chine:** perhaps, likely to (1) decay in the backbone, or (2) die of the glanders

50–51. **lampass:** swelling in the mouth

51. **fashions:** i.e., farcins, a disease in horses causing painful ulcerations, especially on the legs; **windgalls:** tumors on its legs

52. **sped with spavins:** ruined by inflamed cartilage; **rayed with the yellows:** disfigured by jaundice

53. **fives:** avives, a disease causing swelling below the ears; **stark:** entirely; **the staggers:** staggering, giddiness; **begnawn:** gnawed; eaten away

54. **bots:** intestinal worms

54–55. **shoulder-shotten:** lame in the shoulder

55. **near-legged before:** with knock-kneed forelegs

55–56. **half-checked bit:** i.e., faulty **bit**

56. **headstall:** part of the bridle; **sheep's leather:** i.e., inferior **leather,** not the preferable pigskin

59. **pieced:** repaired

60. **crupper:** the strap under the horse's tail that keeps the saddle steady; **velour:** velvet (thus less sturdy than a **leather** crupper) See picture, page 120.

62. **pieced . . . thread:** held together with string

BAPTISTA
Is it new and old too? How may that be?

BIONDELLO Why, is it not news to ⌜hear⌝ of Petruchio's coming?

BAPTISTA Is he come?

BIONDELLO Why, no, sir.

BAPTISTA
What then?

BIONDELLO He is coming.

BAPTISTA When will he be here?

BIONDELLO
When he stands where I am, and sees you there.

TRANIO, ⌜*as* LUCENTIO⌝ But say, what to thine old news?

BIONDELLO Why, Petruchio is coming in a new hat and an old jerkin, a pair of old breeches thrice turned, a pair of boots that have been candle-cases, one buckled, another laced; an old rusty sword ta'en out of the town armory, with a broken hilt, and chapeless; with two broken points; his horse hipped, with an old mothy saddle and stirrups of no kindred, besides possessed with the glanders and like to mose in the chine, troubled with the lampass, infected with the fashions, full of windgalls, sped with spavins, rayed with the yellows, past cure of the fives, stark spoiled with the staggers, begnawn with the bots, ⌜swayed⌝ in the back and shoulder-shotten, near-legged before, and with a half-checked bit and a headstall of sheep's leather, which, being restrained to keep him from stumbling, hath been often burst, and now repaired with knots; one girth six times pieced, and a woman's crupper of velour, which hath two letters for her name fairly set down in studs, and here and there pieced with packthread.

BAPTISTA Who comes with him?

64–65. **caparisoned:** outfitted

65. **stock:** stocking

66. **kersey boot-hose:** coarse wool stocking

67. **list:** strip of cloth

67–68. **humor . . . feather:** One editor explains this obscure phrase as perhaps meaning **forty** ribbons tied together and stuck in the **hat** in a parody of a knight's crest. (See note to 2.1.239 and picture, page 90.)

68. **monster:** beast that combines several forms

71. **humor:** whim, mood; **pricks:** urges

72. **mean-appareled:** dressed poorly

80. **all one:** i.e., the same thing

82. **hold:** bet

86. **gallants:** fine gentlemen

89. **halt:** limp

A horse with bridle and crupper. (3.2.60; 4.1.76)
From Cesare Fiaschi, *Trattato dell'imbrigliare . . .* (1614).

BIONDELLO Oh, sir, his lackey, for all the world caparisoned like the horse: with a linen stock on one leg and a kersey boot-hose on the other, gartered with a red and blue list; an old hat, and the humor of forty fancies pricked in 't for a feather. A monster, a very monster in apparel, and not like a Christian footboy or a gentleman's lackey.

TRANIO, ⌜*as* LUCENTIO⌝
'Tis some odd humor pricks him to this fashion,
Yet oftentimes he goes but mean-appareled.

BAPTISTA
I am glad he's come, howsoe'er he comes.

BIONDELLO Why, sir, he comes not.

BAPTISTA Didst thou not say he comes?

BIONDELLO Who? That Petruchio came?

BAPTISTA Ay, that Petruchio came!

BIONDELLO No, sir, I say his horse comes with him on his back.

BAPTISTA Why, that's all one.

BIONDELLO

Nay, by Saint Jamy.
I hold you a penny,
A horse and a man
Is more than one,
And yet not many.

Enter Petruchio and Grumio.

PETRUCHIO
Come, where be these gallants? Who's at home?

BAPTISTA You are welcome, sir.

PETRUCHIO And yet I come not well.

BAPTISTA And yet you halt not.

TRANIO, ⌜*as* LUCENTIO⌝ Not so well appareled as I wish you were.

PETRUCHIO
Were it better I should rush in thus—

94. **Gentles:** i.e., gentlemen
95. **wherefore:** why
96. **monument:** something that gives warning, a portent
97. **prodigy:** wonder
100. **unprovided:** unprepared
101. **this habit:** these clothes; **estate:** status
102. **solemn:** ceremonial
103. **import:** importance
108. **in some part:** to some extent; **enforcèd to digress:** forced to deviate (from his promise)
113. **unreverent:** unrespectable
117. **Good sooth:** in truth (a mild oath)
121. **accoutrements:** clothes

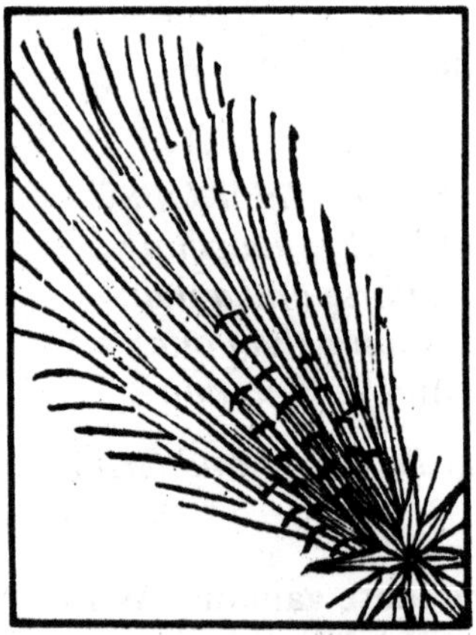

A comet. (3.2.97)
From Hartmann Schedel, *Liber chronicorum* . . . [1493].

But where is Kate? Where is my lovely bride?
How does my father? Gentles, methinks you frown.
And wherefore gaze this goodly company
As if they saw some wondrous monument,
Some comet or unusual prodigy?

BAPTISTA

Why, sir, you know this is your wedding day.
First were we sad, fearing you would not come,
Now sadder that you come so unprovided.
Fie, doff this habit, shame to your estate,
An eyesore to our solemn festival.

TRANIO, ⌜*as* LUCENTIO⌝

And tell us what occasion of import
Hath all so long detained you from your wife
And sent you hither so unlike yourself.

PETRUCHIO

Tedious it were to tell, and harsh to hear.
Sufficeth I am come to keep my word,
Though in some part enforcèd to digress,
Which at more leisure I will so excuse
As you shall well be satisfied with all.
But where is Kate? I stay too long from her.
The morning wears. 'Tis time we were at church.

TRANIO, ⌜*as* LUCENTIO⌝

See not your bride in these unreverent robes.
Go to my chamber, put on clothes of mine.

PETRUCHIO

Not I, believe me. Thus I'll visit her.

BAPTISTA

But thus, I trust, you will not marry her.

PETRUCHIO

Good sooth, even thus. Therefore, ha' done with
  words.
To me she's married, not unto my clothes.
Could I repair what she will wear in me,
As I can change these poor accoutrements,

125. **seal:** i.e., ratify; **the title:** the name of **bride** (line 124); **lovely:** i.e., loving

127. **be it:** i.e., if **it be**

129. **event:** outcome

130. **love:** i.e., Bianca's **love** (The abruptness of the change of subject may reflect some lost lines of text—perhaps an entire scene. In the 1594 *A Shrew*, one finds at this point a comic scene between the Grumio and Biondello characters. It has been suggested that Tranio and Lucentio should not enter until this point, and that the lines earlier in the scene given to Tranio-as-Lucentio should, in fact, be given to Hortensio, for whom they are much more appropriate. See note to 3.2.21, above.)

134. **skills:** i.e., matters; **turn:** purpose

136. **make assurance:** provide guarantees

141. **narrowly:** closely

142. **steal our marriage:** i.e., elope (**marriage** pronounced as a three-syllable word)

145. **That:** i.e., the marriage; **by degrees:** gradually

146. **watch our vantage:** look out for opportunities that favor us

148. **narrow prying:** i.e., overly watchful

149. **quaint:** cunning, crafty

'Twere well for Kate and better for myself.
But what a fool am I to chat with you
When I should bid good morrow to my bride
And seal the title with a lovely kiss!

Petruchio exits, ⌜*with Grumio.*⌝

TRANIO, ⌜*as* LUCENTIO⌝

He hath some meaning in his mad attire.
We will persuade him, be it possible,
To put on better ere he go to church.

BAPTISTA

I'll after him, and see the event of this.

⌜*All except Tranio and Lucentio*⌝ *exit.*

TRANIO

But, sir, ⌜to⌝ love concerneth us to add
Her father's liking, which to bring to pass,
As ⌜I⌝ before imparted to your Worship,
I am to get a man (whate'er he be
It skills not much, we'll fit him to our turn),
And he shall be "Vincentio of Pisa,"
And make assurance here in Padua
Of greater sums than I have promisèd.
So shall you quietly enjoy your hope
And marry sweet Bianca with consent.

LUCENTIO

Were it not that my fellow schoolmaster
Doth watch Bianca's steps so narrowly,
'Twere good, methinks, to steal our marriage,
Which, once performed, let all the world say no,
I'll keep mine own despite of all the world.

TRANIO

That by degrees we mean to look into,
And watch our vantage in this business.
We'll overreach the graybeard, Gremio,
The narrow prying father, Minola,
The quaint musician, amorous Litio,
All for my master's sake, Lucentio.

154. **groom:** man of inferior social position

156. **Curster:** more perverse

158. **dam:** mother (said to be worse than her son, the Devil)

159. **fool:** pitiable creature

161. **Should ask:** i.e., asked; **should:** would

162. **gog's wouns:** i.e., God's wounds (a strong oath)

163. **amazed:** astounded

165. **took:** hit

167. **he:** i.e., Petruchio; **list:** wishes to

169. **for why:** because

170. **vicar:** priest; **cozen:** cheat

172. **health:** toast

173. **aboard:** i.e., on shipboard

174. **quaffed:** drank

Enter Gremio.

TRANIO, ⌜*as* LUCENTIO⌝
Signior Gremio, came you from the church?

GREMIO
As willingly as e'er I came from school.

TRANIO, ⌜*as* LUCENTIO⌝
And is the bride and bridegroom coming home?

GREMIO
A bridegroom, say you? 'Tis a groom indeed,
A grumbling groom, and that the girl shall find.

TRANIO, ⌜*as* LUCENTIO⌝
Curster than she? Why, 'tis impossible.

GREMIO
Why, he's a devil, a devil, a very fiend.

TRANIO, ⌜*as* LUCENTIO⌝
Why, she's a devil, a devil, the Devil's dam.

GREMIO
Tut, she's a lamb, a dove, a fool to him.
I'll tell you, Sir Lucentio: when the priest
Should ask if Katherine should be his wife,
"Ay, by gog's wouns!" quoth he, and swore so loud
That, all amazed, the priest let fall the book,
And as he stooped again to take it up,
This mad-brained bridegroom took him such a cuff
That down fell priest and book, and book and priest.
"Now, take them up," quoth he, "if any list."

TRANIO, ⌜*as* LUCENTIO⌝
What said the wench when he rose again?

GREMIO
Trembled and shook, for why he stamped and swore
As if the vicar meant to cozen him.
But after many ceremonies done,
He calls for wine. "A health!" quoth he, as if
He had been aboard, carousing to his mates
After a storm; quaffed off the muscatel

175. **sops:** cake that had been broken up and soaked in the wine; **sexton:** church officer

177. **his:** i.e., the sexton's; **hungerly:** sparsely

178. **to ask him sops:** i.e., to require **sops**

183. **rout:** crowd

185 SD. **Hortensio:** It is unclear whether Hortensio enters here as "Litio" or as himself.

188. **store:** quantities; **cheer:** food and drink

193. **Make it no wonder:** do not wonder at it

198. **my father:** i.e., my father-in-law, Baptista

And threw the sops all in the sexton's face,
Having no other reason
But that his beard grew thin and hungerly,
And seemed to ask him sops as he was drinking.
This done, he took the bride about the neck
And kissed her lips with such a clamorous smack
That at the parting all the church did echo.
And I, seeing this, came thence for very shame,
And after me I know the rout is coming.
Such a mad marriage never was before! *Music plays.*
Hark, hark, I hear the minstrels play.

Enter Petruchio, Katherine, Bianca, Hortensio, Baptista, ⌜*Grumio, and Attendants.*⌝

PETRUCHIO
Gentlemen and friends, I thank you for your pains.
I know you think to dine with me today
And have prepared great store of wedding cheer,
But so it is, my haste doth call me hence,
And therefore here I mean to take my leave.

BAPTISTA
Is 't possible you will away tonight?

PETRUCHIO
I must away today, before night come.
Make it no wonder. If you knew my business,
You would entreat me rather go than stay.
And, honest company, I thank you all,
That have beheld me give away myself
To this most patient, sweet, and virtuous wife.
Dine with my father, drink a health to me,
For I must hence, and farewell to you all.

TRANIO, ⌜*as* LUCENTIO⌝
Let us entreat you stay till after dinner.

PETRUCHIO It may not be.

GREMIO Let me entreat you.

PETRUCHIO It cannot be.

211–12. **oats . . . horses:** presumably an instance of Grumio's clowning

217. **jogging . . . green:** going while **your boots are** new (an invitation to leave)

219. **like:** i.e., likely; **jolly:** i.e., overbearing

220. **That take . . . roundly:** i.e., in **that you** immediately presume to **take** command **so** completely

222. **What . . . do?:** i.e., what business is it of yours?

223. **stay my leisure:** i.e., wait until I am ready

224. **marry:** i.e., indeed; **begins to work:** perhaps an image from liquor fermenting or the sea foaming; or, perhaps, an ironic comment about Petruchio's attempt to control Kate

230. **domineer:** feast riotously (Dutch *domineren,* to feast luxuriously)

231. **Carouse full measure to:** drink off a vessel full of wine or beer in honor of

KATHERINE Let me entreat you.

PETRUCHIO
I am content.

KATHERINE Are you content to stay?

PETRUCHIO
I am content you shall entreat me stay,
But yet not stay, entreat me how you can.

KATHERINE
Now, if you love me, stay.

PETRUCHIO Grumio, my horse.

GRUMIO Ay, sir, they be ready; the oats have eaten the horses.

KATHERINE Nay, then,
Do what thou canst, I will not go today,
No, nor tomorrow, not till I please myself.
The door is open, sir. There lies your way.
You may be jogging whiles your boots are green.
For me, I'll not be gone till I please myself.
'Tis like you'll prove a jolly surly groom,
That take it on you at the first so roundly.

PETRUCHIO
O Kate, content thee. Prithee, be not angry.

KATHERINE
I will be angry. What hast thou to do?—
Father, be quiet. He shall stay my leisure.

GREMIO
Ay, marry, sir, now it begins to work.

KATHERINE
Gentlemen, forward to the bridal dinner.
I see a woman may be made a fool
If she had not a spirit to resist.

PETRUCHIO
They shall go forward, Kate, at thy command.—
Obey the bride, you that attend on her.
Go to the feast, revel and domineer,
Carouse full measure to her maidenhead,

234. **big:** challenging, defiant

236. **chattels:** property, goods

237. **stuff:** goods

240. **bring mine action:** (1) **bring** legal **action**; (2) attack physically; **he:** i.e., one

246. **buckler:** i.e., defend (A buckler is a small shield. See picture, below.)

248. **Went they not:** i.e., if **they** had **not** gone

251. **mated:** matched, married

254–55. **wants . . . supply:** i.e., are not present to occupy

256. **wants:** are lacking; **junkets:** confections

259. **room:** place

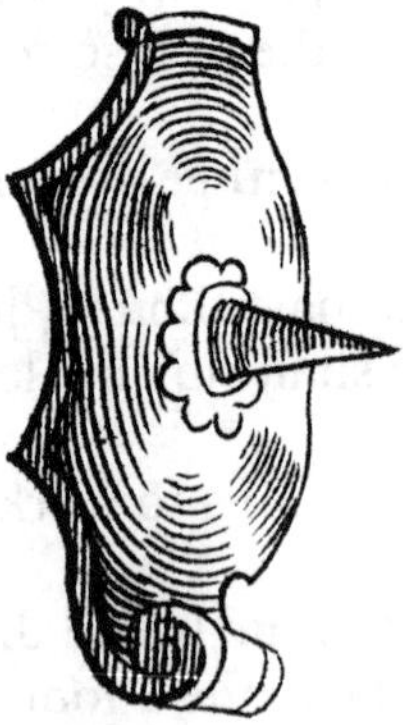

A buckler. (3.2.246)
From Louis de Gaya, *A treatise of the arms* . . . (1678).

Be mad and merry, or go hang yourselves.
But for my bonny Kate, she must with me.—
Nay, look not big, nor stamp, nor stare, nor fret;
I will be master of what is mine own.—
She is my goods, my chattels; she is my house,
My household stuff, my field, my barn,
My horse, my ox, my ass, my anything.
And here she stands, touch her whoever dare.
I'll bring mine action on the proudest he
That stops my way in Padua.—Grumio,
Draw forth thy weapon. We are beset with thieves.
Rescue thy mistress if thou be a man!—
Fear not, sweet wench, they shall not touch thee,
Kate.
I'll buckler thee against a million.

Petruchio and Katherine exit, ⌜*with Grumio.*⌝

BAPTISTA
Nay, let them go. A couple of quiet ones!

GREMIO
Went they not quickly, I should die with laughing.

TRANIO, ⌜*as* LUCENTIO⌝
Of all mad matches never was the like.

LUCENTIO, ⌜*as* CAMBIO⌝
Mistress, what's your opinion of your sister?

BIANCA
That being mad herself, she's madly mated.

GREMIO
I warrant him, Petruchio is Kated.

BAPTISTA
Neighbors and friends, though bride and
bridegroom wants
For to supply the places at the table,
You know there wants no junkets at the feast.
⌜*To Tranio.*⌝ Lucentio, you shall supply the
bridegroom's place,
And let Bianca take her sister's room.

A falconer and his tamed falcon. (4.1.190)
From George Turberville, *The booke of faulconrie or hauking* . . . (1575).

TRANIO, ⌜*as* LUCENTIO⌝
Shall sweet Bianca practice how to bride it?

BAPTISTA, ⌜*to Tranio*⌝
She shall, Lucentio. Come, gentlemen, let's go.

They exit.

THE TAMING OF THE SHREW

ACT 4

4.1 At Petruchio's house in the country, Grumio tells his fellow servant Curtis about the wild journey home to Petruchio's after the wedding. When Petruchio and Katherine arrive, Petruchio attacks his servants verbally and physically. He refuses to let Katherine eat, saying the dinner is burnt and throwing it to the floor. At the end of the scene he confides to the audience that he intends to tame Katherine in the same way that a hunter tames a falcon—by starving it and keeping it sleepless.

---

1. **jades:** worthless horses (See picture, page 66.)
2. **foul ways:** dirty roads
3. **'rayed:** i.e., berayed, dirty
6. **hot:** Proverbial: "**A** small **pot** is **soon hot.**"

10. **taller:** braver, finer (with inevitable wordplay on Grumio's short stature)

10–11. **take cold:** perhaps, suffer from exposure; or, perhaps, become downcast

17–18. **fire, fire . . . water:** an allusion to a catch (i.e., a song written for three voices, sung as a round) called "Scotland's Burning," which includes the words "**Fire, fire, cast on water**!"

⌜*ACT 4*⌝

⌜Scene 1⌝

Enter Grumio.

GRUMIO Fie, fie on all tired jades, on all mad masters, and all foul ways! Was ever man so beaten? Was ever man so 'rayed? Was ever man so weary? I am sent before to make a fire, and they are coming after to warm them. Now were not I a little pot and soon hot, my very lips might freeze to my teeth, my tongue to the roof of my mouth, my heart in my belly, ere I should come by a fire to thaw me. But I with blowing the fire shall warm myself. For, considering the weather, a taller man than I will take cold.—Holla, ho, Curtis!

Enter Curtis.

CURTIS Who is that calls so coldly?

GRUMIO A piece of ice. If thou doubt it, thou mayst slide from my shoulder to my heel with no greater a run but my head and my neck. A fire, good Curtis!

CURTIS Is my master and his wife coming, Grumio?

GRUMIO Oh, ay, Curtis, ay, and therefore fire, fire! Cast on no water.

CURTIS Is she so hot a shrew as she's reported?

GRUMIO She was, good Curtis, before this frost. But thou know'st winter tames man, woman, and

24. **three-inch fool:** another reference to Grumio's short stature (compare **little pot,** line 5)

25–26. **Am I . . . at the least:** probable wordplay on **horn** as erect penis and as the symbol of the cuckold (the husband whose wife is unfaithful) See picture of horned cuckold, page 208.

27. **on thee:** i.e., about you

28. **at hand:** nearby

30. **office:** duty (of lighting a fire)

34. **have thy duty:** i.e., get what is due to you

39. **"Jack boy, ho boy!":** The catch "The Devil Is Dead" begins "**Jack boy, ho boy, news!**"

41. **cony-catching:** deception (Literally, a cony is a rabbit. In **cony-catching,** the cony is the victim of trickery and deception. See picture, page 200.) There is possible wordplay here on *catch,* since Grumio cites catches at lines 17 and 39, and then uses the word *caught* in line 42.

44. **rushes strewed:** i.e., as floor covering

45. **fustian:** coarse-cloth work clothes

46. **officer:** household servant

47. **Jacks:** (1) menservants; (2) large leather drinking cups; **Jills:** (1) women servants; (2) small metal drinking cups

48. **carpets:** probably, woolen table covers

beast, for it hath tamed my old master and my new mistress and myself, fellow Curtis.

⌜CURTIS⌝ Away, you three-inch fool, I am no beast!

GRUMIO Am I but three inches? Why, thy horn is a foot, and so long am I, at the least. But wilt thou make a fire? Or shall I complain on thee to our mistress, whose hand (she being now at hand) thou shalt soon feel, to thy cold comfort, for being slow in thy hot office?

CURTIS I prithee, good Grumio, tell me, how goes the world?

GRUMIO A cold world, Curtis, in every office but thine, and therefore fire! Do thy duty, and have thy duty, for my master and mistress are almost frozen to death.

CURTIS There's fire ready. And therefore, good Grumio, the news!

GRUMIO Why, "Jack boy, ho boy!" and as much news as wilt thou.

CURTIS Come, you are so full of cony-catching.

GRUMIO Why, therefore fire, for I have caught extreme cold. Where's the cook? Is supper ready, the house trimmed, rushes strewed, cobwebs swept, the servingmen in their new fustian, ⌜their⌝ white stockings, and every officer his wedding garment on? Be the Jacks fair within, the Jills fair without, the carpets laid, and everything in order?

CURTIS All ready. And therefore, I pray thee, news.

GRUMIO First, know my horse is tired, my master and mistress fallen out.

CURTIS How?

GRUMIO Out of their saddles into the dirt, and thereby hangs a tale.

CURTIS Let's ha' t, good Grumio.

GRUMIO Lend thine ear.

CURTIS Here.

60. **sensible:** (1) making sense; (2) felt by the senses

62. **Imprimis:** Latin for "first"

63. **foul:** dirty

64. **of:** i.e., on

70. **miry:** swampy; **bemoiled:** muddied

74. **that:** i.e., who

78. **unexperienced:** uninformed

79. **reck'ning:** account

81. **what:** i.e., why

84. **blue coats:** servants' uniforms

85. **indifferent:** equal, i.e., matched

92. **to countenance:** to show respect to (with wordplay on *countenance* as **face** [line 93])

GRUMIO There! ⌜*He slaps Curtis on the ear.*⌝

CURTIS This 'tis to feel a tale, not to hear a tale.

GRUMIO And therefore 'tis called a sensible tale. And this cuff was but to knock at your ear and beseech list'ning. Now I begin: *Imprimis,* we came down a foul hill, my master riding behind my mistress—

CURTIS Both of one horse?

GRUMIO What's that to thee?

CURTIS Why, a horse.

GRUMIO Tell thou the tale! But hadst thou not crossed me, thou shouldst have heard how her horse fell, and she under her horse; thou shouldst have heard in how miry a place, how she was bemoiled, how he left her with the horse upon her, how he beat me because her horse stumbled, how she waded through the dirt to pluck him off me, how he swore, how she prayed that never prayed before, how I cried, how the horses ran away, how her bridle was burst, how I lost my crupper, with many things of worthy memory which now shall die in oblivion, and thou return unexperienced to thy grave.

CURTIS By this reck'ning, he is more shrew than she.

GRUMIO Ay, and that thou and the proudest of you all shall find when he comes home. But what talk I of this? Call forth Nathaniel, Joseph, Nicholas, Phillip, Walter, Sugarsop, and the rest. Let their heads be slickly combed, their blue coats brushed, and their garters of an indifferent knit. Let them curtsy with their left legs, and not presume to touch a hair of my master's horse-tail till they kiss their hands. Are they all ready?

CURTIS They are.

GRUMIO Call them forth.

CURTIS, ⌜*calling out*⌝ Do you hear, ho? You must meet my master to countenance my mistress.

GRUMIO Why, she hath a face of her own.

97. **credit her:** pay respect to her (but "lend her money" in the next line)

106. **spruce:** (1) lively; (2) smart in appearance

111. **Cock's:** i.e., God's or Christ's

117. **loggerheaded:** blockheaded

118. **No attendance:** i.e., no one waiting to serve me

121. **swain:** country bumpkin; **whoreson:** literally, son of a whore; a good-for-nothing

121–22. **malt-horse drudge:** stupid slave (literally, a horse on a treadmill that grinds malt in a brewery)

A malt horse. (4.1.121)
From Georg Andreas Böckler,
Theatrum machinarum novum . . . (1662).

CURTIS Who knows not that?

GRUMIO Thou, it seems, that calls for company to countenance her.

CURTIS I call them forth to credit her.

GRUMIO Why, she comes to borrow nothing of them.

Enter four or five Servingmen.

NATHANIEL Welcome home, Grumio.

PHILLIP How now, Grumio?

JOSEPH What, Grumio!

NICHOLAS Fellow Grumio!

NATHANIEL How now, old lad?

GRUMIO Welcome, you!—How now, you?—What, you!—Fellow, you!—And thus much for greeting. Now, my spruce companions, is all ready and all things neat?

NATHANIEL All things is ready. How near is our master?

⌜GRUMIO⌝ E'en at hand, alighted by this. And therefore be not—Cock's passion, silence! I hear my master.

Enter Petruchio and Katherine.

PETRUCHIO
Where be these knaves? What, no man at door
To hold my stirrup nor to take my horse?
Where is Nathaniel, Gregory, Phillip?

ALL THE SERVANTS Here! Here, sir, here, sir!

PETRUCHIO
"Here, sir! Here, sir! Here, sir! Here, sir!"
You loggerheaded and unpolished grooms.
What? No attendance? No regard? No duty?
Where is the foolish knave I sent before?

GRUMIO
Here, sir, as foolish as I was before.

PETRUCHIO
You peasant swain, you whoreson malt-horse drudge!

123. **park:** grounds

126. **unpinked:** undecorated (literally, without ornamental holes punched in them)

127. **link:** blacking from a torch

128. **sheathing:** being furnished with a sheath

136. **Soud:** Editors vary in their responses to this non-word. Some change it to "food," some suggest that Petruchio is here humming, etc.

139. **When:** i.e., how long do I have to wait

140. **friar of orders gray:** i.e., member of the Franciscan order of friars, whose habits are **gray** or brown (The words are from the bawdy ballad "The Friar and the Nun." See Ross W. Duffin's *Shakespeare's Songbook* [Norton, 2004], pages 155–56, and picture, below.)

144. **mend . . . other:** do better in removing **the other** boot

A Franciscan friar. (4.1.140)
From Niccolo Catalano, *Fiume del terrestre paradiso . . .* (1652).

Did I not bid thee meet me in the park
And bring along these rascal knaves with thee?

GRUMIO

Nathaniel's coat, sir, was not fully made,
And Gabriel's pumps were all unpinked i' th' heel.
There was no link to color Peter's hat,
And Walter's dagger was not come from sheathing.
There were none fine but Adam, Rafe, and Gregory.
The rest were ragged, old, and beggarly.
Yet, as they are, here are they come to meet you.

PETRUCHIO

Go, rascals, go, and fetch my supper in!
The Servants exit.

⌜*Sings.*⌝ *Where is the life that late I led?*
Where are those—

Sit down, Kate, and welcome.
⌜*They sit at a table.*⌝

Soud, soud, soud, soud!

Enter Servants with supper.

Why, when, I say?—Nay, good sweet Kate, be merry.—
Off with my boots, you rogues, you villains! When?

⌜*Sings.*⌝ *It was the friar of orders gray,*
As he forth walkèd on his way—

⌜*Servant begins to remove Petruchio's boots.*⌝

Out, you rogue! You pluck my foot awry.
Take that! ⌜*He hits the Servant.*⌝
And mend the plucking of the other.—
Be merry, Kate.—Some water here! What ho!

Enter one with water.

Where's my spaniel Troilus? Sirrah, get you hence
And bid my cousin Ferdinand come hither.
⌜*A Servant exits.*⌝

152. **it:** i.e., the basin of water

153. **unwilling:** involuntary

154. **beetle-headed:** thickheaded (A beetle was a mallet with a heavy head.)

155. **stomach:** appetite

163. **dresser:** sideboard; or, person who prepared it

165. **trenchers:** wooden platters

166. **joltheads:** blockheads

167. **be . . . straight:** deal **with you** immediately

172. **choler:** i.e., bile, one of the four bodily humors (Excess **choler** was thought to cause an angry temperament.)

175. **it:** i.e., our predisposition to anger

One, Kate, that you must kiss and be acquainted
with.—
Where are my slippers? Shall I have some water?—
Come, Kate, and wash, and welcome heartily.—
You whoreson villain, will you let it fall?
⌜*He hits the Servant.*⌝

KATHERINE
Patience, I pray you, 'twas a fault unwilling.

PETRUCHIO
A whoreson beetle-headed flap-eared knave!—
Come, Kate, sit down. I know you have a stomach.
Will you give thanks, sweet Kate, or else shall I?—
What's this? Mutton?

FIRST SERVANT Ay.

PETRUCHIO Who brought it?

PETER I.

PETRUCHIO 'Tis burnt, and so is all the meat.
What dogs are these? Where is the rascal cook?
How durst you, villains, bring it from the dresser
And serve it thus to me that love it not?
There, take it to you, trenchers, cups, and all!
⌜*He throws the food and dishes at them.*⌝
You heedless joltheads and unmannered slaves!
What, do you grumble? I'll be with you straight.
⌜*The Servants exit.*⌝

KATHERINE
I pray you, husband, be not so disquiet.
The meat was well, if you were so contented.

PETRUCHIO
I tell thee, Kate, 'twas burnt and dried away,
And I expressly am forbid to touch it,
For it engenders choler, planteth anger,
And better 'twere that both of us did fast
(Since of ourselves, ourselves are choleric)
Than feed it with such over-roasted flesh.
Be patient. Tomorrow 't shall be mended,

178 SD. **severally:** i.e., through different entrances

180. **humor:** disposition

183. **continency:** self-restraint

184. **rails . . . rates:** i.e., scolds and berates; **that:** i.e., so that

188. **politicly:** shrewdly

190. **sharp:** hungry; **passing:** completely

191. **stoop:** fly directly to the keeper or to the prey

192. **lure:** the bait held by the keeper

193. **man my haggard:** train my wild hawk (See picture, page 154.)

195. **watch her:** force her to stay awake; **kites:** hawks (See longer note, page 225.)

196. **bate:** beat their wings

197. **meat:** food

203. **hurly:** commotion; **intend:** (will) claim

And for this night we'll fast for company.
Come, I will bring thee to thy bridal chamber.

They exit.

Enter Servants severally.

NATHANIEL Peter, didst ever see the like?
PETER He kills her in her own humor.

Enter Curtis.

GRUMIO Where is he?
CURTIS In her chamber,
Making a sermon of continency to her,
And rails and swears and rates, that she (poor soul)
Knows not which way to stand, to look, to speak,
And sits as one new-risen from a dream.
Away, away, for he is coming hither!

⌜*The Servants exit.*⌝

Enter Petruchio.

PETRUCHIO
Thus have I politicly begun my reign,
And 'tis my hope to end successfully.
My falcon now is sharp and passing empty,
And, till she stoop, she must not be full-gorged,
For then she never looks upon her lure.
Another way I have to man my haggard,
To make her come and know her keeper's call.
That is, to watch her, as we watch these kites
That bate and beat and will not be obedient.
She ate no meat today, nor none shall eat.
Last night she slept not, nor tonight she shall not.
As with the meat, some undeservèd fault
I'll find about the making of the bed,
And here I'll fling the pillow, there the bolster,
This way the coverlet, another way the sheets.
Ay, and amid this hurly I intend

204. **reverend:** respectful
205. **watch:** be kept awake
206. **rail and brawl:** scold and make noise
211. **shew:** reveal (a better way)

4.2 In Padua, Hortensio (as Litio) leads Tranio (as Lucentio) to spy on Bianca and Lucentio-Cambio as the couple kiss and talk of love. Hortensio, doffing his disguise as Litio, then rejects Bianca forever, resolves to marry a wealthy widow who loves him, and sets off to observe Petruchio's taming of Katherine. In the meantime, Biondello has found a traveling merchant whom Tranio persuades to impersonate Lucentio's father, Vincentio.

---

3. **bears . . . hand:** deceives me beautifully
4. **satisfy you in:** convince you of
7. **resolve:** answer
8. **that I profess:** that which I teach; **The Art to Love:** the *Ars Amatoria,* by the Roman poet Ovid
11. **proceeders:** workers (with wordplay on "proceeding" to an academic degree like master of arts, alluded to in line 9); **marry:** i.e., indeed

That all is done in reverend care of her.
And, in conclusion, she shall watch all night,
And, if she chance to nod, I'll rail and brawl,
And with the clamor keep her still awake.
This is a way to kill a wife with kindness.
And thus I'll curb her mad and headstrong humor.
He that knows better how to tame a shrew,
Now let him speak; 'tis charity to shew.

He exits.

⌜Scene 2⌝

Enter Tranio ⌜as Lucentio⌝ and Hortensio ⌜as Litio.⌝

TRANIO, ⌜*as* LUCENTIO⌝
Is 't possible, friend Litio, that mistress Bianca
Doth fancy any other but Lucentio?
I tell you, sir, she bears me fair in hand.

⌜HORTENSIO, *as* LITIO⌝
Sir, to satisfy you in what I have said,
Stand by, and mark the manner of his teaching.

⌜They stand aside.⌝

Enter Bianca ⌜and Lucentio as Cambio.⌝

⌜LUCENTIO, *as* CAMBIO⌝
Now mistress, profit you in what you read?

BIANCA
What, master, read you? First resolve me that.

⌜LUCENTIO, *as* CAMBIO⌝
I read that I profess, *The Art to Love.*

BIANCA
And may you prove, sir, master of your art.

LUCENTIO, ⌜*as* CAMBIO⌝
While you, sweet dear, prove mistress of my heart.

⌜They move aside and kiss and talk.⌝

HORTENSIO, ⌜*as* LITIO⌝
Quick proceeders, marry! Now tell me, I pray,

15. **wonderful:** astounding
18. **scorn:** i.e., scorns
20. **cullion:** low fellow (term of contempt)
24. **lightness:** inconstancy
31. **fondly:** foolishly; **withal:** i.e., with
34. **beastly:** shamelessly
35. **but he:** i.e., except "Cambio"
38. **Ere:** before; **which:** i.e., who (i.e., the widow)
39. **haggard:** a wild female hawk (See picture, below.)

A haggard. (4.1.193; 4.2.39)
From George Turberville, *The booke of faulconrie* . . . (1575).

You that durst swear that your mistress Bianca
Loved ⌜none⌝ in the world so well as Lucentio—

TRANIO, ⌜*as* LUCENTIO⌝
O despiteful love, unconstant womankind!
I tell thee, Litio, this is wonderful!

HORTENSIO
Mistake no more. I am not Litio,
Nor a musician as I seem to be,
But one that scorn to live in this disguise
For such a one as leaves a gentleman
And makes a god of such a cullion.
Know, sir, that I am called Hortensio.

TRANIO, ⌜*as* LUCENTIO⌝
Signior Hortensio, I have often heard
Of your entire affection to Bianca,
And since mine eyes are witness of her lightness,
I will with you, if you be so contented,
Forswear Bianca and her love forever.

HORTENSIO
See how they kiss and court! Signior Lucentio,
Here is my hand, and here I firmly vow
Never to woo her more, but do forswear her
As one unworthy all the former favors
That I have fondly flattered ⌜her⌝ withal.

TRANIO, ⌜*as* LUCENTIO⌝
And here I take the like unfeignèd oath,
Never to marry with her, though she would entreat.
Fie on her, see how beastly she doth court him!

HORTENSIO
Would all the world but he had quite forsworn!
For me, that I may surely keep mine oath,
I will be married to a wealthy widow
Ere three days pass, which hath as long loved me
As I have loved this proud disdainful haggard.
And so farewell, Signior Lucentio.
Kindness in women, not their beauteous looks,

45. **'longeth:** i.e., belongeth

59. **eleven and twenty long:** i.e., exactly right (The allusion is to the card game "Thirty-one.")

60. **charm:** magically silence

63. **ancient angel:** i.e., reliable old man (literally, a coin [**angel**] whose value is above suspicion, unlike that of newer coins)

64. **serve the turn:** suit the purpose

An Italian merchant. (1.1.12; 2.1.345; 4.2.103)
From Jean de Glen, *Des habits, moeurs . . .* (1601).

Shall win my love, and so I take my leave,
In resolution as I swore before.

⌜*Hortensio exits;*
Bianca and Lucentio come forward.⌝

TRANIO
Mistress Bianca, bless you with such grace
As 'longeth to a lover's blessèd case!
Nay, I have ta'en you napping, gentle love,
And have forsworn you with Hortensio.

BIANCA
Tranio, you jest. But have you both forsworn me?

TRANIO
Mistress, we have.

LUCENTIO Then we are rid of Litio.

TRANIO
I' faith, he'll have a lusty widow now
That shall be wooed and wedded in a day.

BIANCA God give him joy.

TRANIO
Ay, and he'll tame her.

BIANCA He says so, Tranio?

TRANIO
Faith, he is gone unto the taming school.

BIANCA
The taming school? What, is there such a place?

TRANIO
Ay, mistress, and Petruchio is the master,
That teacheth tricks eleven and twenty long
To tame a shrew and charm her chattering tongue.

Enter Biondello.

BIONDELLO
O master, master, I have watched so long
That I am dog-weary, but at last I spied
An ancient angel coming down the hill
Will serve the turn.

66. **marcantant:** Biondello's version of *mercatante,* Italian for "merchant"; **pedant:** schoolmaster

72. **give assurance:** i.e., provide guarantees of the dower that Tranio (as Lucentio) has promised

73. **right:** true, real

74 SD. Although the Folio has this character enter and speak under the designation "Pedant," his words (lines 94–95) suggest that he is no schoolmaster, but is rather Biondello's **marcantant,** or merchant. We have therefore followed editor Ann Thompson in emending "Pedant" to "Merchant" throughout. (See picture, page 156.)

77. **far on:** i.e., farther on; **the farthest:** i.e., the end of your journey

81. **What countryman:** i.e., from what country are you

84. **careless:** without regard for

85. **goes hard:** is serious

87. **cause:** situation

88. **Your ships:** i.e., Paduan **ships; stayed:** detained

TRANIO What is he, Biondello?

BIONDELLO
Master, a marcantant, or a pedant,
I know not what, but formal in apparel,
In gait and countenance surely like a father.

LUCENTIO And what of him, Tranio?

TRANIO
If he be credulous, and trust my tale,
I'll make him glad to seem Vincentio
And give assurance to Baptista Minola
As if he were the right Vincentio.
Take ⌜in⌝ your love, and then let me alone.

⌜*Lucentio and Bianca exit.*⌝

Enter a ⌜*Merchant.*⌝

⌜MERCHANT⌝
God save you, sir.

TRANIO, ⌜*as* LUCENTIO⌝ And you, sir. You are welcome.
Travel you far on, or are you at the farthest?

⌜MERCHANT⌝
Sir, at the farthest for a week or two,
But then up farther, and as far as Rome,
And so to Tripoli, if God lend me life.

TRANIO, ⌜*as* LUCENTIO⌝
What countryman, I pray?

⌜MERCHANT⌝ Of Mantua.

TRANIO, ⌜*as* LUCENTIO⌝
Of Mantua, sir? Marry, God forbid!
And come to Padua, careless of your life?

⌜MERCHANT⌝
My life, sir? How, I pray? For that goes hard.

TRANIO, ⌜*as* LUCENTIO⌝
'Tis death for anyone in Mantua
To come to Padua. Know you not the cause?
Your ships are stayed at Venice, and the Duke,
For private quarrel 'twixt your duke and him,

90. **it:** i.e., the death sentence upon citizens of Mantua

91. **but . . . but:** except . . . only

92. **else:** otherwise

94. **bills . . . exchange:** papers to be exchanged **for money**

100. **grave:** worthy and serious

104. **sooth:** truth

107. **all one:** no matter

111. **are like to:** i.e., look **like**

112. **credit:** reputation; **undertake:** take on, assume

114. **take . . . should:** i.e., be careful to assume the proper manner

117. **accept of:** i.e., **accept**

Hath published and proclaimed it openly.
'Tis marvel, but that you are but newly come,
You might have heard it else proclaimed about.

⌜MERCHANT⌝
Alas, sir, it is worse for me than so,
For I have bills for money by exchange
From Florence, and must here deliver them.

TRANIO, ⌜*as* LUCENTIO⌝
Well, sir, to do you courtesy,
This will I do, and this I will advise you.
First tell me, have you ever been at Pisa?

⌜MERCHANT⌝
Ay, sir, in Pisa have I often been,
Pisa renownèd for grave citizens.

TRANIO, ⌜*as* LUCENTIO⌝
Among them know you one Vincentio?

⌜MERCHANT⌝
I know him not, but I have heard of him:
A merchant of incomparable wealth.

TRANIO, ⌜*as* LUCENTIO⌝
He is my father, sir, and sooth to say,
In count'nance somewhat doth resemble you.

BIONDELLO, ⌜*aside*⌝ As much as an apple doth an oyster, and all one.

TRANIO, ⌜*as* LUCENTIO⌝
To save your life in this extremity,
This favor will I do you for his sake
(And think it not the worst of all your fortunes
That you are like to Sir Vincentio):
His name and credit shall you undertake,
And in my house you shall be friendly lodged.
Look that you take upon you as you should.
You understand me, sir. So shall you stay
Till you have done your business in the city.
If this be court'sy, sir, accept of it.

118. **repute:** consider
120. **make . . . good:** carry out the plan
123. **pass assurance of:** formally guarantee

4.3 At Petruchio's home, Grumio torments Katherine by promising her food that he fails to bring. Petruchio then serves Katherine himself, demanding her thanks. The Haberdasher and Tailor bring in the cap and gown that Katherine plans to wear for Bianca's wedding feast, but Petruchio refuses them. Petruchio threatens that she may not return to her father's for Bianca's wedding feast unless Katherine agrees with everything he says, no matter how self-evidently false it is.

---

2. **my wrong:** the **wrong** that I suffer
5. **present:** immediate
8. **needed . . . should:** i.e., **needed** to
9. **meat:** food
11. **spites:** angers; **wants:** deprivations
13. **As who should say:** i.e., **as** if to **say**
16. **so it be:** i.e., so long as it is
17. **neat's:** calf's

⌜MERCHANT⌝
O sir, I do, and will repute you ever
The patron of my life and liberty.
TRANIO, ⌜*as* LUCENTIO⌝
Then go with me, to make the matter good.
This, by the way, I let you understand:
My father is here looked for every day
To pass assurance of a dower in marriage
'Twixt me and one Baptista's daughter here.
In all these circumstances I'll instruct you.
Go with me to clothe you as becomes you.
They exit.

⌜Scene 3⌝

Enter Katherine and Grumio.

GRUMIO
No, no, forsooth, I dare not for my life.
KATHERINE
The more my wrong, the more his spite appears.
What, did he marry me to famish me?
Beggars that come unto my father's door
Upon entreaty have a present alms.
If not, elsewhere they meet with charity.
But I, who never knew how to entreat,
Nor never needed that I should entreat,
Am starved for meat, giddy for lack of sleep,
With oaths kept waking and with brawling fed.
And that which spites me more than all these wants,
He does it under name of perfect love,
As who should say, if I should sleep or eat
'Twere deadly sickness or else present death.
I prithee, go, and get me some repast,
I care not what, so it be wholesome food.
GRUMIO What say you to a neat's foot?

18. **passing:** very
19. **choleric:** liable to promote choler (See note to 4.1.172.)
26. **let . . . rest:** i.e., do without **the mustard**
32. **the very name:** only **the name; meat:** food
33. **Sorrow on thee:** i.e., may **sorrow** come upon **thee**
34. **triumph . . . upon:** are elated . . . about
36. **all amort:** (French: *à la mort*) dejected
37. **what cheer:** i.e., how are you

KATHERINE
'Tis passing good. I prithee let me have it.

GRUMIO
I fear it is too choleric a meat.
How say you to a fat tripe finely broiled?

KATHERINE
I like it well. Good Grumio, fetch it me.

GRUMIO
I cannot tell. I fear 'tis choleric.
What say you to a piece of beef and mustard?

KATHERINE
A dish that I do love to feed upon.

GRUMIO
Ay, but the mustard is too hot a little.

KATHERINE
Why then, the beef, and let the mustard rest.

GRUMIO
Nay then, I will not. You shall have the mustard
Or else you get no beef of Grumio.

KATHERINE
Then both, or one, or any thing thou wilt.

GRUMIO
Why then, the mustard without the beef.

KATHERINE
Go, get thee gone, thou false deluding slave,
⌜*She*⌝ *beats him.*
That feed'st me with the very name of meat.
Sorrow on thee, and all the pack of you
That triumph thus upon my misery.
Go, get thee gone, I say.

Enter Petruchio and Hortensio with meat.

PETRUCHIO
How fares my Kate? What, sweeting, all amort?

HORTENSIO
Mistress, what cheer?

KATHERINE Faith, as cold as can be.

41. **dress thy meat:** prepare your food

44. **is sorted to no proof:** i.e., turn out to produce no good results

46. **stand:** i.e., stay

50. **to blame:** blameworthy, at fault

54. **apace:** right now, immediately

57. **bravely:** splendidly (in our dress)

59. **ruffs:** starched wheel-like collars; **farthingales:** hooped petticoats (See picture, below.)

60. **brav'ry:** splendid dress

61. **knav'ry:** i.e., nonsense

62. **stays thy leisure:** i.e., awaits your pleasure

63. **ruffling:** i.e., ruffled

A woman wearing a farthingale. (4.3.59)
From John Speed, *The theatre of the empire . . .* (1614).

PETRUCHIO
Pluck up thy spirits. Look cheerfully upon me.
Here, love, thou seest how diligent I am,
To dress thy meat myself and bring it thee.
I am sure, sweet Kate, this kindness merits thanks.
What, not a word? Nay then, thou lov'st it not,
And all my pains is sorted to no proof.
Here, take away this dish.

KATHERINE I pray you, let it stand.

PETRUCHIO
The poorest service is repaid with thanks,
And so shall mine before you touch the meat.

KATHERINE I thank you, sir.

HORTENSIO
Signior Petruchio, fie, you are to blame.
Come, Mistress Kate, I'll bear you company.

PETRUCHIO, ⌜*aside to Hortensio*⌝
Eat it up all, Hortensio, if thou lovest me.—
Much good do it unto thy gentle heart.
Kate, eat apace.

⌜*Katherine and Hortensio prepare to eat.*⌝

And now, my honey love,
Will we return unto thy father's house
And revel it as bravely as the best,
With silken coats and caps and golden rings,
With ruffs and cuffs and farthingales and things,
With scarves and fans and double change of brav'ry,
With amber bracelets, beads, and all this knav'ry.
What, hast thou dined? The tailor stays thy leisure
To deck thy body with his ruffling treasure.

Enter Tailor.

Come, tailor, let us see these ornaments.
Lay forth the gown.

Enter Haberdasher.

What news with you, sir?

67. **bespeak:** order

68. **porringer:** porridge bowl

69. **lewd:** low, vulgar; **filthy:** mean, disgusting

70. **cockle:** cockleshell

71. **knack:** knickknack; **toy, trick:** both mean "trifle," something worthless

73. **doth fit the time:** is fashionable now

75. **gentle:** wordplay on **gentlewomen** (line 74)

78. **leave:** permission

87. **custard-coffin:** crust for a custard

92. **masking-stuff:** costumes for maskers (i.e., people who came to parties wearing disguises)

⌜HABERDASHER⌝
Here is the cap your Worship did bespeak.

PETRUCHIO
Why, this was molded on a porringer!
A velvet dish! Fie, fie, 'tis lewd and filthy.
Why, 'tis a cockle or a walnut shell,
A knack, a toy, a trick, a baby's cap.
Away with it! Come, let me have a bigger.

KATHERINE
I'll have no bigger. This doth fit the time,
And gentlewomen wear such caps as these.

PETRUCHIO
When you are gentle, you shall have one too,
And not till then.

HORTENSIO, ⌜*aside*⌝ That will not be in haste.

KATHERINE
Why, sir, I trust I may have leave to speak,
And speak I will. I am no child, no babe.
Your betters have endured me say my mind,
And if you cannot, best you stop your ears.
My tongue will tell the anger of my heart,
Or else my heart, concealing it, will break,
And, rather than it shall, I will be free
Even to the uttermost, as I please, in words.

PETRUCHIO
Why, thou sayst true. It is ⌜a⌝ paltry cap,
A custard-coffin, a bauble, a silken pie.
I love thee well in that thou lik'st it not.

KATHERINE
Love me, or love me not, I like the cap,
And it I will have, or I will have none.
⌜*Exit Haberdasher.*⌝

PETRUCHIO
Thy gown? Why, ay. Come, tailor, let us see 't.
O mercy God, what masking-stuff is here?

93. **demi-cannon:** large cannon

94–96. **up and down . . . shop:** Petruchio here describes an elegant style of dressmaking in which the outer layer of fabric is slashed to reveal the rich lining beneath. The slashes are called "cuts." (See wordplay on "cutting out" vs. "cutting" fabric, lines 133–34 and 151, below.) **carved . . . tart:** i.e., with slits like the upper crust of a pie **censer:** perhaps, incense burner (See picture, page 174.)

98. **like:** i.e., likely

101. **Marry, and did:** i.e., indeed I did; **be remembered:** i.e., remember

102. **mar:** wordplay on the proverbial **"make** [line 99] or **mar"**

103. **hop . . . kennel:** i.e., **hop over every** gutter

104. **custom:** trade, patronage

107. **quaint:** elegant

108. **commendable:** accent on first syllable

109. **Belike:** perhaps; **puppet:** plaything

115. **yard:** yardstick; **quarter:** quarter-yard; **nail:** one-sixteenth yard

116. **nit:** louse egg

117. **Braved:** defied; **with:** i.e., by

119. **be-mete:** intensive form of *mete,* meaning "measure"; i.e., measure thoroughly; beat you

120. **As . . . liv'st:** i.e., remembering this thrashing, you will **think** before chattering as long as you live

What's this? A sleeve? 'Tis like ⌜a⌝ demi-cannon.
What, up and down carved like an apple tart?
Here's snip and nip and cut and slish and slash,
Like to a censer in a barber's shop.
Why, what a devil's name, tailor, call'st thou this?

HORTENSIO, ⌜*aside*⌝
I see she's like to have neither cap nor gown.

TAILOR
You bid me make it orderly and well,
According to the fashion and the time.

PETRUCHIO
Marry, and did. But if you be remembered,
I did not bid you mar it to the time.
Go, hop me over every kennel home,
For you shall hop without my custom, sir.
I'll none of it. Hence, make your best of it.

KATHERINE
I never saw a better-fashioned gown,
More quaint, more pleasing, nor more
commendable.
Belike you mean to make a puppet of me.

PETRUCHIO
Why, true, he means to make a puppet of thee.

TAILOR
She says your Worship means to make a puppet of
her.

PETRUCHIO
O monstrous arrogance! Thou liest, thou thread,
thou thimble,
Thou yard, three-quarters, half-yard, quarter, nail!
Thou flea, thou nit, thou winter cricket, thou!
Braved in mine own house with a skein of thread?
Away, thou rag, thou quantity, thou remnant,
Or I shall so be-mete thee with thy yard
As thou shalt think on prating whilst thou liv'st.
I tell thee, I, that thou hast marred her gown.

123. **had direction:** i.e., was directed
125. **stuff:** material (for the gown)
128. **cut:** See note to lines 94–96, above.
129. **faced:** (1) sewed on trim; (2) defied
131. **Face:** confront; **braved:** made to look splendid
132. **brave:** defy
134. **Ergo:** Latin for "therefore"
136. **note . . . fashion:** written instruction for the style of the gown
138. **lies in 's throat:** tells a serious lie **in 's:** in its
139. **Imprimis:** Latin for "first"
142. **bottom:** ball or skein
144. **small-compassed:** i.e., in the form of a small semicircle
146. **trunk sleeve:** wide **sleeve**
148. **curiously:** exquisitely; **cut:** i.e., slashed
152. **prove upon thee:** i.e., make good in a fight

"A loose-bodied gown." (4.3.139)
From Cesare Vecellio, *Degli habiti antichi* . . . (1590).

TAILOR
Your Worship is deceived. The gown is made
Just as my master had direction.
Grumio gave order how it should be done.

GRUMIO I gave him no order. I gave him the stuff.

TAILOR
But how did you desire it should be made?

GRUMIO Marry, sir, with needle and thread.

TAILOR
But did you not request to have it cut?

GRUMIO Thou hast faced many things.

TAILOR I have.

GRUMIO Face not me. Thou hast braved many men; brave not me. I will neither be faced nor braved. I say unto thee, I bid thy master cut out the gown, but I did not bid him cut it to pieces. *Ergo,* thou liest.

TAILOR Why, here is the note of the fashion to testify.
⌜*He shows a paper.*⌝

PETRUCHIO Read it.

GRUMIO The note lies in 's throat, if he say I said so.

TAILOR ⌜*reads*⌝ "*Imprimis,* a loose-bodied gown—"

GRUMIO Master, if ever I said "loose-bodied gown," sew me in the skirts of it and beat me to death with a bottom of brown thread. I said "a gown."

PETRUCHIO Proceed.

TAILOR ⌜*reads*⌝ "With a small-compassed cape—"

GRUMIO I confess the cape.

TAILOR ⌜*reads*⌝ "With a trunk sleeve—"

GRUMIO I confess two sleeves.

TAILOR ⌜*reads*⌝ "The sleeves curiously cut."

PETRUCHIO Ay, there's the villainy.

GRUMIO Error i' th' bill, sir, error i' th' bill! I commanded the sleeves should be cut out and sewed up again, and that I'll prove upon thee, though thy little finger be armed in a thimble.

154. **An:** i.e., if

154–55. **place where:** a suitable **place**

156. **I . . . thee:** i.e., I'm ready to fight you; **straight:** straightway, immediately; **bill:** (1) note; (2) long-handled weapon

157. **mete-yard:** measuring stick

159. **odds:** i.e., advantage

162. **unto . . . use:** i.e., for your master to use

165. **what's . . . that:** i.e., what do you mean by that

167. **Take up . . . use:** Here (and in lines 163–64) Grumio apparently plays on "**take up**" as meaning "lift up" and "**use**" as meaning "using her sexually."

173. **of:** i.e., at

176. **mean habiliments:** common clothes

180. **peereth in:** i.e., shows through; **habit:** clothes

181. **What:** interjection at the beginning of a question or exclamation

A censer. (4.3.96)
From Giovanni Ferro, *Teatro d'imprese* . . . (1623).

TAILOR This is true that I say. An I had thee in place where, thou shouldst know it.

GRUMIO I am for thee straight. Take thou the bill, give me thy mete-yard, and spare not me.

HORTENSIO God-a-mercy, Grumio, then he shall have no odds.

PETRUCHIO
Well, sir, in brief, the gown is not for me.

GRUMIO You are i' th' right, sir, 'tis for my mistress.

PETRUCHIO
Go, take it up unto thy master's use.

GRUMIO Villain, not for thy life! Take up my mistress' gown for thy master's use?

PETRUCHIO Why, sir, what's your conceit in that?

GRUMIO O, sir, the conceit is deeper than you think for. Take up my mistress' gown to his master's use? O, fie, fie, fie!

PETRUCHIO, ⌜*aside to Hortensio*⌝
Hortensio, say thou wilt see the tailor paid.
⌜*To Tailor.*⌝ Go, take it hence. Begone, and say no more.

HORTENSIO, ⌜*aside to Tailor*⌝
Tailor, I'll pay thee for thy gown tomorrow.
Take no unkindness of his hasty words.
Away, I say. Commend me to thy master.

Tailor exits.

PETRUCHIO
Well, come, my Kate, we will unto your father's,
Even in these honest mean habiliments.
Our purses shall be proud, our garments poor,
For 'tis the mind that makes the body rich,
And as the sun breaks through the darkest clouds,
So honor peereth in the meanest habit.
What, is the jay more precious than the lark
Because his feathers are more beautiful?
Or is the adder better than the eel

186. **furniture:** accessories; **mean array:** ordinary clothes

189. **sport us:** i.e., disport or entertain ourselves

194. **some:** i.e., about

195. **dinner time:** i.e., noon

199. **Look what:** i.e., whatever

200. **still:** always; **crossing:** opposing; **let 't alone:** i.e., abandon preparations for departure

4.4 In Padua, the Merchant impersonating Vincentio visits Baptista with Tranio, who is still disguised as Lucentio. Baptista accepts the Merchant's guarantee of Bianca's dower and sends "Cambio" to Bianca to tell her the marriage plans. Meanwhile, Baptista arranges to visit "Lucentio" and "Vincentio" at their lodging to finalize the marriage contract. Biondello tells Lucentio that all the arrangements have been made for Lucentio to elope with Bianca.

---

0 SD. **booted:** in riding boots

2. **And but:** unless (The Merchant may be practicing his role as Vincentio.)

4. **Near:** i.e., nearly

5. **Pegasus:** i.e., an inn named after the mythical winged horse

Because his painted skin contents the eye?
O no, good Kate. Neither art thou the worse
For this poor furniture and mean array.
If thou ⌜account'st⌝ it shame, lay it on me,
And therefore frolic! We will hence forthwith
To feast and sport us at thy father's house.
⌜*To Grumio.*⌝ Go, call my men, and let us straight to him,
And bring our horses unto Long-lane end.
There will we mount, and thither walk on foot.
Let's see, I think 'tis now some seven o'clock,
And well we may come there by dinner time.

KATHERINE
I dare assure you, sir, 'tis almost two,
And 'twill be supper time ere you come there.

PETRUCHIO
It shall be seven ere I go to horse.
Look what I speak, or do, or think to do,
You are still crossing it.—Sirs, let 't alone.
I will not go today, and, ere I do,
It shall be what o'clock I say it is.

HORTENSIO, ⌜*aside*⌝
Why, so, this gallant will command the sun!
⌜*They exit.*⌝

⌜Scene 4⌝

Enter Tranio ⌜as Lucentio,⌝ and the ⌜Merchant,⌝ booted, and dressed like Vincentio.

TRANIO, ⌜*as* LUCENTIO⌝
⌜Sir,⌝ this is the house. Please it you that I call?

⌜MERCHANT⌝
Ay, what else? And but I be deceived,
Signior Baptista may remember me,
Near twenty years ago, in Genoa,
Where we were lodgers at the Pegasus.

7. **'longeth:** i.e., belongeth
8. **warrant you:** promise I will
10. **schooled:** instructed in his part
12. **throughly:** thoroughly
13. **right:** true
18. **tall:** fine, bold
20. **happily:** opportunely
23. **Give . . . patrimony:** i.e., let what I would inherit from you serve as a dower **for Bianca**
24. **Soft:** i.e., enough, hush
25. **by your leave:** a polite phrase
27. **weighty cause:** serious matter

An Italian gentleman.
From Cesare Vecellio, *Degli habiti antichi* . . . (1590).

TRANIO, ⌜*as* LUCENTIO⌝
'Tis well. And hold your own in any case
With such austerity as 'longeth to a father.

⌜MERCHANT⌝
I warrant you.

Enter Biondello.

But, sir, here comes your boy.
'Twere good he were schooled.

TRANIO, ⌜*as* LUCENTIO⌝
Fear you not him.—Sirrah Biondello,
Now do your duty throughly, I advise you.
Imagine 'twere the right Vincentio.

BIONDELLO Tut, fear not me.

TRANIO, ⌜*as* LUCENTIO⌝
But hast thou done thy errand to Baptista?

BIONDELLO
I told him that your father was at Venice,
And that you looked for him this day in Padua.

TRANIO, ⌜*as* LUCENTIO⌝
Thou'rt a tall fellow. Hold thee that to drink.
⌜*He gives him money.*⌝

Enter Baptista and Lucentio ⌜as Cambio.⌝

Here comes Baptista. Set your countenance, sir.
⌜*Merchant stands*⌝ *bareheaded.*

TRANIO, ⌜*as* LUCENTIO⌝
Signior Baptista, you are happily met.—
Sir, this is the gentleman I told you of.
I pray you stand good father to me now.
Give me Bianca for my patrimony.

⌜MERCHANT, *as* VINCENTIO⌝ Soft, son.—
Sir, by your leave, having come to Padua
To gather in some debts, my son Lucentio
Made me acquainted with a weighty cause
Of love between your daughter and himself.

29, 30. **for:** because of

31. **stay:** delay

32. **in . . . care:** i.e., with the **care** that **a good** father ought to have

33. **matched:** married

37. **curious:** overparticular, too demanding

40. **shortness:** brevity

46. **pass:** transfer to; **dower:** See note to 2.1.363, page 100.

50. **be affied:** may be formally betrothed; **such assurance ta'en: such** guarantees provided

51. **with . . . stand:** accord with what each party has agreed to

53. **Pitchers have ears:** i.e., we might be overheard (proverbial)

54. **heark'ning still:** listening constantly

55. **happily:** perhaps

56. **an it like you:** i.e., if **it** please **you**

57. **lie:** stay

58. **pass:** i.e., transact

And, for the good report I hear of you,
And for the love he beareth to your daughter
And she to him, to stay him not too long,
I am content, in a good father's care,
To have him matched. And if you please to like
No worse than I, upon some agreement
Me shall you find ready and willing
With one consent to have her so bestowed,
For curious I cannot be with you,
Signior Baptista, of whom I hear so well.

BAPTISTA

Sir, pardon me in what I have to say.
Your plainness and your shortness please me well.
Right true it is your son Lucentio here
Doth love my daughter, and she loveth him,
Or both dissemble deeply their affections.
And therefore, if you say no more than this,
That like a father you will deal with him
And pass my daughter a sufficient dower,
The match is made, and all is done.
Your son shall have my daughter with consent.

TRANIO, ⌜*as* LUCENTIO⌝

I thank you, sir. Where then do you know best
We be affied and such assurance ta'en
As shall with either part's agreement stand?

BAPTISTA

Not in my house, Lucentio, for you know
Pitchers have ears, and I have many servants.
Besides, old Gremio is heark'ning still,
And happily we might be interrupted.

TRANIO, ⌜*as* LUCENTIO⌝

Then at my lodging, an it like you.
There doth my father lie, and there this night
We'll pass the business privately and well.
Send for your daughter by your servant here.

⌜*He indicates Lucentio, and winks at him.*⌝

60. **scrivener:** notary public; **presently:** immediately
61. **slender warning:** short notice
62. **pittance:** i.e., refreshment
63. **likes:** pleases; **hie you:** hurry
64. **straight:** straightway, immediately
67. **like:** i.e., likely
71. **mess:** dish; **cheer:** food and drink
72. **better it:** i.e., celebrate more elaborately
79. **’has:** i.e., he has
82. **moralize:** i.e., explain

My boy shall fetch the scrivener presently.
The worst is this: that at so slender warning
You are like to have a thin and slender pittance.

BAPTISTA
It likes me well.—Cambio, hie you home,
And bid Bianca make her ready straight.
And, if you will, tell what hath happenèd:
Lucentio's father is arrived in Padua,
And how she's like to be Lucentio's wife.

⌜*Lucentio exits.*⌝

BIONDELLO
I pray the gods she may, with all my heart.

TRANIO, ⌜*as* LUCENTIO⌝
Dally not with the gods, but get thee gone.—
Signior Baptista, shall I lead the way?
Welcome! One mess is like to be your cheer.
Come, sir, we will better it in Pisa.

BAPTISTA I follow you.

⌜*All but Biondello*⌝ *exit.*

Enter Lucentio.

BIONDELLO Cambio.

LUCENTIO What sayst thou, Biondello?

BIONDELLO You saw my master wink and laugh upon you?

LUCENTIO Biondello, what of that?

BIONDELLO Faith, nothing; but 'has left me here behind to expound the meaning or moral of his signs and tokens.

LUCENTIO I pray thee, moralize them.

BIONDELLO Then thus: Baptista is safe, talking with the deceiving father of a deceitful son.

LUCENTIO And what of him?

BIONDELLO His daughter is to be brought by you to the supper.

93. **assurance:** legal settlement

93–94. **Take . . . of her:** i.e., make sure **of her**

94. **cum . . . solum:** "with the exclusive right to print" (Latin), a formula often appearing on the title pages of books in this period (Biondello plays with the formula as a description of legal marriage.)

97. **that:** i.e., what, **that** which

101. **tarry:** wait

105–6. **against you come:** in preparation for your coming

106. **appendix:** appendage (spouse)

108. **wherefore:** why

110. **Hap what hap may:** i.e., whatever may happen; **roundly . . . her:** perhaps, approach her boldly

111. **shall go hard:** i.e., will not be for lack of effort

111 SD. For Sly's comments on the action at this point in *A Shrew,* see "Framing Dialogue," D, page 242, below.

4.5 Katherine now gives assent to every word Petruchio says. On their way to her father's, they meet the true Vincentio, who is going to Padua to visit his son. They travel together to Padua.

1–2. **our father's:** i.e., Baptista's

3. **goodly:** beautifully

LUCENTIO And then?

BIONDELLO The old priest at Saint Luke's Church is at your command at all hours.

LUCENTIO And what of all this?

BIONDELLO I cannot tell, ⌜except⌝ they are busied about a counterfeit assurance. Take you assurance of her *cum privilegio ad imprimendum solum.* To th' church take the priest, clerk, and some sufficient honest witnesses.

If this be not that you look for, I have no more to say,
But bid Bianca farewell forever and a day.

LUCENTIO Hear'st thou, Biondello?

BIONDELLO I cannot tarry. I knew a wench married in an afternoon as she went to the garden for parsley to stuff a rabbit, and so may you, sir. And so adieu, sir. My master hath appointed me to go to Saint Luke's to bid the priest be ready to come against you come with your appendix.

He exits.

LUCENTIO
I may, and will, if she be so contented.
She will be pleased. Then wherefore should I doubt?
Hap what hap may, I'll roundly go about her.
It shall go hard if "Cambio" go without her.

He exits.

⌜Scene 5⌝

Enter Petruchio, Katherine, Hortensio, ⌜and Servants.⌝

PETRUCHIO
Come on, i' God's name, once more toward our father's.
Good Lord, how bright and goodly shines the moon!

KATHERINE
The moon? The sun! It is not moonlight now.

8. **list:** choose; or, please

9. **Or e'er I:** before I ever will

12. **crossed:** opposed, contradicted

16. **rush candle:** cheap **candle** made by dipping a **rush** in grease or fat

26. **go thy ways:** i.e., well done; **field:** i.e., battlefield

27–28. **Thus . . . bias:** Petruchio claims that Katherine is now acting naturally, no longer being perverse. (In the game of bowls, the ball is weighted so that it follows a curved path [its **bias**]; **against the bias,** thus, means "off its natural course." See picture, below.) **unluckily:** unhappily; or, perhaps, unsuccessfully

29. **soft:** i.e., wait a minute

The game of bowls. (4.5.27–28)
From *Le centre de l'amour* . . . [1650?].

PETRUCHIO
I say it is the moon that shines so bright.
KATHERINE
I know it is the sun that shines so bright.
PETRUCHIO
Now, by my mother's son, and that's myself,
It shall be moon, or star, or what I list,
Or e'er I journey to your father's house.
⌜*To Servants.*⌝ Go on, and fetch our horses back
again.—
Evermore crossed and crossed, nothing but crossed!
HORTENSIO, ⌜*to Katherine*⌝
Say as he says, or we shall never go.
KATHERINE
Forward, I pray, since we have come so far,
And be it moon, or sun, or what you please.
And if you please to call it a rush candle,
Henceforth I vow it shall be so for me.
PETRUCHIO I say it is the moon.
KATHERINE I know it is the moon.
PETRUCHIO
Nay, then you lie. It is the blessèd sun.
KATHERINE
Then God be blest, it ⌜is⌝ the blessèd sun.
But sun it is not, when you say it is not,
And the moon changes even as your mind.
What you will have it named, even that it is,
And so it shall be so for Katherine.
HORTENSIO
Petruchio, go thy ways, the field is won.
PETRUCHIO
Well, forward, forward. Thus the bowl should run,
And not unluckily against the bias.
But soft! Company is coming here.

Enter Vincentio.

30–31. **where away:** i.e., **where** are you going

33. **fresher:** more radiant

34. **war . . . red:** language typical of love poetry of the period as it described womanly beauty

36. **become:** adorn

42. **Whither away:** i.e., where are you going

44–45. **whom . . . thee:** i.e., to whom you have been given by Fortune **Allots:** i.e., allot

46. **how now:** i.e., what's going on

51. **green:** i.e., young, fresh

52. **reverend father:** i.e., old man worthy of respect

54. **withal:** in addition

58. **encounter:** i.e., greeting; **amazed:** astounded

⌜*To Vincentio.*⌝ Good morrow, gentle mistress, where away?—
Tell me, sweet Kate, and tell me truly, too,
Hast thou beheld a fresher gentlewoman?
Such war of white and red within her cheeks!
What stars do spangle heaven with such beauty
As those two eyes become that heavenly face?—
Fair lovely maid, once more good day to thee.—
Sweet Kate, embrace her for her beauty's sake.

HORTENSIO, ⌜*aside*⌝
He will make the man mad, to make the woman of him.

KATHERINE
Young budding virgin, fair and fresh and sweet,
Whither away, or ⌜where⌝ is thy abode?
Happy the parents of so fair a child!
Happier the man whom favorable stars
⌜Allots⌝ thee for his lovely bedfellow.

PETRUCHIO
Why, how now, Kate? I hope thou art not mad!
This is a man—old, wrinkled, faded, withered—
And not a maiden, as thou sayst he is.

KATHERINE
Pardon, old father, my mistaking eyes
That have been so bedazzled with the sun
That everything I look on seemeth green.
Now I perceive thou art a reverend father.
Pardon, I pray thee, for my mad mistaking.

PETRUCHIO
Do, good old grandsire, and withal make known
Which way thou travelest. If along with us,
We shall be joyful of thy company.

VINCENTIO
Fair sir, and you, my merry mistress,
That with your strange encounter much amazed me,
My name is called Vincentio, my dwelling Pisa,

68. **by this:** by now
69. **esteem:** repute
71. **so qualified:** with such qualities; **beseem:** suit, become
74. **honest:** honorable, worthy
75. **of:** i.e., at, with
76. **else:** instead
77. **pleasant:** merry; **break a jest:** play a joke
80. **hereof:** of it
81. **merriment:** joke; **jealous:** suspicious
82. **in heart:** in good spirits
83. **Have to:** i.e., now for; **froward:** perverse
84. **untoward:** stubborn, intractable

And bound I am to Padua, there to visit
A son of mine which long I have not seen.

PETRUCHIO
What is his name?

VINCENTIO Lucentio, gentle sir.

PETRUCHIO
Happily met, the happier for thy son.
And now by law as well as reverend age,
I may entitle thee my loving father.
The sister to my wife, this gentlewoman,
Thy son by this hath married. Wonder not,
Nor be not grieved. She is of good esteem,
Her dowry wealthy, and of worthy birth;
Beside, so qualified as may beseem
The spouse of any noble gentleman.
Let me embrace with old Vincentio,
And wander we to see thy honest son,
Who will of thy arrival be full joyous.

VINCENTIO
But is this true, or is it else your pleasure,
Like pleasant travelers, to break a jest
Upon the company you overtake?

HORTENSIO
I do assure thee, father, so it is.

PETRUCHIO
Come, go along and see the truth hereof,
For our first merriment hath made thee jealous.
⌜*All but Hortensio*⌝ *exit.*

HORTENSIO
Well, Petruchio, this has put me in heart!
Have to my widow, and if she ⌜be⌝ froward,
Then hast thou taught Hortensio to be untoward.
He exits.

THE TAMING OF THE SHREW

ACT 5

5.1 After Bianca has secretly married Lucentio, Petruchio, Katherine, and Lucentio's father arrive at Lucentio's lodging. They are rebuffed by the Merchant impersonating Vincentio. Vincentio denounces as frauds the Merchant and then Tranio, who turns up still disguised as Lucentio. As Vincentio is about to be carried off to jail by an officer, the true Lucentio arrives with his bride, successfully begs his father's pardon for the secret marriage, and explains the disguises.

---

0 SD. **Gremio . . . before:** Presumably this Folio direction means that Gremio enters first. He apparently sees none of what happens in lines 1–7. (See his comment at line 8.) It has been argued that he simply fails to recognize Lucentio, but note that he does not mention Bianca's entrance or exit.

5. **see . . . back:** i.e., **see** you married

10. **bears more toward:** is closer to

13. **shall command your welcome:** i.e., have the power to order that you be given **welcome**

14. **cheer is toward:** refreshment can be expected

⌜ACT 5⌝

⌜Scene 1⌝

Enter Biondello, Lucentio ⌜*as himself,*⌝ *and Bianca. Gremio is out before* ⌜*and stands to the side.*⌝

BIONDELLO Softly and swiftly, sir, for the priest is ready.

LUCENTIO I fly, Biondello. But they may chance to need thee at home. Therefore leave us.

⌜*Lucentio exits with Bianca.*⌝

BIONDELLO Nay, faith, I'll see the church a' your back, and then come back to my ⌜master's⌝ as soon as I can. ⌜*He exits.*⌝

GREMIO I marvel Cambio comes not all this while.

Enter Petruchio, Katherine, Vincentio, Grumio, with Attendants.

PETRUCHIO

Sir, here's the door. This is Lucentio's house.
My father's bears more toward the marketplace.
Thither must I, and here I leave you, sir.

VINCENTIO

You shall not choose but drink before you go.
I think I shall command your welcome here,
And by all likelihood some cheer is toward.

⌜*He*⌝ *knocks.*

20, 22. **withal:** i.e., with

28. **frivolous circumstances:** i.e., silly details

38. **flat:** downright

41. **cosen:** cheat

42. **under my countenance:** i.e., by exploiting my good name

44. **good shipping:** i.e., **good** luck

46. **undone:** ruined

GREMIO, ⌜*coming forward*⌝
They're busy within. You were best knock louder.

⌜*Merchant*⌝ *looks out of the window.*

⌜MERCHANT, *as* VINCENTIO⌝ What's he that knocks as he would beat down the gate?

VINCENTIO Is Signior Lucentio within, sir?

⌜MERCHANT, *as* VINCENTIO⌝ He's within, sir, but not to be spoken withal.

VINCENTIO What if a man bring him a hundred pound or two to make merry withal?

⌜MERCHANT, *as* VINCENTIO⌝ Keep your hundred pounds to yourself. He shall need none so long as I live.

PETRUCHIO, ⌜*to Vincentio*⌝ Nay, I told you your son was well beloved in Padua.—Do you hear, sir? To leave frivolous circumstances, I pray you tell Signior Lucentio that his father is come from Pisa and is here at the door to speak with him.

⌜MERCHANT, *as* VINCENTIO⌝ Thou liest. His father is come from Padua and here looking out at the window.

VINCENTIO Art thou his father?

⌜MERCHANT, *as* VINCENTIO⌝ Ay, sir, so his mother says, if I may believe her.

PETRUCHIO, ⌜*to Vincentio*⌝ Why, how now, gentleman! Why, this is flat knavery, to take upon you another man's name.

⌜MERCHANT, *as* VINCENTIO⌝ Lay hands on the villain. I believe he means to cosen somebody in this city under my countenance.

Enter Biondello.

BIONDELLO, ⌜*aside*⌝ I have seen them in the church together. God send 'em good shipping! But who is here? Mine old master Vincentio! Now we are undone and brought to nothing.

47. **crack-hemp:** i.e., rogue (literally, someone who will stretch the hangman's rope)

48. **I may choose:** i.e., go my own way

56. **marry:** indeed

67. **fine villain:** splendidly dressed rogue; **doublet:** jacket

68. **hose:** breeches; **copatain:** high-crowned

69. **undone:** ruined, destroyed

69–70. **play the good husband:** i.e., conserve, save money

75. **habit:** clothes

76. **'cerns:** i.e., concerns

78. **maintain:** afford

Men in doublet and hose. (IND.2.9; 5.1.67–68)
From [Robert Greene,] *A quip for an vpstart courtier . . .* (1620).

VINCENTIO, ⌜*to Biondello*⌝ Come hither, crack-hemp.

BIONDELLO I hope I may choose, sir.

VINCENTIO Come hither, you rogue! What, have you forgot me?

BIONDELLO Forgot you? No, sir. I could not forget you, for I never saw you before in all my life.

VINCENTIO What, you notorious villain, didst thou never see thy ⌜master's⌝ father, Vincentio?

BIONDELLO What, my old worshipful old master? Yes, marry, sir. See where he looks out of the window.

VINCENTIO Is 't so indeed? *He beats Biondello.*

BIONDELLO Help, help, help! Here's a madman will murder me. ⌜*Biondello exits.*⌝

⌜MERCHANT, *as* VINCENTIO⌝ Help, son! Help, Signior Baptista! ⌜*He exits from window.*⌝

PETRUCHIO Prithee, Kate, let's stand aside and see the end of this controversy. ⌜*They move aside.*⌝

Enter ⌜Merchant⌝ with Servants, ⌜and⌝ Baptista ⌜and⌝ Tranio ⌜disguised as Lucentio.⌝

TRANIO, ⌜*as* LUCENTIO⌝ Sir, what are you that offer to beat my servant?

VINCENTIO What am I, sir? Nay, what are you, sir! O immortal gods! O fine villain! A silken doublet, a velvet hose, a scarlet cloak, and a copatain hat! O, I am undone, I am undone! While I play the good husband at home, my son and my servant spend all at the university.

TRANIO, ⌜*as* LUCENTIO⌝ How now, what's the matter?

BAPTISTA What, is the man lunatic?

TRANIO, ⌜*as* LUCENTIO⌝ Sir, you seem a sober ancient gentleman by your habit, but your words show you a madman. Why, sir, what 'cerns it you if I wear pearl and gold? I thank my good father, I am able to maintain it.

82. **his name:** i.e., Tranio's **name**

95. **forthcoming:** produced (at the time of his trial)

100–101. **cony-catched:** deceived and victimized (See note to 4.1.41, and picture, below.)

102. **right:** true

105. **thou . . . say:** i.e., you might as well **say**

108. **dotard:** foolish old man

109. **haled:** molested

A cony. (4.1.41; 5.1.100–101)
From the title page of Robert Greene, *Notable discouery of coosenage . . . practised by . . . connie-catchers* . . . (1592).

VINCENTIO Thy father! O villain, he is a sailmaker in Bergamo.

BAPTISTA You mistake, sir, you mistake, sir! Pray, what do you think is his name?

VINCENTIO His name? As if I knew not his name! I have brought him up ever since he was three years old, and his name is Tranio.

⌜MERCHANT, *as* VINCENTIO⌝ Away, away, mad ass! His name is Lucentio and he is mine only son, and heir to the lands of me, Signior Vincentio.

VINCENTIO Lucentio? O, he hath murdered his master! Lay hold on him, I charge you in the Duke's name. O, my son, my son! Tell me, thou villain, where is my son Lucentio?

TRANIO, ⌜*as* LUCENTIO⌝ Call forth an officer.

⌜*Enter an Officer.*⌝

Carry this mad knave to the jail.—Father Baptista, I charge you see that he be forthcoming.

VINCENTIO Carry me to the jail?

GREMIO Stay, officer. He shall not go to prison.

BAPTISTA Talk not, Signior Gremio. I say he shall go to prison.

GREMIO Take heed, Signior Baptista, lest you be cony-catched in this business. I dare swear this is the right Vincentio.

⌜MERCHANT, *as* VINCENTIO⌝ Swear, if thou dar'st.

GREMIO Nay, I dare not swear it.

TRANIO, ⌜*as* LUCENTIO⌝ Then thou wert best say that I am not Lucentio.

GREMIO Yes, I know thee to be Signior Lucentio.

BAPTISTA Away with the dotard, to the jail with him.

VINCENTIO Thus strangers may be haled and abused.—O monstrous villain!

Enter Biondello, Lucentio and Bianca.

111. **spoiled:** ruined

112 SD. **exit . . . be:** For Sly's comments on the action at this point in *A Shrew,* see "Framing Dialogue," E, page 243, below.

119. **Right:** true

121. **counterfeit supposes:** false impersonations; **eyne:** i.e., eyes

122. **packing:** plotting, conspiracy; **with a witness:** i.e., **with a** vengeance

124. **faced and braved:** i.e., defied

128. **state:** status

129. **countenance:** i.e., position and reputation

131. **Unto:** i.e., at

Cupid, the god of love. (5.1.127)
From August Casimir Redel, *Apophtegmata symbolica* . . . [n.d.].

BIONDELLO O, we are spoiled, and yonder he is! Deny him, forswear him, or else we are all undone.

Biondello, Tranio, and ⌜*Merchant*⌝ *exit as fast as may be.*

LUCENTIO
Pardon, sweet father. ⌜*Lucentio and Bianca*⌝ *kneel.*

VINCENTIO Lives my sweet son?

BIANCA
Pardon, dear father.

BAPTISTA How hast thou offended?
Where is Lucentio?

LUCENTIO Here's Lucentio,
Right son to the right Vincentio,
That have by marriage made thy daughter mine
While counterfeit supposes bleared thine eyne.

GREMIO
Here's packing, with a witness, to deceive us all!

VINCENTIO
Where is that damnèd villain, Tranio,
That faced and braved me in this matter so?

BAPTISTA
Why, tell me, is not this my Cambio?

BIANCA
Cambio is changed into Lucentio.

LUCENTIO
Love wrought these miracles. Bianca's love
Made me exchange my state with Tranio,
While he did bear my countenance in the town,
And happily I have arrivèd at the last
Unto the wishèd haven of my bliss.
What Tranio did, myself enforced him to.
Then pardon him, sweet father, for my sake.

VINCENTIO I'll slit the villain's nose that would have sent me to the jail!

BAPTISTA But do you hear, sir, have you married my daughter without asking my goodwill?

138–39. **Go to:** i.e., don't worry

139. **will in:** i.e., **will** go **in**

140. **sound the depth:** explore deeply (literally, drop a plumb line and weight into water to determine its **depth**)

143. **My cake is dough:** proverbial for "I've failed"

144. **Out . . . but:** without **hope of** anything except

146. **ado:** fuss

156. **Better . . . late:** Petruchio combines two proverbs—"**Better once than never**" (i.e., "Better late than never") and "It is **never too late** to mend."

156 SD. See "Framing Dialogue," F, page 243, below.

5.2 Three couples attend the wedding banquet—Lucentio and Bianca, Petruchio and Katherine, and Hortensio and the Widow. Petruchio is repeatedly teased about being married to a shrew. In retaliation Petruchio wagers with Lucentio and Hortensio that if they all summon their wives to them, his Katherine will be the most obedient in responding. When Bianca and the Widow refuse to come at all and Katherine promptly appears, Petruchio wins, and then he sends Katherine to bring the other wives to their husbands. When they return, Petruchio tells Katherine to instruct the other wives in their wifely duty. Katherine delivers a long speech in praise of women's submission to their husbands. Petruchio kisses Katherine, and they go off to bed.

---

0 SD. **banquet:** dessert and wine (See lines 9–10, below.)

1. **At last, though long:** i.e., **at long last**

VINCENTIO Fear not, Baptista, we will content you. Go to. But I will in to be revenged for this villainy.

He exits.

BAPTISTA And I to sound the depth of this knavery.

He exits.

LUCENTIO Look not pale, Bianca. Thy father will not frown. *They exit.*

GREMIO

My cake is dough, but I'll in among the rest,
Out of hope of all but my share of the feast.

⌜*He exits.*⌝

KATHERINE Husband, let's follow to see the end of this ado.

PETRUCHIO First kiss me, Kate, and we will.

KATHERINE What, in the midst of the street?

PETRUCHIO What, art thou ashamed of me?

KATHERINE ⌜No,⌝ sir, God forbid, but ashamed to kiss.

PETRUCHIO

Why, then, let's home again. ⌜*To Grumio.*⌝ Come, sirrah, let's away.

KATHERINE

Nay, I will give thee a kiss. ⌜*She kisses him.*⌝
Now pray thee, love, stay.

PETRUCHIO

Is not this well? Come, my sweet Kate.
Better once than never, for never too late.

They exit.

⌜Scene 2⌝

Enter Baptista, Vincentio, Gremio, the ⌜*Merchant,*⌝ *Lucentio, and Bianca;* ⌜*Hortensio*⌝ *and* ⌜*the*⌝ *Widow,* ⌜*Petruchio and Katherine;*⌝ *Tranio, Biondello,* ⌜*and*⌝ *Grumio,* ⌜*with*⌝ *Servingmen bringing in a banquet.*

LUCENTIO

At last, though long, our jarring notes agree,

3. **'scapes:** i.e., escapes; **overblown:** i.e., past

9. **My banquet:** i.e., the pastries, fruit, and wine I am here serving

10. **great good cheer:** i.e., the wedding feast

13, 14. **affords:** provides from its own resources

15. **would:** wish

16. **fears:** is afraid of (The widow takes **fears** to mean "frightens.")

17. **afeard:** afraid

21. **Roundly:** bluntly

23. **Thus I conceive by him:** i.e., I come to this understanding through observing him (Petruchio plays on **conceive** as "become pregnant.")

And time it is when raging war is ⌜done⌝
To smile at 'scapes and perils overblown.
My fair Bianca, bid my father welcome,
While I with selfsame kindness welcome thine.
Brother Petruchio, sister Katherina,
And thou, Hortensio, with thy loving widow,
Feast with the best, and welcome to my house.
My banquet is to close our stomachs up
After our great good cheer. Pray you, sit down,
For now we sit to chat as well as eat. ⌜*They sit.*⌝

PETRUCHIO
Nothing but sit and sit, and eat and eat!

BAPTISTA
Padua affords this kindness, son Petruchio.

PETRUCHIO
Padua affords nothing but what is kind.

HORTENSIO
For both our sakes I would that word were true.

PETRUCHIO
Now, for my life, Hortensio fears his widow!

WIDOW
Then never trust me if I be afeard.

PETRUCHIO
You are very sensible, and yet you miss my sense:
I mean Hortensio is afeard of you.

WIDOW
He that is giddy thinks the world turns round.

PETRUCHIO
Roundly replied.

KATHERINE Mistress, how mean you that?

WIDOW Thus I conceive by him.

PETRUCHIO
Conceives by me? How likes Hortensio that?

HORTENSIO
My widow says, thus she conceives her tale.

30. **his:** i.e., his own (Petruchio's)

34. **mean . . . you:** (1) temperate compared to you; (2) nasty, where you are concerned

37. **marks:** i.e., coins (A "mark" was worth 13 shillings.) **put her down:** defeat her

38. **office:** duty, privilege (Hortensio plays with the words "put her down" in the sexual sense.)

39. **Ha' to:** i.e., here's to

41. **butt together:** knock heads

42. **body:** i.e., person

43. **horn:** symbol of a cuckold (See picture, below.)

47. **Have at you for:** i.e., I challenge you to

A cuckold. (4.1.25; 5.2.43)
From *Bagford Ballads* (printed in 1878).

PETRUCHIO
Very well mended. Kiss him for that, good widow.

KATHERINE
"He that is giddy thinks the world turns round"—
I pray you tell me what you meant by that.

WIDOW
Your husband being troubled with a shrew
Measures my husband's sorrow by his woe.
And now you know my meaning.

KATHERINE
A very mean meaning.

WIDOW Right, I mean you.

KATHERINE
And I am mean indeed, respecting you.

PETRUCHIO To her, Kate!

HORTENSIO To her, widow!

PETRUCHIO
A hundred marks, my Kate does put her down.

HORTENSIO That's my office.

PETRUCHIO
Spoke like an officer! Ha' to thee, lad.
⌜He⌝ drinks to Hortensio.

BAPTISTA
How likes Gremio these quick-witted folks?

GREMIO
Believe me, sir, they butt together well.

BIANCA
Head and butt! An hasty-witted body
Would say your head and butt were head and horn.

VINCENTIO
Ay, mistress bride, hath that awakened you?

BIANCA
Ay, but not frighted me. Therefore I'll sleep again.

PETRUCHIO
Nay, that you shall not. Since you have begun,
Have at you for a ⌜bitter⌝ jest or two.

48. **bird:** i.e., target; **shift my bush:** i.e., go elsewhere, leave

51. **prevented me:** stopped me in advance

53. **health:** toast

54. **slipped:** loosed

56. **something:** i.e., somewhat

58. **deer . . . bay:** The image is perhaps of the cornered animal defending itself against the attacking hounds (see picture, page 212); or, perhaps, Tranio is picturing Kate as a deer cornering the hunter.

60. **gird:** biting remark

62. **galled:** scratched, irritated

65. **in good sadness:** i.e., seriously

66. **veriest shrew:** i.e., **shrew** in the truest sense, **the** most complete **shrew**

67. **for assurance:** i.e., to put it to the test

BIANCA

Am I your bird? I mean to shift my bush,
And then pursue me as you draw your bow.—
You are welcome all.

Bianca, ⌜Katherine, and the Widow⌝ exit.

PETRUCHIO

She hath prevented me. Here, Signior Tranio,
This bird you aimed at, though you hit her not.—
Therefore a health to all that shot and missed.

TRANIO

O, sir, Lucentio slipped me like his greyhound,
Which runs himself and catches for his master.

PETRUCHIO

A good swift simile, but something currish.

TRANIO

'Tis well, sir, that you hunted for yourself.
'Tis thought your deer does hold you at a bay.

BAPTISTA

O, O, Petruchio! Tranio hits you now.

LUCENTIO

I thank thee for that gird, good Tranio.

HORTENSIO

Confess, confess! Hath he not hit you here?

PETRUCHIO

He has a little galled me, I confess.
And as the jest did glance away from me,
'Tis ten to one it maimed you two outright.

BAPTISTA

Now, in good sadness, son Petruchio,
I think thou hast the veriest shrew of all.

PETRUCHIO

Well, I say no. And therefore, ⌜for⌝ assurance,
Let's each one send unto his wife,
And he whose wife is most obedient
To come at first when he doth send for her
Shall win the wager which we will propose.

75. **of:** i.e., on

84. **be your half:** assume **half** your bet

96. **forthwith:** immediately

98. **must needs: must** necessarily, **must** of necessity

A deer at bay. (5.2.58)
From George Turberville, *The noble art of . . . hunting . . .* (1611).

HORTENSIO
Content, what's the wager?
LUCENTIO Twenty crowns.
PETRUCHIO Twenty crowns?
I'll venture so much of my hawk or hound,
But twenty times so much upon my wife.
LUCENTIO
A hundred, then.
HORTENSIO Content.
PETRUCHIO A match! 'Tis done.
HORTENSIO Who shall begin?
LUCENTIO That will I.
Go, Biondello, bid your mistress come to me.
BIONDELLO I go. *He exits.*
BAPTISTA
Son, I'll be your half Bianca comes.
LUCENTIO
I'll have no halves. I'll bear it all myself.

Enter Biondello.

How now, what news?
BIONDELLO Sir, my mistress sends you word
That she is busy, and she cannot come.
PETRUCHIO
How? "She's busy, and she cannot come"?
Is that an answer?
GREMIO Ay, and a kind one, too.
Pray God, sir, your wife send you not a worse.
PETRUCHIO I hope better.
HORTENSIO
Sirrah Biondello, go and entreat my wife
To come to me forthwith. *Biondello exits.*
PETRUCHIO O ho, entreat her!
Nay, then, she must needs come.

111. **there an end:** proverbial for "**there** is no more to say"

112. **holidam:** a confusion of "holidom," meaning a relic or the state of holiness, with "holidame," or the Virgin Mary

115. **conferring:** conversing, talking

116. **deny:** i.e., refuse

117. **Swinge me them:** beat them

118. **straight:** immediately

119. **wonder:** miracle

120. **bodes:** foretells, presages

HORTENSIO I am afraid, sir,
Do what you can, yours will not be entreated.

Enter Biondello.

Now, where's my wife?

BIONDELLO
She says you have some goodly jest in hand.
She will not come. She bids you come to her.

PETRUCHIO Worse and worse. She will not come!
O vile, intolerable, not to be endured!—
Sirrah Grumio, go to your mistress,
Say I command her come to me. ⌜*Grumio*⌝ *exits.*

HORTENSIO
I know her answer.

PETRUCHIO What?

HORTENSIO She will not.

PETRUCHIO
The fouler fortune mine, and there an end.

Enter Katherine.

BAPTISTA
Now by my holidam, here comes Katherina!

KATHERINE
What is your will, sir, that you send for me?

PETRUCHIO
Where is your sister, and Hortensio's wife?

KATHERINE
They sit conferring by the parlor fire.

PETRUCHIO
Go fetch them hither. If they deny to come,
Swinge me them soundly forth unto their husbands.
Away, I say, and bring them hither straight.
⌜*Katherine exits.*⌝

LUCENTIO
Here is a wonder, if you talk of a wonder.

HORTENSIO
And so it is. I wonder what it bodes.

122. **awful rule: rule** by commanding respect or awe; **right:** proper

123. **what not:** i.e., anything and everything

124. **fair befall thee:** i.e., good fortune come to you

128. **as:** i.e., **as** though

132. **froward:** perverse

136. **bauble:** showy trifle

137. **cause:** reason

138. **pass:** state of affairs

139. **duty:** obedience

143. **laying:** betting

Hitting "the white." (5.2.203)

From Gilles Corrozet, *Hecatongraphie* . . . (1543).

PETRUCHIO
Marry, peace it bodes, and love, and quiet life,
An awful rule, and right supremacy,
And, to be short, what not that's sweet and happy.

BAPTISTA
Now fair befall thee, good Petruchio!
The wager thou hast won, and I will add
Unto their losses twenty thousand crowns,
Another dowry to another daughter,
For she is changed as she had never been.

PETRUCHIO
Nay, I will win my wager better yet,
And show more sign of her obedience,
Her new-built virtue and obedience.

Enter Katherine, Bianca, and Widow.

See where she comes, and brings your froward wives
As prisoners to her womanly persuasion.—
Katherine, that cap of yours becomes you not.
Off with that bauble, throw it underfoot.
⌜*She obeys.*⌝

WIDOW
Lord, let me never have a cause to sigh
Till I be brought to such a silly pass.

BIANCA
Fie, what a foolish duty call you this?

LUCENTIO
I would your duty were as foolish too.
The wisdom of your duty, fair Bianca,
Hath cost me ⌜a⌝ hundred crowns since suppertime.

BIANCA
The more fool you for laying on my duty.

PETRUCHIO
Katherine, I charge thee tell these headstrong women
What duty they do owe their lords and husbands.

152. **Fie, fie . . . :** For the parallel (but interestingly different) speech given by Kate in *A Shrew*, see Longer Notes, page 225, below.

155. **meads:** meadows

156. **Confounds thy fame:** i.e., spoils your reputation

157. **meet:** appropriate

158. **moved:** angry; **fountain:** spring of water collecting in a natural basin

159. **ill-seeming:** of evil appearance or aspect; **thick:** viscid

162–70. **Thy husband . . . debt:** See Paul's Letter to the Ephesians 5.22–28 ("Wives, submit yourselves unto your husbands, . . . for the husband is the head of the wife, even as Christ is the head of the Church . . ."). In the Geneva Bible, the marginal gloss adds "So the husband ought to nourish, govern, and defend his wife from perils." **To watch:** i.e., to keep watch throughout **at thy hands:** i.e., from your **hands**

171–76. **Such duty . . . lord:** See 1 Peter 2.13–3.7: "Submit yourselves to every ordinance of man for the Lord's sake: whether it be to the king . . . or unto governors. . . . Likewise, ye wives, be in subjection to your own husbands. . . ."

177. **simple:** foolish

WIDOW

Come, come, ⌜you're⌝ mocking. We will have no telling.

PETRUCHIO

Come on, I say, and first begin with her.

WIDOW She shall not.

PETRUCHIO

I say she shall.—And first begin with her.

KATHERINE

Fie, fie! Unknit that threat'ning unkind brow,
And dart not scornful glances from those eyes
To wound thy lord, thy king, thy governor.
It blots thy beauty as frosts do bite the meads,
Confounds thy fame as whirlwinds shake fair buds,
And in no sense is meet or amiable.
A woman moved is like a fountain troubled,
Muddy, ill-seeming, thick, bereft of beauty,
And while it is so, none so dry or thirsty
Will deign to sip or touch one drop of it.
Thy husband is thy lord, thy life, thy keeper,
Thy head, thy sovereign, one that cares for thee,
And for thy maintenance commits his body
To painful labor both by sea and land,
To watch the night in storms, the day in cold,
Whilst thou liest warm at home, secure and safe,
And craves no other tribute at thy hands
But love, fair looks, and true obedience—
Too little payment for so great a debt.
Such duty as the subject owes the prince,
Even such a woman oweth to her husband;
And when she is froward, peevish, sullen, sour,
And not obedient to his honest will,
What is she but a foul contending rebel
And graceless traitor to her loving lord?
I am ashamed that women are so simple
To offer war where they should kneel for peace,

179. **sway:** power
182. **Unapt:** unsuited
183. **conditions:** qualities
185. **unable:** helpless
186. **big:** self-important
187. **heart:** courage; **haply:** perhaps
188. **bandy:** exchange (literally, hit back and forth)
190. **as weak:** i.e., **as weak** as **straws; past compare:** beyond comparison
191. **That seeming . . . least are:** perhaps, "in that we pretend **to be most** (i.e., strong) when **we are** actually weak"
192. **vail your stomachs:** i.e., subdue your pride; **no boot:** i.e., bootless, futile
195. **may it:** i.e., if **it may**
197. **ha 't:** have it (i.e., you win)
198. **a good hearing:** i.e., good to hear; **toward:** compliant, cooperative
201. **We three:** i.e., Petruchio, Hortensio, Lucentio; **sped:** done for
203. **the white:** the bull's eye (i.e., won the woman prized by all, Bianca, whose name in Italian means "white") See picture, page 216.
204. **God:** i.e., I pray **God** to
206. **shrow:** an archaic spelling of *shrew*
206 SD. For conclusion of "Framing Dialogue" in *A Shrew*, see G, page 244, below.

Or seek for rule, supremacy, and sway
When they are bound to serve, love, and obey.
Why are our bodies soft and weak and smooth,
Unapt to toil and trouble in the world,
But that our soft conditions and our hearts
Should well agree with our external parts?
Come, come, you froward and unable worms!
My mind hath been as big as one of yours,
My heart as great, my reason haply more,
To bandy word for word and frown for frown;
But now I see our lances are but straws,
Our strength as weak, our weakness past compare,
That seeming to be most which we indeed least are.
Then vail your stomachs, for it is no boot,
And place your hands below your husband's foot;
In token of which duty, if he please,
My hand is ready, may it do him ease.

PETRUCHIO
Why, there's a wench! Come on, and kiss me, Kate.
⌜*They kiss.*⌝

LUCENTIO
Well, go thy ways, old lad, for thou shalt ha 't.

VINCENTIO
'Tis a good hearing when children are toward.

LUCENTIO
But a harsh hearing when women are froward.

PETRUCHIO Come, Kate, we'll to bed.
We three are married, but you two are sped.
⌜*To Lucentio.*⌝ 'Twas I won the wager, though you hit the white,
And being a winner, God give you good night.
Petruchio ⌜*and Katherine*⌝ *exit.*

HORTENSIO
Now, go thy ways, thou hast tamed a curst shrow.

LUCENTIO
'Tis a wonder, by your leave, she will be tamed so.
⌜*They exit.*⌝

Longer Notes

Ind.1.14. **boy:** Scholars point out that this is the only instance in Shakespeare's plays where *boy*, used as a term of address, is directed to a female character. Ann Thompson, editor of the NCS *Taming of the Shrew*, noting that in the anonymous *Taming of a Shrew* (1594), Sly is thrown out of the tavern by a Tapster, not a Hostess, suggests that *boy* may here "indicate the original casting" in *The Shrew*. (The Hostess would, of course, have been personated on the stage by a male, but not necessarily by a boy.) See Appendix, "Framing Dialogue in *The Taming of a Shrew* (1594)," pages 233ff.

1.1.213. **colored hat and cloak:** Tranio is presumably wearing blue servants' garb, which is therefore "colored" in the most obvious sense of this word. This creates a puzzle about Lucentio's reference to his **hat and cloak** as **colored.** Even if Lucentio is somehow referring to the sumptuary laws that governed the colors permitted to each social class (as some editors have suggested), that does not explain why Lucentio refers to his own garb as "colored." The answer here may be found in the *Oxford English Dictionary*'s attribution to Samuel Johnson of a definition of *colored* as "diversified with a variety of hues." On this definition, Lucentio might be drawing a distinction between Tranio's blue livery and his own variegated outfit, an elegant cloak and hat in "a variety of hues."

1.2.288 SD. **They exit:** Sly's first comment on the play in *A Shrew* (See C in "Framing Dialogue," page 241) follows soon after the exit of the Grumio character, Sander, whom Sly sees as the play's Fool (i.e., the designated comic figure who plays with language and who has license to speak impertinently to his master). This belief on Sly's part is made clear in his later comment when, on seeing Sander enter, Sly says "Look, Sim, the Fool is come again now." (See D in "Framing Dialogue, page 242.) In terms of several plot events in the two plays (including Ferando-Petruchio's and Kate's first meeting and the marriage agreement between Kate's father and Ferando-Petruchio), the bit of framing dialogue at C, page 241, would be placed after 2.1 in *The Shrew.* However, the connection between Sly's lines here and the exit of Sander-Grumio suggests to us that were it in *The Shrew,* it would be placed at the end of Act 1, scene 2 (just after 1.2.288 SD, *They exit*), where its concluding lines—"My lord, here comes the players again." SLY "O, brave! Here's two fine gentlewomen"—lead naturally into *The Shrew*'s Act 2, scene 1, *"Enter Katherine and Bianca."*

2.1.363. **dower:** This word had three possible meanings in Shakespeare's day. It could occasionally mean money that the husband brings to the bride's family. More often, it meant the same thing as *dowry,* the money or goods that the bride brings to the husband. When Shakespeare uses the word *dower,* he almost always uses it in this popular sense—i.e., as synonymous with *dowry* (as in, for example, King Lear's words to Cordelia: "Thy truth, then, be thy dower"—and to Burgundy: "What in the least / Will you require in present dower with her?" [1.1.120, 217–18]). In *Taming of the Shrew,* however, he uses it throughout with its third meaning: the portion of the deceased husband's estate legally remaining in the possession of his widow. (In only one other play, *Henry VI, Part 3,* does he use *dower* in this sense, when he has Lady Grey refer to her dead husband's lands as her "dower" [3.2.72].) In the Petruchio-Kate plot, the word *dower* does not occur. Instead, Baptista promises a large *dowry* with Katherine, against which Petruchio promises "I'll assure her of / Her widowhood [i.e., dower or jointure] . . . / In all my lands and leases whatsoever" (2.1.130–32). In the plot involving Bianca and her suitors, in contrast, no dowry is mentioned; instead, the suitors, and the supposed father of one of the suitors, must "assure" Bianca of a large *dower*—property to be left to her at her husband's death (2.1.363; 2.1.411; 4.4.46).

4.1.195. **kites:** In Shakespeare's other plays, a kite is a vicious predatory bird. When Lear's daughter Goneril turns on him, for example, and demands he dismiss his attendants, he calls her "detested kite" (1.4.274); when Antony is furious with Cleopatra for letting Caesar's messenger kiss her hand, he calls her "Ah, you kite!" (3.13.111). In *Taming,* however, the word appears to name one among several kinds of hawks that are trained in falconry.

5.2.152. **Fie, fie:** Kate's speech to the other women in *A Shrew* is based on the theological premise that God created woman as inferior to man and that woman, through Eve, brought sin into the world:

> Then you that live thus by your pampered wills,
> Now list to me and mark what I shall say.
> The eternal power that with his only breath
> Shall cause this end and this beginning frame,
> Not in time, nor before time, but with time,
>   confused,
> For all the course of years, of ages, months,
> Of seasons temperate, of days and hours,
> Are tuned and stopped, by measure of his hand.
> The first world was a form without a form,

A heap confused, a mixture all deformed,
A gulf of gulfs, a body bodiless,
Where all the elements were orderless,
Before the great commander of the world,
The King of Kings, the glorious God of heaven,
Who in six days did frame his heavenly work,
And made all things to stand in perfect course.
Then to his image he did make a man,
Old Adam, and from his side asleep
A rib was taken, of which the Lord did make
The woe of man so termed by Adam then,
Woman, for that by her came sin to us,
And for her sin was Adam doomed to die.
As Sara to her husband, so should we
Obey them, love them, keep and nourish them,
If they by any means do want our helps,
Laying our hands under their feet to tread,
If that by that we might procure their ease,
And for a precedent I'll first begin,
And lay my hand under my husband's feet.

She lays her hand under her husband's feet.

Textual Notes

The reading of the present text appears to the left of the square bracket. The earliest sources of readings not in F, the First Folio text (upon which this edition is based), are indicated as follows: **Q** is *The Taming of a Shrew* 1594; **F2** is the Second Folio of 1632; **F3** is the Third Folio of 1663–64; **F4** is the Fourth Folio of 1685. **Ed.** is an earlier editor of Shakespeare, beginning with Rowe in 1709. No sources are given for emendations of punctuation or for corrections of obvious typographical errors, like turned letters that produce no known word. **SD** means stage direction; **SP** means speech prefix; **uncorr.** means the first or uncorrected state of the First Folio; **corr.** means the second or corrected state of the First Folio; ~ stands in place of a word already quoted before the square bracket; ^ indicates the omission of a punctuation mark.

Ind.1 Ind.1] Ed.; *Actus primus. Scœna Prima.* F

0. SD *Enter Begger and Hostes, Christophero Sly.* F

1. SP SLY] Ed.; *Begger* F

3 *and hereafter.* SP SLY] Ed.; *Beg.* F

9. Saint] Ed.; S. F

17. Breathe] Ed.; Brach F

22, 30. SP FIRST HUNTSMAN] Ed.; *Hunts.* F

44. SP THIRD HUNTSMAN] This ed.; *1. Hun.* F

72. SP THIRD HUNTSMAN] This ed.; *1. Hunts.* F

83. SD *1 line earlier in* F

87. SP FIRST PLAYER] Ed.; *2. Player.* F

93. SP SECOND PLAYER] Ed.; *Sincklo. (the name of an actor in Shakespeare's company)* F

105. SP FIRST PLAYER] Ed.; *Plai.* F

Ind.2 18. Sly's] Ed.; Sies F
26 *and hereafter.* SP SERVINGMAN] Ed.; *Man.* (*man., M.*) F
94. Greete] Ed.; Greece F
100. SD *1 line earlier in* F
111. Alice] *Alce* F
139–40. I will. Let them play it. Is not] I will let them play, it is not F
144. a] a a F

1.1 0. SD *Tranio*] *Triano* F
13. Vincentio] Ed.; *Vincentio's* F
14. brought] brough F
17–18. study∧ / Virtue] Ed.; ~, / ~ F
25. *Mi perdonato*] Ed.; *Me Pardonato* F
33. Ovid∧] ~; F
45. SD *2 lines later in* F
45. SD *suitors*] This ed.; *sister* F; *suitor* F2
92. resolved] resould F
147. SD *Gremio . . . onstage.*] *Exeunt ambo. Manet Tranio and Lucentio* F
164. *captum*] F2; *captam* F
213. colored] Conlord F
242. Ay, sir] Ed.; I sir F
254. your] F2; you F
258. SD *speak*] Ed.; *speakes* F

1.2 26. *Con tutto il cuore ben trovato*] Ed.; *Contutti le core bene trobatto* F
27. *ben*] Ed.; *bene* F
27. *molto*] Ed.; *multo* F
28. *honorato*] Ed.; *honorata* F
28. *signor*] Ed.; *signior* F
47. 'twixt] twixr F
53. grows. But . . . few,] ~∧ ~ . . . ~. F
74. me, were] ~. ~ F
74. she as] Ed.; she is as F
122. me and other] Ed.; me. Other F

140. SD 2 *lines earlier in* F
140. SD *disguised*] *disgused* F
174. me] Ed.; one F
186. dowry] F (corr.); dowric F (uncorr.)
192. Antonio's] *Butonios* F
221. SD *disguised as Lucentio*] Ed.; *braue* F
229. sir] F (corr.); fir F (ucorr.)
237. streets] streers F
260. The] F (corr.); Tne F (uncorr.)
269. first] F (corr.); sirst F (uncorr.)
273. feat] Ed.; seeke F
288. *ben*] F2; *Been* F

2.1 8. thee] F2; *omit* F
21. SD *1 line earlier in* F
79–80. wooing. Neighbor, this] Ed.; wooing neighbors: this F
83. you] Ed.; *omit* F
95. a suitor] as utor F
109. Pisa. By] Ed.; ~∧ ~ F
176. SD *1 line earlier in* F
262. askance] Ed.; a sconce F
270. than] rhen F
293. SD *3 lines earlier in* F
293. SD *Tranio*] *Trayno* F
320. goodnight] godnight F
349. in] Ed.; me F
422. SD *1 line earlier in* F

3.1 30. *hic*] *hie* F
30, 35, 45. *Sigeia*] F2; *sigeria* F
46. *steterat*] F2; *staterat* F
51. How] Ed.; *Luc.* How F
54. SP BIANCA In] Ed.; In F
55. SP LUCENTIO] Ed.; *Bian.* F
57. SP BIANCA] Ed.; *Hort.* F
77. *A re*] Q; *Are* F
78. *B mi*] Ed.; *Beeme* F

79. *C fa ut*] Q; *C favt* F
84. change] F2; charge F
84. odd] Ed.; old F
84. SD *Servant*] Ed.; *Messenger* F
85. SP SERVANT] Ed.; *Nicke.* F

3.2
14. man,] ~; F
29. thy] F2; *omit* F
30. old] Ed.; *omit* F
33. hear] Q; heard F
54. swayed] Ed.; Waid F
129. SD *Exit.* F
130. to] Ed.; *omit* F
132. I] F2; *omit* F
155. grumbling] grumlling F
184. SD *1 line later in* F
202. SP GREMIO] F2; *Gra.* F

4.1
24. SP CURTIS] Q; *Gru.* F
45. their] F3; the F
98. SD *1 line earlier in* F
110. SP GRUMIO] F3; *Gre.* F
180. SD *Enter Curtis*] *Enter Curtis a Seruant.* F, *1 line later*

4.2
4. SP HORTENSIO] F2; *Luc.* F
6. SP LUCENTIO] F2; *Hor.* F
7. you? First . . . that.] Ed.; ~∧ ~, . . . ~? F
8. SP LUCENTIO] F2; *Hor.* F
8. profess,] ~∧ F
10. prove] ptoue F
13. none] Ed.; me F
31. her] F3; them F
35. forsworn!] ~∧ F
68. countenance] eountenance F
72. Minola∧] ~. F
74. Take] F2; *Par.* Take F
74. in] Ed.; me F
74. SD *and hereafter. Merchant*] Ed.; *Pedant* F (*Ped.* in SPs)

4.3 4.3. Ed.; *Actus Quartus, Scena Prima.* F
65. SD *1 line earlier in* F
67. SP HABERDASHER] Ed.; *Fel.* F
86. a] Q; *omit* F
93. a] Q; *omit* F
115. yard,] ~ ∧ F
187. account'st] Ed.; accountedst F
195. And] Aud F

4.4 0. SD *booted, and*] F *at line 19* SD *repeats the Pedant-Merchant's entrance: "Enter . . . Pedant booted and bare headed."*
1. Sir] Ed.; Sirs F
4. Genoa,] ~. F
5. Where] Ed.; *Tra.* Where F
8. SD *1 line earlier in* F
18. SD *1 line later in* F
19. SD *See note to* 4.4.0 SD.
67. SD *Exit.* F *1 line later*
69. SD *Enter Peter.* F
73. SD *Enter Lucentio.*] Ed.; *Enter Lucentio and Biondello.* F
92. except] F2; expect F
97. for] fot F

4.5 21. is] Q; in F
42. where] F2; whether F
45. Allots] Q; A lots F
83. be] F2; *omit* F

5.1 0. SD *Bianca*] *Bianea* F
4. SD *Exit.* F
6. master's] Ed.; mistris F
14. SD *He knocks.*] Ed.; *Knock.* F
46. brought] brough F
54. master's] F2; Mistris F
67. doublet] doubtlet F
85. Tranio] Tronio F
110. SD *2 lines earlier in* F
110. SD *Bianca*] *Biancu* F

125. SP BAPTISTA] *Bvp.* F
143. dough, but] doug, hbut F
150. No] Mo F
156. never,] ueuer, F

5.2

5.2. Ed.; *Actus Quintus* F
0. SD *Enter Baptista, Vincentio, Gremio, the Pedant, Lucentio, and Bianca. Tranio, Biondello Grumio, and Widdow: The Seruingmen with Tranio bringing in a Banquet.* F
2. done] Ed.; come F
39. thee] F (the)
42. butt!] ~ ∧ F
47. bitter] Ed.; better F
54. SP TRANIO] *Tri.* F
64. two] F (too)
67. for] F2; sir F
100. SD *1/2 line earlier in* F
142. a] Ed.; fiue F
147. you're] F3; your F
152. threat'ning] thretaning F
164. maintenance∧] ~. F
200. we'll] weee'le F

Appendix: Framing Dialogue in *The Taming of a Shrew* (1594)

The relationship between *A Shrew* and *The Shrew* has puzzled scholars and others from the very beginning. The two plays were both performed before 1594. For many years editors believed that *A Shrew* was written first, by an anonymous author or group of authors, and then expanded by Shakespeare into *The Shrew*. That opinion is no longer held, and it is thought today that both *A Shrew* and *The Shrew* are versions of Shakespeare's original play. In this scenario, the "taming" plot of *A Shrew* is, to a limited extent, a reconstruction from memory of Shakespeare's original play, containing a few passages that show verbal resemblances to *The Shrew*; the "Bianca" subplot, in contrast, has been completely rewritten, incorporating passages from plays by Christopher Marlowe. *A Shrew* contains material that has disappeared from the version of the play printed in the First Folio in 1623 as *The Shrew*: primarily, much of Sly's commentary on the action of the play-within-the-play, the conclusion of the Christopher Sly frame, and one scene that covers the time of the first off-stage wedding. Those who argue that *The Shrew* as it appears in the Folio is defective point not only to these missing pieces but also to a host of loose ends and confusions in the play that are barely noticed in performance but are obvious to any editor who has tried to make sense of this text. To many editors, these omissions indicate deliberate changes (probably made by Shakespeare as he revised the play). Given the fact, though, that other Folio plays have parts missing unintentionally (for example, the opening Prologue to *Romeo and Juliet* did not make it into the 1623 Folio), we would argue that it is just as likely that the manuscript used to print Folio *The Shrew* was itself defective. We are aware that this is all guesswork, but it is guesswork founded on persuasive supporting evidence and arguments. Whatever the connection between the two plays, it is helpful to be aware of the contents of *A Shrew* as one studies or performs *The Shrew.*

Like Shakespeare's *The Taming of the Shrew* (1623), *A Shrew* opens with two scenes that feature Christopher Sly, along with a nobleman and the nobleman's servants. The passages from *A Shrew* printed below are taken from the 1594 quarto, with the spelling and punctuation modernized. Added stage directions are in half-square brackets.

A. [Compare *The Shrew,* Induction, scene 1.]

Enter a Tapster, beating out of his doors Sly, drunken.

TAPSTER
You whoreson drunken slave, you had best be gone,
And empty your drunken paunch somewhere else,
For in this house thou shalt not rest tonight.
Tapster exits.

SLY Tilly vally, by crisee, Tapster, I'll feeze you anon. Fill 's the t'other pot and all's paid for, look you, I do drink it of mine own instigation. *Omne bene.* Here I'll lie awhile. Why, Tapster, I say, fill 's a fresh cushion here. Heigh ho, here's good warm lying.
He falls asleep.

Enter a Nobleman and his men from hunting.

LORD
Now that the gloomy shadow of the night,
Longing to view Orion's drizzling looks,

Leaps from th' Antarctic world unto the sky
And dims the welkin with her pitchy breath,
And darksome night o'ershades the crystal heavens,
Here break we off our hunting for tonight.
Couple up the hounds and let us hie us home,
And bid the huntsman see them meated well,
For they have all deserved it well today.
But soft, what sleepy fellow is this lies here?
Or is he dead? See one what he doth lack.

SERVINGMAN

My lord, 'tis nothing but a drunken sleep.
His head is too heavy for his body,
And he hath drunk so much that he can go no further.

LORD

Fie, how the slavish villain stinks of drink!—
Ho, sirrah, arise. What, so sound asleep?—
Go take him up and bear him to my house,
And bear him easily for fear he wake,
And in my fairest chamber make a fire,
And set a sumptuous banquet on the board,
And put my richest garments on his back.
Then set him at the table in a chair.
When that is done, against he shall awake,
Let heavenly music play about him still.
Go two of you away and bear him hence,
And then I'll tell you what I have devised.
But see in any case you wake him not.

Exit two with Sly.

Now take my cloak and give me one of yours.

⌜*The lord and a servant take each other's cloaks. The lord puts on the servant's cloak.*⌝

All fellows now, and see you take me so,
For we will wait upon this drunken man
To see his countenance when he doth awake
And find himself clothed in such attire,
With heavenly music sounding in his ears,

And such a banquet set before his eyes,
The fellow sure will think he is in heaven.
But we will be about him when he wakes,
And see you call him "lord" at every word,—
And offer thou him his horse to ride abroad,—
And thou his hawks and hounds to hunt the deer,—
And I will ask what suits he means to wear.
And whatsoe'er he saith, see you do not laugh,
But still persuade him that he is a lord.

Enter one ⌜a Messenger.⌝

MESSENGER
An it please your Honor, your players be come
And do attend your Honor's pleasure here.

LORD
The fittest time they could have chosen out.
Bid one or two of them come hither straight.
⌜Messenger exits.⌝
Now will I fit myself accordingly,
For they shall play to him when he awakes.

Enter two of the Players ⌜Sander and Tom⌝ with packs at their backs, and a Boy.

Now, sirs, what store of plays have you?

SANDER Marry, my lord, you may have a tragical or a commodity, or what you will.

THE OTHER A comedy, thou shouldst say. Zounds, thou 'lt shame us all.

LORD And what's the name of your comedy?

SANDER Marry, my lord, 'tis called "The Taming of a Shrew." 'Tis a good lesson for us, my lord, for us that are married men.

LORD
"The Taming of a Shrew." That's excellent sure.
Go see that you make you ready straight,
For you must play before a lord tonight.

Say you are his men and I your fellow.
He's something foolish, but whatsoe'er he says,
See that you be not dashed out of countenance.
⌜*To Boy.*⌝ And, sirrah, go you make you ready straight,
And dress yourself like some lovely lady,
And when I call, see that you come to me,
For I will say to him thou art his wife.
Dally with him and hug him in thine arms,
And if he desire to go to bed with thee,
Then feign some 'scuse and say thou wilt anon.
Be gone, I say, and see thou doest it well.

BOY
Fear not, my lord, I'll dandle him well enough,
And make him think I love him mightily.

Boy exits.

LORD, ⌜*to Sander and Tom*⌝
Now, sirs, go you and make you ready too,
For you must play as soon as he doth wake.

SANDER O, brave, sirrah Tom, we must play before a foolish lord! Come, let's go make us ready. Go get a dishclout to make clean your shoes, and I'll speak for the properties.—My lord, we must have a shoulder of mutton for a property, and a little vinegar to make our devil roar.

LORD Very well. ⌜*To a Servingman.*⌝ Sirrah, see that they want nothing.

They all exit.

B. [Compare *The Shrew,* Induction, scene 2.]

Enter two with a table and a banquet on it, and two other, with Sly asleep in a chair, richly appareled, and the music playing.

ONE ⌜SERVINGMAN⌝ So, sirrah, now go call my lord and tell him that all things is ready as he willed it.

ANOTHER ⌜SERVINGMAN⌝ Set thou some wine upon the board, and then I'll go fetch my lord presently.

He exits.

Enter the lord and his men.

LORD How now, what, is all things ready?

ONE ⌜SERVINGMAN⌝ Ay, my lord.

LORD
Then sound the music, and I'll wake him straight,
And see you do as erst I gave in charge.
⌜*To Sly.*⌝ My lord, my lord.—He sleeps soundly.—My lord!

SLY Tapster, gi 's a little small ale. Heigh, ho!

LORD, ⌜*as Sim*⌝
Here's wine, my lord, the purest of the grape.

SLY For which lord?

LORD, ⌜*as Sim*⌝ For your Honor, my lord.

SLY Who, I? Am I a lord?
Jesus, what fine apparel have I got!

LORD, ⌜*as Sim*⌝
More richer far your Honor hath to wear,
And if it please you I will fetch them straight.

WILLIAM ⌜A SERVINGMAN⌝
And if your Honor please to ride abroad,
I'll fetch you lusty steeds more swift of pace
Than wingèd Pegasus in all his pride,
That ran so swiftly over the Persian plains.

TOM ⌜A SERVINGMAN⌝
And if your Honor please to hunt the deer,
Your hounds stands ready coupled at the door,
Who in running will o'ertake the roe
And make the long-breathed tiger broken-winded.

SLY
By the mass, I think I am a lord indeed!
⌜*To the lord.*⌝ What's thy name?

LORD, ⌜*as Sim*⌝ Simon, an it please your Honor.

SLY "Simon."
That's as much to say "Si mi on" or Simon.
Put forth thy hand and fill the pot.
Give me thy hand, Sim. Am I a lord indeed?

LORD, ⌜*as Sim*⌝
Ay, my gracious lord, and your lovely lady
Long time hath mournèd for your absence here.
And now with joy behold where she doth come
To gratulate your Honor's safe return.

Enter the Boy in woman's attire.

SLY Sim, is this she?

LORD, ⌜*as Sim*⌝ Ay, my lord.

SLY
Mass, 'tis a pretty wench. What's her name?

BOY, ⌜*as Wife*⌝
O, that my lovely lord would once vouchsafe
To look on me, and leave these frantic fits,
Or were I now but half so eloquent
To paint in words what I'll perform in deeds,
I know your Honor then would pity me.

SLY
Hark you, mistress, will you eat a piece of bread?
Come, sit down on my knee.—Sim, drink to her, Sim,
For she and I will go to bed anon.

LORD, ⌜*as Sim*⌝
May it please you, your Honor's players be come
To offer your Honor a play.

SLY
A play, Sim? O, brave! Be they my players?

LORD, ⌜*as Sim*⌝ Ay, my lord.

SLY Is there not a Fool in the play?

LORD, ⌜*as Sim*⌝ Yes, my lord.

SLY When will they play, Sim?

LORD, ⌜*as Sim*⌝
Even when it please your Honor. They be ready.

BOY, ⌜*as Wife*⌝

My lord, I'll go bid them begin their play.

SLY Do, but look that you come again.

BOY, ⌜*as Wife*⌝

I warrant you, my lord, I will not leave you thus.

Boy exits.

SLY

Come, Sim, where be the players? Sim, stand by
Me and we'll flout the players out of their coats.

LORD, ⌜*as Sim*⌝

I'll call them, my lord.—Ho, where are you there?

Sound trumpets.

SYNOPSIS 1. [Compare *The Shrew,* 1.1, 1.2, 2.1.]

Enter two young Gentlemen ⌜ *Polidor and Aurelius*⌝, *and a man* ⌜*Valeria*⌝ *and a Boy.*

In these scenes, Aurelius and his manservant Valeria are welcomed to Athens by Polidor, who is in love with Alfonso's third daughter. Aurelius sees Alfonso's second daughter, Phylena, and immediately falls in love with her. He learns from Polidor that the father will not allow the two younger daughters to be wooed or married until the oldest, Kate, finds a husband. Polidor sends for Ferando, a man whom he thinks would be a good match for Kate. Aurelius, in the meantime, arranges to exchange garments and positions in life with his servant Valeria in order to see Phylena. When Ferando and his servant Sander enter, the men learn that Alfonso has already paid Ferando six thousand crowns to win Kate's love and persuade her to marry. After a brief scolding match between Kate and Ferando, Alfonso is told by Ferando that he has won Kate's love, and Alfonso sets the following Sunday for their wedding day. Sander plays the Fool with Ferando and then with Polidor's boy. Ferando sets off for his country home, while Aurelius, disguised as Valeria, goes to Alfonso's house as a musician.

C. [See *The Shrew,* 1.2.288 SD
and longer note to 1.2.288 SD.]

Then Sly speaks.

SLY Sim, when will the Fool come again?
LORD, ⌜*as Sim*⌝ He'll come again, my lord, anon.
SLY Gi 's some more drink here. Zounds, where's the tapster? Here, Sim, eat some of these things.
LORD, ⌜*as Sim*⌝ So I do, my lord.
SLY Here, Sim, I drink to thee.
LORD, ⌜*as Sim*⌝ My lord, here comes the players again.
SLY O, brave! Here's two fine gentlewomen.

SYNOPSIS 2. [Compare *The Shrew,* 3.1–4.4.]

Valeria attempts to instruct Kate in playing the lute; then Alfonso's younger daughters are wooed by their suitors. The wedding day arrives, and Ferando enters "basely attired, and a red cap on his head." Alfonso, Kate, and others cannot believe that he plans to be married in such clothing, but he says "take me thus or not at all," and they all leave for the church. A comic scene between "Polidor's boy and Sander" covers the time the wedding is taking place. Ferando enters with others after the wedding and insists, over Kate's and Alfonso's protests, that he and Kate will not stay for the wedding dinner but will go immediately to his home. After Ferando, Kate, and Sander exit, Alfonso is assured that Aurelius's wealthy father will soon appear to back his son's marriage proposal. The scene then shifts to Ferando's home, where Ferando sends back the food and tells the audience about his plan to tame Kate: "Nor sleep nor meat shall she enjoy tonight / I'll mew her up as men do mew their hawks, / And make her gently come unto the lure." Back at Alfonso's home, Aurelius and Valeria have found a merchant to impersonate Aurelius's wealthy father. At Ferando's, Sander taunts Kate with talk of food. Aurelius brings his pretend father to meet Alfonso and to promise to give Aurelius lands and property, which Alfonso matches with an increased dowry. A haberdasher brings a cap to Kate, but Ferando sends away the man and the cap; a tailor arrives with a gown, but, after being denigrated by Ferando, it is sent away; Ferando tells Kate they will go to her father's, but only when Kate allows Ferando to declare the time of day to be whatever he chooses. Alfonso's two younger daughters and their lovers declare their love in high-flown language. They exit for their weddings.

D. [See *The Shrew,* 4.4.111 SD.]

SLY Sim, must they be married now?
LORD, ⌜*as Sim*⌝ Ay, my lord.

Enter Ferando and Kate and Sander.

SLY Look, Sim, the Fool is come again now.

SYNOPSIS 3. [Compare *The Shrew,* 4.5–5.1.112.]

On the way to Alfonso's home, Ferando persuades Kate to call the sun the moon. They meet Aurelius's real father, en route to see his son, and they both greet him as if he were a young maiden. He leaves them, convinced that they are mad, but Ferando is delighted with Kate's obedience. At Alfonso's, the weddings are over when Aurelius's real father enters. Aurelius begs his forgiveness, but the father orders the arrest of the counterfeit father and Valeria, who run away.

E. [See *The Shrew,* 5.1.112 SD.]

Then Sly speaks.

SLY I say we'll have no sending to prison.
LORD, ⌜*as Sim*⌝ My lord, this is but the play. They're but in jest.
SLY I tell thee, Sim, we'll have no sending to prison, that's flat. Why, Sim, am not I Don Christo Vary? Therefore I say they shall not go to prison.
LORD, ⌜*as Sim*⌝ No more they shall not, my lord. They be run away.
SLY Are they run away, Sim? That's well. Then gi 's some more drink, and let them play again.
LORD, ⌜*as Sim, giving him drink*⌝ Here, my lord.
Sly drinks and then falls asleep.

SYNOPSIS 4. [Compare *The Shrew,* 5.1.113–56 SD.]

Aurelius's father is enraged against Valeria, Aurelius, and Alfonso. All the principal characters kneel to him and beg his forgiveness. He forgives them and accepts the marriage. They all exit.

F. [See *The Shrew,* 5.1.156 SD.]

Sly sleeps.

LORD Who's within there? Come hither, sirs. My lord's asleep again. Go take him easily up,
And put him in his own apparel again,

And lay him in the place where we did find him,
Just underneath the alehouse side below.
But see you wake him not in any case.

BOY It shall be done, my lord.—Come help to bear him hence.

Exit.

SYNOPSIS 5 [Compare *The Shrew,* 5.2.]

Aurelius, Ferando, and Polidor set up a trial of their wives. Each sends for his wife, but only Kate responds by coming. Ferando sends Kate to fetch the other two wives. When they all appear, he orders Kate to "tell unto these headstrong women / What duty wives do owe unto their husbands." (For Kate's speech, which differs interestingly from that of Katherine in *The Shrew,* see longer note to 5.2.152, page 225.) With Ferando having won the wager and received additional money as dowry from Alfonso, the three couples exit, along with the other players of "The Taming of a Shrew."

G. [See *The Shrew,* 5.2.206 SD.]

Then enter two bearing of Sly in his own apparel again, and leaves him where they found him, and then goes out. Then enter the Tapster.

TAPSTER

Now that the darksome night is overpast
And dawning day appears in crystal sky,
Now must I haste abroad. But, soft! Who's this?
What, Sly! O, wondrous! Hath he lain here all night?
I'll wake him. I think he's starved by this,
But that his belly was so stuffed with ale.
What, how, Sly! Awake for shame.

SLY Sim, gi 's some more wine. What's all the players gone? Am not I a lord?

TAPSTER

A lord with a murrain! Come, art thou drunken still?

SLY Who's this? Tapster, O Lord, sirrah, I have had the bravest dream tonight that ever thou heardest in all thy life.

TAPSTER

Ay, marry, but you had best get you home,
For your wife will curse you for dreaming here tonight.

SLY

Will she? I know now how to tame a shrew.
I dreamt upon it all this night till now,
And thou hast waked me out of the best dream
That ever I had in my life! But I'll to my
Wife presently and tame her too,
An if she anger me.

TAPSTER

Nay, tarry, Sly, for I'll go home with thee
And hear the rest that thou hast dreamt tonight.

They exit.

The Taming of the Shrew: A Modern Perspective

Karen Newman

In sermons preached from the pulpit, in exhortations urged from the magistrate's bench, in plays and popular pastimes, in morning and evening prayers at home, in early printed books rehearsing seemly female conduct, the tripartite ideal of women's chastity, silence, and obedience was proclaimed far and wide in early modern England. Shakespeare's heroine, Kate, in *The Taming of the Shrew* refuses to abide by these Renaissance ideals of womanly submission. Her self-confidence and independence, which the male characters disparage by calling her a "devil," threaten the hierarchical organization of Renaissance society in which women were believed inferior. The price of Kate's resistance is summed up in Hortensio's taunt, "No mates for you, / Unless you were of gentler, milder mold" (1.1.59–61).

Instead of wooing Kate, the suitors pursue her more tractable sister, Bianca, whom they admire for her silence, mildness, and sobriety. But in Bianca's dealings with her two suitors (disguised as tutors), even she shows herself less docile than she seems. As many readers of *The Taming of the Shrew* have noted, if in the end one shrew is tamed, two more reveal themselves: Bianca and the widow refuse to do their husbands' bidding at the very moment Kate has ostensibly learned to obey. In the play, the gulf between Renaissance ideals of a submissive femininity and the realities of women's behavior is wide.

Recently, commentators have turned to the work of social historians to explain *The Taming of the Shrew*'s presentation of the female characters' transgression of Renaissance standards for women's behavior. They point out that during the period from 1560 until the English Civil War, England suffered a "crisis of order" brought about by enormous economic, demographic, and political changes that produced acute anxiety about conventional hierarchies.[1] Groups that had traditionally been subject to the authority of others—merchants and actors, servants and apprentices—were enabled by rapid change to enter social spheres that had been customarily closed to them. Such shifts threatened perceived hierarchies in Tudor and Stuart England: men complained of upstart courtiership, of a socially mobile middle class, of "masterless men," and of female rebellion. Since public and domestic authority in Elizabethan England was vested in men—in fathers, husbands, masters, teachers, magistrates, lords—Elizabeth I's rule inevitably produced anxiety about women's roles.[2]

Arraignments for scolding, shrewishness, and bastardy, as well as witchcraft persecutions, crowd the historical record.[3] Although men were occasionally charged with scolding, shrewishness was a predominately female offense. Punishment for such crimes and for related offenses involving sexual misbehavior or "domineering" wives who "beat" or "abused" their husbands often involved public humiliation: the ducking stool, "carting," and/or reproof by means of the skimmington or charivari (an informal ritual in which the accused woman or her surrogate was put in a scold's collar or paraded through the village or town in a cart accompanied by a procession of neighbors banging pots and pans). In Shakespeare's play we can observe traces of such practices when Baptista, Kate's father, exhorts Bianca's suitors to court Kate instead and Gremio exclaims, "To cart her, rather. She's too rough for me" (1.1.55). Anxiety about changing social relations prompted the labeling of old behaviors in new ways that made criminals of women whose actions threatened patriarchal authority.

But history alone cannot account for Shakespeare's presentation of the shrew-taming plot. Literary history—generic models and conventions, both popular and elite—shaped the way Shakespeare represents the play's characters and action. Popular medieval *fabliaux* and Tudor jest books and pamphlets recount tales of shrew-taming that furnished patterns from which Shakespeare drew. These and the oral folktales on which they are based include incidents similar to the plot of *The Taming of the Shrew:* a father with two daughters, one curst (i.e., bad-tempered) and spurned, the other mild and sought after; a suitor determined to tame the shrew; a farcical wedding scene; quarrels of the sort Kate and Petruchio have at his country house and on the road to Padua; and a bet on the most obedient wife. An often-cited example is the anonymous ballad *A Merry Jest of a Shrewd and Curst Wife Lapped in Morel's Skin for her Good Behavior* (c. 1550), in which a father has two daughters, one curst, the other docile. When a wooer seeks the shrewish daughter's hand, the father warns him against this "devilish fiend of hell." Unmoved, he marries her and proceeds to tame her by means of beatings and torture: after cudgeling her bloody, he wraps her in a salted morel skin. The ballad ends conventionally with a meal at which father, mother, and neighbors admire the once-shrewish wife's obedience and with a challenge to the audience: "He that can charm a shrewd wife / Better than thus, Let him come to me and fetch ten pound / And a golden purse."

Though the basic situation of *The Taming of the Shrew* resembles that of *A Merry Jest,* in Shakespeare's play Petruchio avoids physical violence. Instead of beating Kate, he resorts to more civilized coercion: public humiliation at their wedding, starvation, sleep deprivation, and verbal bullying, all administered with the utmost courtesy and pretended kindness. The less violent but equally coercive taming strategies that Shakespeare has Petruchio employ can be linked to a humanist tradition represented by Juan Luis Vives, Erasmus, and later Protestant reformers, who recommend persuasion, not brutality, as the means of inculcating wifely obedience. But even the popular tradition offers analogues less grisly than *A Merry Jest.* For example, in the early broadside *The Taming of a Shrew or the only way to make a Bad Wife Good: At least, to keep her quiet, be she bad or good,* a father counsels his newly married son not to chide his wife and to give her reign over the household to prevent marital strife.

In both popular and elite materials on marriage and education, taming or educating a wife is likened to the training or domestication of animals—unbroken horses, intractable cats, untamed hawks, even wild beasts. Implied in this comparison is the view that women are themselves unmanageable creatures whom only rigorous training and violence, or the continued threat of violence, can render submissive. Popular folktales and *fabliaux,* marital handbooks, sermons, and educational treatises all resort to the language and vocabularies of animal taming. In *The Taming of the Shrew,* Shakespeare has Petruchio compare taming Kate to training a falcon, and he peppers Petruchio's speech with the technical language of hawk taming.

The humanist writers also sought to inculcate obedience through a less dehumanizing but perhaps more powerfully manipulative method. Following such earlier writers as Saint Paul, they set up an analogy in which marriage and the family are likened to the government of the kingdom. The family is represented as a little world organized like the larger world of the state or commonwealth, and the wife's duty to obey her husband is equated with the subject's duty to obey the prince. Wifely obedience, according to this model, is exacted not through violence but through strategies of molding the wife into a fit subject. In early modern England, the family was the basic unit of production as well as consumption, the site of the pooling and distribution of resources and of the reproduction of proper subjects for the commonwealth. In such a world, managing femininity had important political as well as social and economic consequences: in Elizabethan England a woman who murdered her spouse was tried not for murder as was her male counterpart but for treason, and her punishment was correspondingly more severe.

Kate's speech at the end of the play on the status of wives as subjects most forcefully illustrates this rationalization of wifely subjection:

> Such duty as the subject owes the prince,
> Even such a woman oweth to her husband;
> And when she is froward, peevish, sullen, sour,
> And not obedient to his honest will,
> What is she but a foul contending rebel
> And graceless traitor to her loving lord?
> (5.2.171–76)

No lines in the play have been more variously interpreted than this final speech in which Kate advocates women's submission to their husbands' wills. Some critics have accepted Kate's speech simply as testimony that she has been tamed; others argue that it must be understood ironically as pretense, a strategy for living peaceably in patriarchal culture. Although either interpretation can be supported by the text and by a director's choices in the theater, what is perhaps most striking about Kate's final speech is that at the very moment the ideology of women's silence and submission is most forcefully articulated, we find a woman (or at any rate, a boy playing a woman's part, since on the Elizabethan stage all women's parts were played by boy actors) speaking forcefully and in public the longest speech in the play, at the most dramatic moment in the action. In short, Kate's speaking as she does contradicts the very sentiments she affirms.

Not only does Shakespeare's shrew-taming plot depend on generic models—*fabliaux,* folktales, educational treatises, sermons and the like—but the subplot—the wooing of Bianca—also depends on literary models, in particular George Gascoigne's *Supposes* (1566), a translation of the Italian comedy *I Suppositi* (1509) by the Italian poet and playwright Lodovico Ariosto (1474–1533). Ariosto's play was modeled on the classical new comic tradition generally traced to the Greek playwright Menander (4th century B.C.E.) and made available to the Renaissance through his Latin imitators Plautus (254?–184 B.C.E.) and Terence (185–159 B.C.E.).[4] Typically, the plot structure of new comedy involves young people whose desire for one another is opposed by the young man's father, or by a pimp, or by some other representative of an older generation. The plot depends on a trick or twist usually involving money and perpetrated by a servant or slave that allows the lovers to be united. In the Greco-Roman tradition, the female character is often an unmarriageable slave or courtesan, and the resolution sometimes entails mistaken identity—the woman is discovered to be a citizen lost or sold into slavery at birth, in which case the play can end in marriage.

Early Renaissance versions of such comedies transform the social and sexual relations typical of new-comic plots: the young woman is typically marriageable, the opposition is often her father, and the sexual intrigue usually ends in marriage. Shakespeare and the English playwrights modify this structure further by melding it with the romance tradition of the chaste lover (like Lucentio) who wishes only for marriage from the start. In addition, in *The Taming of the Shrew* Shakespeare adds a rival for Bianca's hand (Hortensio) to enhance the romantic plot by allowing her a choice between possible husbands. New comedy typically follows the unities of time and place: the lovers are already at odds with some authority at the outset, and the play enacts only the intrigue that brings them together. Shakespeare, however, dramatizes the entire action, from Lucentio's falling in love and wooing Bianca through the intrigue that leads to their marriage and on to the celebratory feast at the end.

In *The Taming of the Shrew,* Shakespeare carefully interweaves his main plot and his subplot: Lucentio sees and loves Bianca (1.1); Petruchio vows to marry Kate (1.2); Petruchio woos her (2.1); Lucentio and Hortensio woo Bianca (3.1). The plots diverge at the marriage of Kate and Petruchio (3.2), briefly to reunite (after the taming scenes at Petruchio's house and Lucentio's gulling of Baptista) on the journey back to Padua when Kate calls Lucentio's father a "young budding virgin" (4.5.41). That "mistaken" identity in turn prepares for another, Tranio's refusal to recognize Vincentio in 5.1, a complication resolved by the appearance of the young lovers as husband and wife. The two plots are united again in the conventional comic feast and wager that end the play.

The convention of mistaken identity, which Shakespeare inherited from his classical and Italian predecessors, is not only a plot device in the play but also works thematically to undermine notions of an essential self or a fixed identity. In the Induction (an eighteenth-century editorial appellation, since the Sly incidents are simply part of Act 1 in the First Folio [1623], the earliest printed edition of *The Taming of the Shrew*), Sly is persuaded he is a lord instead of a tinker; in the opening scene of the play proper, Lucentio and Tranio exchange identities as master and servant. Kate is transformed after enduring the irrational world of Petruchio's country house, where she is denied food, sleep, and the fashionable accoutrements of her social class until

> she (poor soul)
> Knows not which way to stand, to look, to speak,
> And sits as one new-risen from a dream.
> (4.1.184–86)

In the tradition of Shakespeare's later romantic comedies, she subsequently "discovers" a new identity as obedient wife.[5] Bianca and the widow, who begin by conforming to oppressive codes of womanly duty, reveal their independence. The Merchant assumes the identity of Vincentio, while Vincentio is "mistaken" for a "fair lovely maid." Mistaken identity works literally in the disguise plots of the Induction and the Bianca-Lucentio action and figuratively in the taming plot, in which Petruchio plays at antic ruffian and Kate at submissive wife.

The Induction, with its duping of the tinker Sly, is linked to yet another folklore tradition, the motif of the "sleeper awakened" found in many versions throughout the Middle Ages and Renaissance. Usually the story ends with the Sly character returned to his beggarly identity, as in a play published in 1594, the anonymous *A Pleasant Conceited Historie, called The taming of a Shrew.* In the anonymous play, the Sly action is completed with an epilogue in which Sly awakes after the comedy to rediscover himself a tinker and vows to return home to tame his own shrewish wife. Unusually, in *The Taming of the Shrew* there is no such epilogue and no return to the Christopher Sly action. (See Appendix, "Framing Dialogue in *The Taming of a Shrew* [1594]," pages 233–34, above, for a discussion of the relation of Shakespeare's *The Taming of the Shrew* and the anonymous play.)

The Taming of the Shrew has been popular onstage since its earliest production, though, like many of Shakespeare's plays, in radically altered forms. By the early seventeenth century it had already prompted a sequel, John Fletcher's *The Woman's Prize; or the Tamer Tamed* (c. 1611). In the twentieth and twenty-first centuries, it has inspired successful musical, popular film, and television adaptations, and numerous stage productions. And the play continues to be a staple in both secondary and postsecondary school curricula. The play's contemporary success depends first on comic virtuosity, but in a time of rapid social change when traditional gender roles are being challenged and the malleability of identity is increasingly acknowledged, audiences take pleasure in *The Taming of the Shrew*'s representation of the instability both of conventional gender hierarchies and of human identity itself.

---

1. See particularly Lawrence Stone, *The Causes of the English Revolution, 1529–1642* (New York: Harper & Row, 1972) and his *Crisis of the English Aristocracy, 1558–1641* (Oxford: Clarendon Press, 1965).

2. On the anxiety produced by Elizabeth, see Louis Montrose, "'Shaping Fantasies': Gender and Power in Elizabethan Culture," *Representations,* no. 1 (1983): 61–94; however, see also Leah Marcus, *Puzzling Shakespeare: Local Reading and Its Discontents* (Berkeley:

University of California Press, 1988), ch. 2, in which she shows how Elizabeth represented herself as both prince and father to her people.

3. See David Underdown, "The Taming of the Scold: The Enforcement of Patriarchal Authority in Early Modern England," in *Order and Disorder in Early Modern England,* edited by Anthony Fletcher and John Stevenson, (Cambridge: Cambridge University Press, 1985), pp. 116–35.

4. "New" is a misnomer since "new comedy" is dubbed "new" only in relation to the "old" comic tradition represented by Aristophanes (448?–380? B.C.E.).

5. On Kate's development and *Shrew* as romantic comedy, see John Bean, "Comic Structure and the Humanizing of Kate in *The Taming of the Shrew,*" in *The Woman's Part,* edited by Carolyn Ruth Swift Lenz, Gayle Greene, and Carol Thomas Neely, (Urbana: University of Illinois Press, 1980), pp. 65–78.

Further Reading

The Taming of the Shrew

Abbreviations: *MM* = *Measure for Measure*; *MV* = *The Merchant of Venice*; *Ado* = *Much Ado about Nothing; The Shrew* = *The Taming of the Shrew*; *A Shrew* = *The Taming of a Shrew*

Amussen, Susan. *An Ordered Society: Gender and Class in Early Modern England.* New York: Blackwell, 1988.

Amussen studies English villagers between the years 1560 and 1725, initially dividing the ideology of family from its material reality. Beginning with ideology, she identifies popular uses of the analogy between the family and the state and of conceptions of authority. Focusing mainly on the town of Norfolk, Amussen scrutinizes townspeople's expectations of one another in order to better understand gender and class hierarchies and how people lived within an assumed congruence between family and state institutions. She uses household manuals and political treatises to present the dogma behind family hierarchy and then examines family economics to reveal familial material existence. While the former discloses a staunch patriarchal hierarchy in the family unit, one that is used as a model for the political framework, Amussen finds a striking difference in the economic reality of families, in which women often have a great deal of responsibility for family finances and are trusted partners in matters of pastoral economics or even executors of their husbands' wills. The subordination of wife to husband appears clear in theory but not in practice. Nonetheless, strong bonds of deference and responsibility in the patriarchal system held together family, town, county, and nation and were plainly showcased by the hierarchical seating in local churches. Early modern England ushered in challenges to authority that were economic (through population growth and inflation), political (through the Civil War between Parliamentarians and Royalists), familial (through industrialization, which changed the family from a unit of joint production and consumption to one that only consumed together), and social (through rejection of local notables by the townspeople). Thus authority changed with the Restoration. The prosecution of moral disorder ceased after the Restoration not because class and gender tensions ended but because "order no longer depended on the reiteration of an ideal of the family as the only apparently unchanging institution, as it had in the early seventeenth century." The elites traded the Puritan vision of a unified morality for a capitalist ideal in which they could hold their position at the top. Ultimately, the lack of recorded moral disorder after the Restoration represented not equanimity between the genders and classes but polarization of roles and "containment by a careful local elite."

Aspinall, Dana E., ed. *The Taming of the Shrew: Critical Essays.* Shakespeare Criticism. New York: Routledge, 2002.

In addition to an extract from Arthur Quiller-Couch's introduction to his 1923 edition of *The Shrew*, Aspinall reprints the following critical appraisals: Robert B. Heilman, "The Taming Untamed, or, The Return of the Shrew" (1966); Jeanne Addison Roberts, "Horses and Hermaphrodites: Metamorphoses in [*The Shrew*]" (1983); David Daniell, "The Good Marriage of Katherine and Petruchio" (1984); Margie Burns, "The Ending of [*The Shrew*]" (1986); Margaret L. Mikesell, "'Love wrought these miracles': Marriage and Genre in [*The Shrew*]" (1990); Lynda E. Boose, "Scolding Brides and

Bridling Scolds: Taming the Woman's Unruly Member" (1991); Juliet Dusinberre, "[*The Shrew*]: Women, Acting, and Power" (1993); Lena Cowen Orlin, "The Performance of Things in [*The Shrew*]" (1993); Michael Shapiro, "Framing the Taming: Metatheatrical Awareness of Female Impersonation in [*The Shrew*]" (1993); Laurie E. Maguire, "Cultural Control in [*The Shrew*]" (1997); Thomas Moisan, "'What's that to you?' or, Facing Facts: Anti-Paternalist Chords and Social Discords in [*The Shrew*]" (1997); and Natasha Korda, "Household Kates: Domesticating Commodities in [*The Shrew*]" (1996). The collection concludes with reprints of theater studies and reviews of the play on stage, screen, and television: Jan MacDonald, "'An Unholy Alliance': William Poel, Martin Harvey, and [*The Shrew*]" (1982); Patty S. Derrick, "[*The Shrew*], Presented by Three Rivers Shakespeare Festival at the Stephen Foster Theatre, Pittsburgh, PA, June 30–July 16, 1994"; Margaret Loftus Ranald, "The Performance of Feminism in [*The Shrew*]" (1994); Nicholas De Jongh, "Review of Gale Edwards's [*The Shrew*], Royal Shakespeare Company" (*Evening Standard* [April 24, 1995]); Ann C. Christensen, "Petruchio's House in Postwar Suburbia: Reinventing the Domestic Woman (Again)" (1997); and Barbara Hodgdon, "Katherina Bound, or Play(K)ating the Strictures of Everyday Life" (extracted from her 1998 *The Shakespeare Trade: Performances and Appropriations*). Aspinall's introductory discussion of the critical and theatrical reception of *The Shrew* maps out "a chronological overview of the stipulations and qualities inherent in [the] three issues which so preoccupy and vex" critics: (1) the play's "rough-and-tumble treatment of the . . . 'curst shrew' Katherine and . . . of all potentially unruly wives," (2) the role of the Induction, and (3) the relationship of *A Shrew* to *The Shrew*. Aspinall emphasizes the wide range of responses to Katherine's final speech (the longest in the play) and Petruchio's "hearty response" to it, because "[i]t is here . . . that the play becomes most resonant in our own culture as we enter a new century of critical inquiry." While cultural and political interests have informed Shakespeare scholarship since the 1960s, "virtually unique" to *The Shrew* is the way "even the most cursory of research . . . reveals that much discussion of the play assumes a cultural or political bent from the start."

Bean, John C. "Comic Structure and the Humanizing of Kate in *The Taming of the Shrew*." In *The Woman's Part: Feminist Criticism of Shakespeare*, edited by Carolyn Ruth Swift, Gayle Greene, and Carol Thomas Neely, pp. 65–78. Urbana: University of Illinois Press, 1980.

Bean characterizes critics of *The Shrew* as either revisionists (in their belief that Katherine delivers her final speech ironically and remains untamed) or anti-revisionists (in their belief that Katherine is tamed "through the reductive procedures of rollicking, old-fashioned farce"). Objecting to both these positions, Bean argues that "what we should emphasize . . . is the emergence of a humanized heroine against the background of depersonalized farce unassimilated from the play's fabliau sources. If we can appreciate the liberal element in Kate's last speech—the speech that strikes modern sensibilities as advocating male tyranny—we can perhaps see that Kate is tamed not in the automatic manner of behavioral psychology but the spontaneous manner of the later romantic comedies where characters lose themselves in chaos and emerge, as from a dream, liberated into the bonds of love." In making his case, Bean contrasts *The Shrew* with the brutality of the folktales presented by Jan H. Brunvand (see below) and of *A Shrew*. Contrasting the last speeches of the heroine in the two plays, Bean can point to the misogyny of *A Shrew*'s version, with woman being presented as the source of sin, and to the emphasis in *The Shrew*'s version on "reciprocity of duties in marriage." Through the latter Bean believes that Shakespeare is complicating the tradition of farce that he inherited by introducing into it the humanist conception of marriage as a union bound together "by the mutual obligations of love." As his sources for this view of marriage, Bean cites the Catholic Erasmus and Juan Luis Vives and the Protestant Heinrich Bullinger and Robert Cleaver. Bean finds romantic elements in the taming, chiefly in the role-playing of Petruchio on the occasion of his wedding and in his language games later in the play, both of which lead Katherine into chaos, from which she emerges through the discovery of her own imagination. Bean also notes the persistence of farce in Shakespeare's play, in Petruchio's "beating of servants, his throwing of food and bedding, his railing at the tailor" and in Katherine's "being compelled to come on stage at the end of play, to stomp obediently on her new hat, and to lecture on cue about the duties of wives." It is against this background of farce that, Bean says, we see her emerge as a romantic character.

Brunvand, Jan Harold. "The Folktale Origin of *The Taming of the Shrew.*" *Shakespeare Quarterly* 17 (1966): 345–59.

Brunvand contends that "examination of the background of . . . folktale tradition coupled with study of a few key texts can prove quite conclusively that Shakespeare's taming plot, which has not been traced successfully in its entirety to any known printed version, must have come ultimately from oral tradition." While no oral text has been reported from England, such texts have been reported from the countries surrounding it—Scotland, Ireland, Norway, Sweden, Denmark,

Germany. Shakespeare's play shares with a Danish folktale three of the four elaborations on the basic plot of taming that distinguish the particular subtype of the folktale found throughout northern Europe: "several details about the bridegroom's arrival at the wedding (riding a nag, wearing old clothes, etc.) [3.2.42–62], the absurd statements to which the wife must agree [4.3.194–202; 4.5.1–45], the incident with the bent green branch [in the folktale, but not the play], and a wager on the wives' obedience [5.2.67–128]." It is only in northern European versions that the wife must agree to the husband's absurd statements before he will take her back to her father's home. These versions, like Shakespeare's play, also feature a cash wager that is laid only after dinner. Then "the wives are called in successively and further demands are made on them. Often in the tales the wives must either enter in some stage of undress or remove some clothing in front of the men, just as in Shakespeare's play Kate must remove her cap and throw it to the floor." Brunvand also purports to show that the shorter play *A Shrew* must derive from Shakespeare's play by demonstrating that the latter is closer to its folktale origin than the former. Only Shakespeare's play contains these four folktale traits: "warnings to the suitor about the shrewish girl, the man's arrival at the wedding on an old sick horse, his bad behavior there, and the wife kissing her husband as a proof of her taming."

Bullough, Geoffrey, ed. *Narrative and Dramatic Sources of Shakespeare*, vol. 1, pp. 57–160. New York: Columbia University Press, 1957.

Bullough tracks the many possible sources for *The Shrew* and prints two sources and an analogue, attempting to account for the relation of each to Shakespeare's play. The first source is George Gascoigne's 1566 play *Supposes*, published in 1575, and no doubt a source for Shakespeare, who took the names Petruc(h)io and Litio, as well as suggestions about the play's disguises and subterfuge, from Gascoigne. The analogue is from Goulart's *Thrésor d'Histoires Admirables et Memorables*, as translated by Edward Grimestone in 1607, which contains a story of Philip, duke of Burgundy's deception of a drunken artisan that is roughly analogous to the Lord's trick on the tinker Sly in Shakespeare's play. The second alleged source Bullough prints is the play *A Shrew*, printed in 1594, and thought by Bullough possibly to be "Shakespeare's first shot at the theme" and thus a source for *The Shrew.* (It now seems more likely that the 1594 play and the 1623 *Shrew* derive in some way from an earlier Shakespearean treatment.) Bullough also re-creates for his reader the long histories of parts of Shakespeare's play. Versions of the beggar transported to wealth are found in *The Arabian Nights*, in Goulart, in a 1570 jestbook by Richard Edwardes, in Sir Richard Barckley's *A Discourse of the Felicitie of Man* (1598), in one of the ballads in Bishop Thomas Percy's collection, and in Robert Burton's *Anatomy of Melancholy* (1621). Literary representations of marital conflict date from Plautus in classical drama through Geoffrey Chaucer's "The Wife of Bath's Prologue and Tale" and such Tudor jestbooks as *A Hundred Mery Talys* (from around 1525) and *Tales and Quick Answers* (1567), as well as *The Ballad of the Curst Wife Wrapt in a Morell's Skin* [i.e., the skin of a dead horse] (from around 1550).

Enterline, Lynn. "The Cruelties of Character in *The Taming of the Shrew.*" Chapter 4 in *Shakespeare's Schoolroom: Rhetoric, Discipline, Emotion*, pp. 95–119. Philadelphia: University of Pennsylvania Press, 2012.

Two questions inform Enterline's study of Shakespeare's "career-long fascination" with the classical curriculum and humanist pedagogy of the early modern grammar school: "How did [such] training influence what counted as genteel masculinity in the period?" and "How did early modern pedagogy affect experiences of sexuality and desire?" Throughout the book, Enterline underscores "the significant difference between what humanists claimed their [pedagogical] methods would achieve [the formation of proper English gentlemen who would benefit the commonwealth] and what the texts of at least one former schoolboy reveal about the institution's unintended literary and social consequences." When read in light of Baptista's pledge to afford his children "good bringing-up" (1.1.94–101), *The Shrew*'s many references to classical authors (especially Ovid), "overt interest in grammar school lessons," and themes of "shrew" and "swine" taming (both topics associated with educational aims of the time) reveal it to be "one of Shakespeare's most sustained engagements with the social aims, rhetorical techniques, and affective contradictions of early modern pedagogy." Approaching the play through three Ovidian texts—*Heroides, Ars amatoria,* and *Metamorphoses*—Enterline traces their subversive influence on the social transformations of Bianca, Sly, and Katherine, three marginalized figures (as women and as a member of the lower class) who are, nevertheless, awarded the benefits of a grammar school education, something none would have been expected to receive. In the first case, the female student Bianca evinces a better grasp of Latin grammar and schoolroom practice than does her male tutor (3.1.33–38, 44–47; 4.2.6–10); in the second, the deluded beggar proves as comfortable with blank verse as does the capricious lord (Ind.2.68–75); and in the third, Katherine reveals a rhetorical facility and gift for public oratory that rival, if not surpass, the taming master Petruchio's. Each plot in this play about mastery "raises complex questions . . . about rhetoric's practical efficacy in 'training up' subjects to occupy different social stations by learning acceptable verbal, corporal, and affective behavior." The vivid descriptions of Ovidian violence and pain that prompt Sly's transformation from beggar to lord (Ind.2.50–60) remind us that "grammar school practice . . . produced both writers and audiences for a commercial theater in which cruelty became central to representations of emotion and character." Katherine's final speech of submission is, perhaps, best appreciated as an oration delivered before her peers and a "master," the culmination of the "training up" envisioned by humanist schoolmasters, and thus indicative of "a performer performing." Such rhetorical training encouraged a "habit of alterity," the ability to impersonate other voices by imitating and embodying passions that were not one's own. As *The Shrew* attests, "when Shakespeare creates the convincing effects of character and emotion for which he is so often singled out as a precursor of 'modern' subjectivity, he signals his debt to the Latin institution that granted him the cultural capital of an early modern gentleman precisely when undercutting the socially normative categories schoolmasters invoked as their educational goal."

Henderson, Diana E. "The Return of the Shrew: New Media, Old Stories, and Shakespearean Comedy." Chapter 3 in *Collaborations with the Past: Reshaping Shakespeare across Time and Media*, pp. 155–201. Ithaca: Cornell University Press, 2006.

Henderson examines the diachronic collaborations over the past two hundred years between Shakespeare and major novelists, actors, theater directors, and filmmakers who, in reshaping his plays, have also re-created modern Anglo-American culture. Her "cross-medial" study of "Shake-shiftings" addresses the political, economic, psychological, formal, and technical forces "that serendipitously transform imagination into memory." The chapter on *The Shrew* examines five filmed/televised productions to illustrate how "modern collaborators with the camera dramatize and finesse the difficulties of (yet again) taming a shrew": the Mary Pickford–Douglas Fairbanks film directed by Sam Taylor (1929), the Elizabeth Taylor–Richard Burton screen version directed by Franco Zeffirelli (1967), Jonathan Miller's BBC-Time/Life production (1980), the televised docudrama *Kiss Me, Petruchio* starring Raúl Juliá and Meryl Streep (1981), and Gil Junger's *10 Things I Hate about You* (1999). The "throughline" shared by these very different screen *Shrews* "is their resort to some mode of justification for collaborating with this overtly tricky [and for many critics and audiences, 'archaic and benighted'] text in the first place: the layers they add and the solutions they find vary, from medial to psychological to narrative re-vision, but all implicitly acknowledge . . . [that t]he greater the perceived difficulty in making the audience laugh, the greater the urgency of Shake-shifting." Throughout the chapter, but particularly in reference to Miller's production, Henderson cites Freud's clinical essay "A Child Is Being Beaten" (1919)—"the comedy's uncanny double"—to shed light on how, through their use of the camera, certain films and videos "wrestle with the possibilities of narrative rupture and psychological depth." The author concludes that Zeffirelli's choices to "use rather than paper over [the play's] narrative gaps and silences" result in "the most layered and lasting of cinematic *Shrews*." [The chapter incorporates a revision of "'A Shrew for the Times,' Revisited," in *Shakespeare, the Movie, II: Popularizing the Plays on Film, TV, Video, and DVD,* edited by Richard Burt and Lynda Boose, pp. 120–39 (New York: Routledge, 2003).]

"Homily on Obedience" (1559). In *Elizabethan Backgrounds,* edited by Arthur F. Kinney, pp. 44–70. Hamden, Conn.: Archon, 1975.

Read from pulpits throughout the realm, this homily or sermon forcefully portrays the Elizabethan state's doctrine of hierarchy and authority. According to the homily, God has created perfect order across his whole creation, from heaven (with its orders of archangels and angels) through the air (with the sun, moon, and stars, in their orderly progress around the Earth, and even with the different orders of birds), the water (with all kinds of fishes in the seas and rivers), the land (with its trees, plants, seeds, and animals of all kinds), the year (with its seasons), the human body (with its soul, heart, mind, and limbs in necessary order), and human society (where God, says the homily, creates some of high status and some of low, some rich and some poor). Any threat whatsoever to this divinely created social order is represented (in a slippery-slope argument) as the potential source of chaos—"all abuse, carnal libertie, enormitie, synne, and Babilonical confusion," in which "no man shall ryde or go by the hyghway unrobbed, no man shall slepe in his owne house or bed unkylled, no man shal kepe his wife, children and possessions in quietnes." The emphasis falls heavily on God's appointment of Queen Elizabeth and her "supreme and higher officers" and on their function as a bulwark against such chaos. The homily infers from this alleged divine selection of the queen that opposition to her will be punished by divine vengeance through the agency of those appointed by God: "ther is no power but of god: the powers that be, be ordeined of god, whosoever therfore withstandeth the power, withstandeth the ordinaunce of god, but they that resiste or are against, shal receive to themselves damnacion, for rulers are not feareful to them that do good, but to them that do evil. . . . But an if thou doe what which is evil, then feare, for he beareth not the sweorde for naughte, for he is the minister of God, to take vengeaunce on hym that doeth evil." The examples of Christ and his apostles and of David are adduced to persuade English subjects never to resist the power of state authority, but to accept even gross injustice, as did these biblical models. Finally the homily is careful to distinguish between, on the one hand, the alleged direct appointment of Elizabeth and her officials by God and, on the other hand, the pope's claim to be God's delegate in making similar appointments, a claim the homily is concerned to repudiate.

Kahn, Coppélia. "*The Taming of the Shrew*: Shakespeare's Mirror of Marriage." In *The Authority of Experience*, edited by Arlyn Diamond and Lee Edwards, pp. 84–100. Amherst: University of Massachusetts Press, 1977.

For Kahn, Shakespeare creates in Petruchio the stereotype of male dominance, while fashioning Katherine realistically and sympathetically as initially "a woman trapped in the self-destructive role of shrew by her male guardians." While Shakespeare may subscribe to the principle of gender hierarchy, he is skeptical of the practice, and his play exposes the division of power and status according to sex alone as irrational and ultimately illusory. As farce the play satirizes men's attitudes toward women by exaggerating to a ridiculous extent the reach and force of male dominance so that it seems a childish fantasy of omnipotence. This fantasy plays out in all the noise and violence of Petruchio—his stamping, shouting, beating of servants, and throwing of food and dishes to the floor. He plays lord over nature, exhibiting violence that is legitimized by his society. In the quieter language games at the end of the play, his dominance is revealed to defy reason. Katherine verbally accepts his power to call the sun the moon and have her name it so, but in her capitulation she clearly indicates that she thinks him mad. Implicitly she "reassures him that she will give him obedience if that is what he must have, but . . . warns him that she, in turn, must retain her intellectual freedom. . . . Though Kate is clever enough to use his verbal strategies against him, she is trapped in her own cleverness. Her only way of maintaining her inner freedom is by outwardly denying it," as in her famous speech to Bianca and the widow, understood by Kahn to be delivered ironically. At its conclusion the play appears to replace the fantasy of male dominance with "a contrary myth: that only a woman has the power to authenticate a man, by acknowledging him *her* master. Petruchio's mind may change even as the moon, but what is important is that Kate confirm those changes; moreover, that she do so willingly and consciously. Such voluntary surrender is, paradoxically, part of the myth of female power, which assigns to woman the crucial responsibility for creating a mature and socially respectable man. . . . Shakespeare reveals the dependency which underlies mastery, the strength behind submission."

Kidnie, Mary Jane. *The Taming of the Shrew.* Shakespeare Handbooks. New York: Palgrave Macmillan, 2006.

The core of Kidnie's handbook, a performance-oriented introduction to *The Shrew*, is a scene-by-scene commentary (Chapter 2) that encourages readers to "envisage the words . . . unfurling in performance," thereby opening up the "environment for which [the play was] written and [offering] an experience as close as possible to an audience's progressive experience of a production." Other chapters address the authority of the dramatic text and early performances, sources and cultural context, key stage and cinematic revivals, and major trends in modern critical approaches. In addition to passages from sermons, treatises, and pamphlets of the period, the chapter on cultural context includes extracts from three sources and analogues for the three separate strands of Shakespeare's play: Gascoigne's *Supposes* (1556) for the disguise plot, the ballad "A Merry Jest of a Shrewd and Curst Wife" (c. 1550) for the central taming plot, and the anonymous *A Shrew* (1594) for the Sly induction scenes. The key productions receiving special attention in Chapters 4 and 5 are David Garrick's adaptation *Catharine and Petruchio* (1754), the Sam Taylor (1929) and Franco Zeffirelli (1967) films, Charles Marowitz's *The Shrew* (1974), Jonathan Miller's BBC-Time/Life version (1980), Richard Monette's staging for the Stratford Festival of Canada (1988), and Gil Junger's *10 Things I Hate about You* (1999). Kidnie shapes her critical assessment of *The Shrew* (Chapter 6) around three sets of twentieth-century responses to the central "taming" plot: readings of it as a romantic comedy, as "a form of overt ideological display" rooted in the patriarchal order of early modern England, and "trickster" readings, which argue that Shakespeare's play "only *seems* to affirm male privilege and female subjection." In modern critical discourse, *The Shrew*—like *MV* and *MM*—has become a "problem comedy," its final moments leaving us "with unresolved concerns about the prevailing structure of power." The play remains one of Shakespeare's most frequently staged comedies, "not despite, but because of, its controversial staging of a battle of the sexes."

Newman, Karen. "Renaissance Family Politics and Shakespeare's *The Taming of the Shrew.*" *English Literary Renaissance* 16 (1986): 86–100.

Newman argues that dramatic representation, whether on the stage in plays or elsewhere, has the power to expose as unnatural historical gender and class hierarchies that we might otherwise be persuaded to understand as being part of nature. Of chief concern is the dominance of male over female, and the moment crucial to Newman's analysis is Katherine's delivery of her long speech about wives' necessary submission to the wills of their husbands in the last scene of *The Shrew*. Newman's method is to contrast the play with an account of an early seventeenth-century court case brought by a small-town tanner against his neighbors. When the drunken tanner was physically and verbally abused by his wife, his neighbors sought to restore the hierarchy of males over females in their town by publicly ridiculing the tanner and his wife: one of the male neighbors, dressed as the tanner's wife, was carried around so that he could abuse his fellow townsmen. The tanner brought a suit against his neighbors, but his wife is never heard from; she is denied any voice. However, in *The Shrew*, even from the beginning of the play-within-the-play performed for the formerly drunken tinker Christopher Sly, the shrew Katherine is given a voice and therefore has the power to represent in her speeches the gender hierarchy against which she struggles. Her speeches "deform language by sub-verting it, that is, by turning it inside out so that metaphors, puns and other forms of wordplay manifest their veiled equivalences: the meaning of woman as treasure, of wooing as a civilized and acceptable disguise for sexual exploitation, of the objectification and exchange of women. Kate's having the last word contradicts the very sentiments she speaks; rather than resolve the play's action, her monologue simply displays the fundamental contradiction presented by a female dramatic protagonist, between woman as a sexually desirable, silent object and women of words, women with power over language who disrupt, or at least italicize, women's place and part in culture."

Novy, Marianne. "Patriarchy and Play in *The Taming of the Shrew*." *English Literary Renaissance* 9 (1979): 264–80.

Novy responds to the playfulness of Petruchio, but without losing sight of him as the embodiment of patriarchy, with his commitment to the authority of fathers over families, husbands over wives, and generally men over women. Even before Petruchio's appearance on stage, the play confronts its audience with the representation of social hierarchy as a game when the Induction's Lord changes places with the beggar Sly and when the gentleman Lucentio and his servant Tranio exchange clothes and social roles. Two features of game-playing feature in the first encounter of Petruchio and Katherine: he "behaves according to 'the fiction, the sentiment of "as if"'" when he invents a Katherine renowned across her social circle for her virtues and beauty, and she behaves as if playing a game in her verbal competition to best him with puns. He continues with his game beyond their private conversation when he represents the two of them as complicit in pretending to observers that she is still a shrew, even though she, he claims, is none. At their wedding, Petruchio exploits the power conferred on him by the patriarchal social order by playfully laughing at the conventions of this order in his manner and dress, but Katherine, in the subordinate position, worries about society's judgment of her. This inequality persists in the scene with the tailor and haberdasher, when Petruchio can scorn social conventions governing female attire that Katherine is anxious to observe. Not until Petruchio begins playfully to use language later in the play does he offer Katherine an opportunity, which she eventually accepts, to join him in his game, as together they imaginatively re-create the words in terms that they share. "Faced with irrational demands, she has experienced the benefit of seeing them as part of a game and playing along. . . . Her education in folly has taught her how to live with relative comfort in a patriarchal culture." This language game provides a perspective from which the audience can interpret her final speech as a performance rather than as a sincere expression of belief. The final scene "presents their marriage as a private world, a joke that the rest of the characters miss, a game that excludes all but the two of them."

Paster, Gail Kern. "The Humor of It: Bodies, Fluids, and Social Discipline in Shakespearean Comedy." In *A Companion to Shakespeare's Works*, edited by Richard Dutton and Jean Howard, 3:47–66, esp. 58–65. Malden, Mass.: Blackwell, 2003.

The second-century Galen's doctrine of the four humors—the bodily fluids of blood, phlegm, yellow bile, and black bile; their accompanying qualities (either hot or cold, moist or dry); and the behaviors resulting from particular combinations (sanguine, phlegmatic, choleric, and melancholic)—offered Shakespeare and his contemporaries "a theory of personality, behavior, status, gender, age, and ethnicity that had the distinct advantage of being rooted in what they believed to be indisputable facts about the human body and its relation to the natural world." Classical humoralism did not distinguish between the psychological and the physiological; moreover, as understood in the traditional society of early modern England, it "reflect[ed] hierarchical social [and gender] values and could be used powerfully to naturalize them." Paster applies Galenic humoral theory across Shakespeare's comedies, with special attention to *The Shrew.* The play's "underlying interest in social regulation of the natural and the appropriateness of the means for doing so" allows Paster to focus on the lowborn Sly and the choleric but wellborn Katherine, the two bodies "most conspicuously subject to humoral manipulation in all of Shakespearean comedy." In the case of Sly, the Lord's trick offers him "a dream of social elevation against the 'humor' of lowness"; the "sensual inducements" afforded him are "intended literally to warm [the beggar] into activity from the lethargy associated with lowness and drink"; even the entertainment provided by the itinerant actors is "presented . . . in humoral terms" (Ind.2.130–38). Whatever threat Sly's humoral manipulation poses to hierarchical tradition is "fragmentary" because we never see the final effect of the "taming" inner play on him. Unlike Sly and the Lord, both Katherine and her tamer Petruchio "are constructed as humoral subjects prone to [choler and violence,] . . . socially outrageous behaviors produced by chronic humoral imbalance." The challenge to tame Katherine presents Petruchio with the opportunity to alter himself materially, not merely by marrying a wealthy heiress but also by "expending [his own choleric temper] against a socially sanctioned target," the unruly woman. His abuse of Katherine thus points up the "ideological underpinnings of the play's humoral logic in which both protagonists undergo humoral reformation, but only the woman's reformation is called a taming." The defining moment of Katherine's humoral reprogramming comes when she loses her relationship to her environment in the sun and moon scene sequence of 4.5. By denying the empirical evidence of her senses and her own independent judgment, she "agrees in effect to perceive the world through the spectacles of [Petruchio's willfully changeable] humor" (4.5.21–25). Whether her words here and in her final speech in Act 5 are a strategic means of self-preservation—and whether we interpret the "ratification of male dominance" as ironic—the taming of Katherine, when read in light of humoral theory, becomes "more than tragicomic." [The revised essay is incorporated as part of Chapter 2, "Love Will Have Heat," in Paster's 2004 *Humoring the Body: Emotions and the Shakespearean Stage* (Chicago: University of Chicago Press).]

Ryan, Kiernan. "'A kind of history': *The Taming of the Shrew.*" Chapter 2 in *Shakespeare's Comedies,* pp. 19–38. New York: Palgrave Macmillan, 2009.

Ryan focuses on the playwright's ten "farcical and festive Elizabethan comedies" as the first phase of "a kind of comedy which Shakespeare quite consciously brought to an end with *Twelfth Night* and to which he never returned." (He assigns the problem plays and romances to subsequent phases of Shakespearean comedy.) Ryan begins and ends his analysis of *The Shrew* with a close reading of Katherine's final speech, arguing that disparagement of it as a "patriarchal apologia" fails to see how it uses "the template of the taming game in order to subvert the assumptions on which the rules of that game rest." In support of this claim, the author devotes the middle sections of the chapter to an examination of (1) the "proleptic parody" of the Induction, (2) the foil function of the Lucentio-Bianca subplot, (3) the essential parity of Katherine and Petruchio (see 2.1.138–43, 190–282; 3.2.157–58, 251–52), and (4) the horseplay of the abortive honeymoon at Petruchio's countryhouse, wherein we see male and female shrews as "mirror-images of each other." Katherine's collusion in Petruchio's "*reductio ad absurdum* of male supremacy" (4.5.21–25, 30–53) is further evidence that this husband and wife are "a double-act." As their good-natured bantering about whether to kiss demonstrates (5.1.147–56), the couple's "intimate tenderness" has been "won through, not by bowing to convention but by flouting it together." Katherine's "scripted" and extreme argument on behalf of husbands "crowns the comedy's sly undoing of the discourse of male domination" even as it illustrates "how deeply entrenched that discourse remains in the minds and hearts of women as well as men." In Ryan's reading, the play emerges not as "a repellant patriarchal parable" but as "the much more complex, exhilarating engagement with gender, love and marriage most people instinctively know it to be."

Schalkwyk, David. "Performance and Imagination: *The Taming of the Shrew* and *A Midsummer Night's Dream.*" Chapter 2 in *Shakespeare, Love, and Service,* pp. 57–79. Cambridge: Cambridge University Press, 2008.

In this study of the "conjunctive play of love and service" in the Shakespeare canon, Schalkwyk examines how "the social, structural interactions of service inform the personal, affective [interplay] of love" in relationships marked by differences of rank, gender, and sexual identity. The author invokes the precept central to the Protestant ideology of service—namely, that it is "not a form of bondage but perfect freedom if perceived and experienced in the right way"—in order to tie the psychology of service to both love and theatrical performance: If reciprocated, love may be seen as mutual service; if not, it becomes "a form of asymmetrical devotion to the other who occupies the place of master or sovereign. . . . Both service and love are peculiarly performative insofar as they are capable of creating their own worlds or projective valuation through imaginative or aspect-perception." As evidenced by the Induction (which "reveal[s] *all* the players [to be] servants"—see especially Ind.1.82), the self-reflexive theatricality "of the player as the double embodiment of service as representing actor and represented character [is] nowhere more evident in Shakespeare than in [*The Shrew*]." To demonstrate the performative implications of service and love in the play, Schalkwyk considers three passages/episodes: (1) Grumio's linguistic subversion of his master Petruchio's commands (1.2.1–19)—an exchange that assumes greater complexity if read "as the representation by servants of a bit of stock master-servant intercourse; (2) the "ironical interplay of clothing and service" that informs the "monstrous sartorial transformation of a servant by an outlandish master" (3.2); and (3) Kate's final speech (5.2.152–95), its "framework of reciprocal service and love . . . qualified by the [self-reflexive theatrical tenor] of the play as a whole." Unlike *Ado*, which ultimately celebrates communal integration, the ending of *The Shrew* shuns social inclusiveness "for a private arrangement that hovers between virtue and necessity, paradoxically forging the only space in which the reciprocity of love and service may . . . be viable, if only through the fantasy of delight offered by the (in)subordinate servant-player." [The chapter incorporates a revision of "Love and Service in *The Taming of the Shrew* and *All's Well That Ends Well*," *International Yearbook* 5 (2005): 3–43.]

Underdown, David. *Revel, Riot and Rebellion: Popular Politics and Culture in England, 1603–1660*. New York: Oxford University Press, 1985.

Underdown investigates and explains the behavior of English common people (that is, people below the rank of gentry) during the civil wars and revolutions of 1640–60. With the aid of political and military documents from the years leading up to, during, and after the civil wars and Restoration, Underdown asserts that civil war allegiances of the common people are products of regional and cultural differences shaped by a complex interweaving of localism, class, religion, environment, industry, and tradition. Reaching back to the prewar period, Underdown notes that the traditional patriarchal hierarchy of God, kingdom, and family is challenged by the forces of population growth, inflation, and industrialization of agricultural society. These forces stratify the classes, oppress the common people, and create a cultural and religious conflict between the community-oriented, traditional "Cavalier" Royalists and the individualist, devout "Roundhead" Puritan Parliamentarians. Prompted by the brutality of both the Royalist and Parliamentary soldiers, common people formed the massive popular movement of the "Clubmen," whose goal was to end the war. Common people voiced their displeasure in less organized ways through riots sparked by lack of food, loss of traditions, and taxation. Underdown argues that such movements point to the civil war as empowering the lower sphere of English people to make decisions in government matters. He offers a complex and multifaceted account of the civil war that dethroned the monarchy and produced an egalitarian parliament. This Puritan parliament championed gender and class equality and food justice, which came at the price of a loss of order, hierarchy, tradition, and stability. Popular opinion toward the "upside-down" and "divisive" Puritans became hostile, and widespread celebrations erupted upon the Restoration of the monarchy. A cautious conservatism threatened to erase newly established equalities. The civil wars brought about inversions of patriarchy, but in the end these "foundered on the stubborn resilience of traditional culture." However, after the Restoration, "the frequency of prosecution of both witches and scolds declined." Owing to improved economic conditions and the "emerging conception of the affective family," physical violence against women was no longer tolerated, but "women lost most of the vestiges of economic and personal independence some had acquired in the unstable years before 1660." The early beginnings of the fall of patriarchy as a theory of government are present in the civil war period but not fully actualized until after 1688.

Underdown, David. "The Taming of the Scold: The Enforcement of Patriarchal Authority in Early Modern England." In *Order and Disorder in Early Modern England*, pp. 116–35. Cambridge: Cambridge University Press, 1985.

According to Underdown, fears of an impending breakdown in the established patriarchal social order were widespread in early modern England. This anxiety displayed itself in a vast literature rife with references to rebellious wives and hectored husbands. In order to determine whether this "threat" to the social order was real or imagined, Underdown sketches a historical context of disobedient wives, rising accusations of witchcraft, and single women refusing service. He notes that until the middle of the sixteenth century punishment of disobedient women was in the hands of the manor or ecclesiastical courts and consisted generally of penance or small fines. However, in the latter half of the century, these offending women become a more important concern. Generally the women accused of being scolds were "poor, social outcasts, widows or otherwise lacking the protection of a family, [or] newcomers to communities." They began to be forced to wear the scold's bridle or brank—"an iron collar with a bit to prevent the victim from talking." Wives believed to be unfaithful or abusive to their husbands were also targets. They now could be bound to the cucking-stool—"the see-saw-like contraption in which the victim was seated in order to be ducked in pond or river." Or both they and their husbands could be the victims of the elaborate shaming rituals of the charivari, in which they were led about in a procession of their neighbors beating pots and pans, or the skimmington—in which they were confronted by a neighbor wearing horns and others making noise with kitchen utensils, including the skimming ladle. From his study of surviving documents, Underdown learns that prosecution and persecution of women was more common in agricultural communities with dairies than in those with crops. He notes that in the former women enjoyed greater economic power, not only making the butter and cheese but also bringing them to market. The entrance of women into the economy of these regions coincides with other stressors, such as excessive population growth, inflation, land shortage, the rise of capitalism, poverty, and vagrancy, and seems to have contributed to anxiety about their continued submission to male authority and to the strained gender relations that distinguish the early modern period.

Wayne, Valerie. "Refashioning the Shrew." *Shakespeare Studies* 17 (1985): 159–87.

Wayne situates Shakespeare's Katherine in *The Shrew* in a rich context of medieval and Shakespearean drama. The figure of the shrew or scold, Wayne discovers, is widespread, appearing in relation to accounts of Noah and the flood in a wide variety of postbiblical sources: "in the fourth-century Gnostic *Book of Noria*, in the Koran, and in a tenth-century Mohammedan account, as well as in the Caedmonian manuscript, two

Wogul folk tales, a Russian redaction of the *Revelations of Methodius*, Enikel's *Weltchronik* of the thirteenth century, and Queen Mary's Psalter, and on Swedish church walls of the fourteenth century." Wayne pays particular attention to the figure in the so-called Towneley cycle by the Wakefield Master, particularly in the Noah play and the famous *Second Shepherds' Play*, and, in addition to *The Shrew*, in Shakespeare's *The Comedy of Errors* (Adriana), *Othello* (Emilia), and *The Winter's Tale* (Paulina). Wayne sees some connection between the character Gill in *The Second Shepherds' Play* and Katherine in *The Shrew* insofar as both appear to collude with their husbands in elaborate schemes to take material advantage of their immediate social groups, being unsuccessful in the medieval play and successful in the Shakespearean one. By defining the scold or shrew as necessarily a married woman, Wayne finds that Katherine largely falls outside the social category because she is not even fully married at the end of the play when she exits with Petruchio to consummate their marriage. Wayne characterizes Petruchio as "not an object of wrath [like the husband of the conventional shrew], but an agent of concord. . . . He has only to show himself superior to the other men in Padua, especially Kate's father, in his understanding of her needs and wants and how to deal with them, and the shrew is already on her way to submission." He thus begins to resolve the problem of shrewishness "before it arises." In Act 4 he becomes a parody of the shrew, but his disorderly conduct, while domestic, is not marital: "it is not aimed at Kate." The irony that arises from Katherine's final speech can be understood in terms of the humanist Juan Luis Vives's maxim "A good woman by lowely obeysaunce ruleth her husbande," and "Petruchio is in on the joke." An audience may nonetheless feel cheated by the play's ending, because "it provides us with absolutely no help in dealing with the inequities of the world of the play."

Wootton, David, and Graham Holderness, eds. *Gender and Power in Shrew-Taming Narratives, 1500–1700.* New York: Palgrave Macmillan, 2010.

This anthology of eleven essays explores "the various dramatic, poetic and narrative versions of the popular 'taming of the shrew' story, from the Middle Ages to the Restoration, in light of new historical work on the place of early modern women in society." The essays are the following: Anna Bayman and George Southcombe, "Shrews in Pamphlets and Plays"; Sandra Clark, "Shrews, Marriage and Murder"; Holly A. Crocker, "Engendering Shrews: Medieval to Early Modern"; Richard Madelaine, "'He speaks very shrewishly': Apprentice-training and *The Taming of the Shrew*"; Leah S. Marcus, "The Shrew as Editor / Editing *Shrews*"; Margaret Maurer and Barry Gaines, "Putting the Silent Woman Back into the Shakespearean *Shrew*"; Helmer J. Helmers, "Unknown Shrews: Three Transformations of *The/A Shrew*"; Charles Conaway, "'Ye sid ha taken my Counsel sir': Restoration Satire and Theatrical Authority"; Graham Holderness, "'Darkenes was before light': Hierarchy and Duality in [*A Shrew*]"; Jan Purnis, "The Gendered Stomach in [*The Shrew*]"; and David Wootton, "*The Tamer Tamed*, or None Shall Have Prizes: 'Equality' in Shakespeare's England." Graham Holderness's introduction outlines two opposing views of *The Shrew* dominant in scholarship of the 1980s and early '90s: "knowledge" readings, which discern "reciprocal accommodations and free mutuality between the sexes," and "power" readings, which consider the play (and the "taming trope" itself) barbaric and "beyond redemption." The reassessment of early modern gender relations in more recent historiography and cultural criticism does not deny "the depth and extent of patriarchal oppression" in the sixteenth and seventeenth centuries; it does, however, insist on the "contestedness [and instability] of English patriarchy within the early modern home," where women wielded more domestic authority than previously believed. The essays gathered here attempt to bridge the gulf between "knowledge" and "power" readings of the play, while also seeking to extend "the semiotic and chronological range" of the term "shrew," which could be used of either a man or a woman, and which "could attract positive as well as negative valencies." In her afterword titled "'Thus have I politicly ended my reign,'" Ann Thompson responds to the preceding essays, comments on several recent productions in which gender and class conflicts are front and center, and confirms what she had suggested in her 1984 Cambridge edition: *The Shrew* should be redefined as a "problem play."

Shakespeare's Language

Abbott, E. A. *A Shakespearian Grammar.* New York: Haskell House, 1972.

This compact reference book, first published in 1870, helps with many difficulties in Shakespeare's language. It systematically accounts for a host of differences between Shakespeare's usage and sentence structure and our own.

Blake, Norman. *Shakespeare's Language: An Introduction.* New York: St. Martin's Press, 1983.

This general introduction to Elizabethan English discusses various aspects of the language of Shakespeare and his contemporaries, offering possible meanings for hundreds of ambiguous constructions.

Dobson, E. J. *English Pronunciation, 1500–1700.* 2 vols. Oxford: Clarendon Press, 1968.

This long and technical work includes chapters on spelling (and its reformation), phonetics, stressed vowels, and consonants in early modern English.

Hope, Jonathan. *Shakespeare's Grammar.* London: Arden Shakespeare, 2003.

Commissioned as a replacement for Abbott's *Shakespearian Grammar,* Hope's book is organized in terms of the two basic parts of speech, the noun and the verb. After extensive analysis of the noun phrase and the verb phrase come briefer discussions of subjects and agents, objects, complements, and adverbials.

Houston, John. *Shakespearean Sentences: A Study in Style and Syntax.* Baton Rouge: Louisiana State University Press, 1988.

Houston studies Shakespeare's stylistic choices, considering matters such as sentence length and the relative positions of subject, verb, and direct object. Examining plays throughout the canon in a roughly chronological, developmental order, he analyzes how sentence structure is used in setting tone, in characterization, and for other dramatic purposes.

Onions, C. T. *A Shakespeare Glossary.* Oxford: Clarendon Press, 1986.

This revised edition updates Onions's standard, selective glossary of words and phrases in Shakespeare's plays that are now obsolete, archaic, or obscure.

Robinson, Randal. *Unlocking Shakespeare's Language: Help for the Teacher and Student.* Urbana, Ill.: National Council of Teachers of English and the ERIC Clearinghouse on Reading and Communication Skills, 1989.

Specifically designed for the high-school and undergraduate college teacher and student, Robinson's book addresses the problems that most often hinder present-day readers of Shakespeare. Through work with his own students, Robinson found that many readers today are particularly puzzled by such stylistic characteristics as subject-verb inversion, interrupted structures, and compression. He shows how our own colloquial language contains comparable structures, and thus helps students recognize such structures when they find them in Shakespeare's plays. This book supplies worksheets—with examples from major plays—to illuminate and remedy such problems as unusual sequences of words and the separation of related parts of sentences.

Williams, Gordon. *A Dictionary of Sexual Language and Imagery in Shakespearean and Stuart Literature.* 3 vols. London: Athlone Press, 1994.

Williams provides a comprehensive list of words to which Shakespeare, his contemporaries, and later Stuart writers gave sexual meanings. He supports his identification of these meanings by extensive quotations.

Shakespeare's Life

Baldwin, T. W. *William Shakspere's Petty School.* Urbana: University of Illinois Press, 1943.

Baldwin here investigates the theory and practice of the petty school, the first level of education in Elizabethan England. He focuses on that educational system primarily as it is reflected in Shakespeare's art.

Baldwin, T. W. *William Shakspere's Small Latine and Lesse Greeke.* 2 vols. Urbana: University of Illinois Press, 1944.

Baldwin attacks the view that Shakespeare was an uneducated genius—a view that had been dominant among Shakespeareans since the eighteenth century.

Instead, Baldwin shows, the educational system of Shakespeare's time would have given the playwright a strong background in the classics, and there is much in the plays that shows how Shakespeare benefited from such an education.

Beier, A. L., and Roger Finlay, eds. *London 1500–1700: The Making of the Metropolis.* New York: Longman, 1986.

Focusing on the economic and social history of early modern London, these collected essays probe aspects of metropolitan life, including "Population and Disease," "Commerce and Manufacture," and "Society and Change."

Bentley, G. E. *Shakespeare's Life: A Biographical Handbook.* New Haven: Yale University Press, 1961.

This "just-the-facts" account presents the surviving documents of Shakespeare's life against an Elizabethan background.

Chambers, E. K. *William Shakespeare: A Study of Facts and Problems.* 2 vols. Oxford: Clarendon Press, 1930.

Analyzing in great detail the scant historical data, Chambers's complex, scholarly study considers the nature of the texts in which Shakespeare's work is preserved.

Cressy, David. *Education in Tudor and Stuart England.* London: Edward Arnold, 1975.

This volume collects sixteenth-, seventeenth-, and early eighteenth-century documents detailing aspects of formal education in England, such as the curriculum, the control and organization of education, and the education of women.

Dutton, Richard. *William Shakespeare: A Literary Life.* New York: St. Martin's Press, 1989.

Not a biography in the traditional sense, Dutton's very readable work nevertheless "follows the contours of Shakespeare's life" as it examines Shakespeare's career as playwright and poet, with consideration of his patrons, theatrical associations, and audience.

Honan, Park. *Shakespeare: A Life.* New York: Oxford University Press, 1998.

Honan's accessible biography focuses on the various contexts of Shakespeare's life—physical, social, political, and cultural—to place the dramatist within a lucidly described world. The biography includes detailed examinations of, for example, Stratford schooling, theatrical politics of 1590s London, and the careers of Shakespeare's associates. The author draws on a wealth of established knowledge and on interesting new research into local records and documents; he also engages in speculation about, for example, the possibilities that Shakespeare was a tutor in a Catholic household in the north of England in the 1580s and that he acted particular roles in his own plays, areas that reflect new, but unproven and debatable, data—though Honan is usually careful to note where a particular narrative "has not been capable of proof or disproof."

Schoenbaum, S. *William Shakespeare: A Compact Documentary Life.* New York: Oxford University Press, 1977.

This standard biography economically presents the essential documents from Shakespeare's time in an accessible narrative account of the playwright's life.

Shakespeare's Theater

Bentley, G. E. *The Profession of Player in Shakespeare's Time, 1590–1642.* Princeton: Princeton University Press, 1984.

Bentley readably sets forth a wealth of evidence about performance in Shakespeare's time, with special attention to the relations between player and company, and the business of casting, managing, and touring.

Berry, Herbert. *Shakespeare's Playhouses.* New York: AMS Press, 1987.

Berry's six essays collected here discuss (with illustrations) varying aspects of the four playhouses in which Shakespeare had a financial stake: the Theatre in Shoreditch, the Blackfriars, and the first and second Globe.

Berry, Herbert, William Ingram, and Glynne Wickham, eds. *English Professional Theatre, 1530–1660.* Cambridge: Cambridge University Press, 2000.

Wickham presents the government documents designed to control professional players, their plays, and playing places. Ingram handles the professional actors, giving as representative a life of the actor Augustine Phillips, and discussing, among other topics, patrons, acting companies, costumes, props, playbooks, provincial playing, and child actors. Berry treats the twenty-three different London playhouses from 1560 to 1660 for which there are records, including four inns.

Cook, Ann Jennalie. *The Privileged Playgoers of Shakespeare's London.* Princeton: Princeton University Press, 1981.

Cook's work argues, on the basis of sociological, economic, and documentary evidence, that Shakespeare's audience—and the audience for English Renaissance drama generally—consisted mainly of the "privileged."

Greg, W. W. *Dramatic Documents from the Elizabethan Playhouses.* 2 vols. Oxford: Clarendon Press, 1931.

Greg itemizes and briefly describes almost all the play manuscripts that survive from the period 1590 to around 1660, including, among other things, players' parts. His second volume offers facsimiles of selected manuscripts.

Gurr, Andrew. *Playgoing in Shakespeare's London.* Cambridge: Cambridge University Press, 1987.

Gurr charts how the theatrical enterprise developed from its modest beginnings in the late 1560s to become a thriving institution in the 1600s. He argues that there were important changes over the period 1567–1644 in the playhouses, the audience, and the plays.

Harbage, Alfred. *Shakespeare's Audience.* New York: Columbia University Press, 1941.

Harbage investigates the fragmentary surviving evidence to interpret the size, composition, and behavior of Shakespeare's audience.

Hattaway, Michael. *Elizabethan Popular Theatre: Plays in Performance.* London: Routledge & Kegan Paul, 1982.

Beginning with a study of the popular drama of the late Elizabethan age—a description of the stages, performance conditions, and acting of the period—this volume concludes with an analysis of five well-known plays of the 1590s, one of them (*Titus Andronicus*) by Shakespeare.

Shapiro, Michael. *Children of the Revels: The Boy Companies of Shakespeare's Time and Their Plays.* New York: Columbia University Press, 1977.

Shapiro chronicles the history of the amateur and quasi-professional child companies that flourished in London at the end of Elizabeth's reign and the beginning of James's.

The Publication of Shakespeare's Plays

Blayney, Peter W. M. *The First Folio of Shakespeare.* Hanover, Md.: Folger, 1991.

Blayney's accessible account of the printing and later life of the First Folio—an amply illustrated catalogue to a 1991 Folger Shakespeare Library exhibition—analyzes the mechanical production of the First Folio, describing how the Folio was made, by whom and for whom, how much it cost, and its ups and downs (or, rather, downs and ups) since its printing in 1623.

Hinman, Charlton. *The Norton Facsimile: The First Folio of Shakespeare.* 2nd ed. New York: W. W. Norton, 1996.

This facsimile presents a photographic reproduction of an "ideal" copy of the First Folio of Shakespeare; Hinman attempts to represent each page in its most fully corrected state. This second edition includes an important new introduction by Peter W. M. Blayney.

Hinman, Charlton. *The Printing and Proof-Reading of the First Folio of Shakespeare.* 2 vols. Oxford: Clarendon Press, 1963.

In the most arduous study of a single book ever undertaken, Hinman attempts to reconstruct how the Shakespeare First Folio of 1623 was set into type and run off the press, sheet by sheet. He also provides almost all the known variations in readings from copy to copy.

Werstine, Paul. *Early Modern Playhouse Manuscripts and the Editing of Shakespeare.* Cambridge: Cambridge University Press, 2012.

Werstine examines in detail nearly two dozen texts associated with the playhouses in and around Shakespeare's time, conducting the examination against the background of the two idealized forms of manuscript that have governed the editing of Shakespeare from the twentieth into the twenty-first century—Shakespeare's so-called foul papers and the so-called promptbooks of his plays. By comparing the two extant texts of John Fletcher's *Bonduca,* one in manuscript and the other printed in 1647, Werstine shows that the term "foul papers" that is found in a note in the *Bonduca* manuscript does not refer, as editors have believed, to a species of messy authorial manuscript but is instead simply a designation for a manuscript, whatever its features, that has served as the copy from which another manuscript has been made. By surveying twenty-one texts with theatrical mark-up, he demonstrates that the playhouses used a wide variety of different kinds of manuscripts and printed texts but did not use the highly regularized promptbooks of the eighteenth-century theaters and later. His presentation of the pecularities of playhouse texts provides an empirical basis for inferring the nature of the manuscripts that lie behind printed Shakespeare plays.

Key to Famous Lines and Phrases

No profit grows where is no pleasure ta'en.
In brief, sir, study what you most affect.
[Tranio—1.1.39–40]

I come to wive it wealthy in Padua;
If wealthily, then happily in Padua.
[Petruchio—1.2.76–77]

. . . nothing comes amiss, so money comes withal.
[Grumio—1.2.83]

Old fashions please me best. [Bianca—3.1.83]

Who wooed in haste and means to wed at leisure.
[Katherine—3.2.11]

This is a way to kill a wife with kindness.
[Petruchio—4.1.208]

Our purses shall be proud, our garments poor,
For 'tis the mind that makes the body rich . . .
[Petruchio—4.3.177–78]

THE FOLGER SHAKESPEARE LIBRARY